"Those familiar with previous editions of this excellent text will find the 7th edition extensively revised. However, the focus on the human element of managing effectively across national and cultural contexts, a highlight of previous editions, has been maintained. This new edition provides immediate and practical guidance for managers. This application to practice, drawn from extensive research and the experiences of managers, is what sets this book apart. Anyone interested in knowing how to function effectively in a global business environment should keep this volume close at hand."

David C. Thomas, PhD, Professor of International Business,
Australian School of Business, Author of
Cross-Cultural Management: Essential Concepts

"Professors Harry Lane and Martha Maznevski are two of the most skilled, experienced, and insightful cross-cultural educators of our time. The seventh edition of *International Management Behavior* is subtitled *Global and Sustainable Leadership*, a topic that resonates well with what I consider important to convey to a student of today. Lane and Maznevski epitomize the subtitle by leading the way in sharing their teaching. We are provided with meaningful models which not only illustrate the text but are also bound to generate exciting discussions in class. This book is not to be missed!"

Lena Zander, Professor, Uppsala University, Sweden

"I recall when I encountered the first edition of *International Management Behavior*. It was like a cool drink on a hot day. The world suddenly seemed a better place. As I review the 7th edition, I marvel that the book still packs a punch and maintains what made it a stand-out book from the start — its overwhelmingly positive view of the world and of the potential for skilled managers to make a profound and positive difference. The changes in this edition are both needed and welcome; the world is rapidly changing and this edition has responded in kind. Anyone who absorbs and applies the wisdom between its covers will be well prepared to take their place among the best global managers."

Allan Bird, Brodsky Professor in Global Business,
D'Amore-McKim School of Business, Northeastern University

"Since its first publication in 1988, *International Management Behavior* has been an indispensable resource for faculty teaching a wide variety of courses in international management, cross-cultural management and international organizational behavior. IMB has a number of strengths. It was one of the first texts to take a process and interactive approach to international management behavior. Its 'MBI–Map–Bridge–Integrate framework' foresaw research that was to come much later and has stood the test of time. The fact that its authors are active researchers as well as closely engaged with the world of practice makes this text current, rigorous and relevant. I recommend it unreservedly!"

Nakiye A. Boyacigiller, Professor of Management, Sabanci University,
Istanbul, Turkey, President-elect, Academy of International Business

International Management Behavior

International Management Behavior
Global and Sustainable Leadership

Seventh Edition

Henry W. Lane

Professor of International Business and Strategy, D'Amore-McKim School of Business, Northeastern University, and Professor Emeritus, Richard Ivey School of Business, University of Western Ontario

Martha L. Maznevski

Professor of Organizational Behavior and International Management, IMD, Lausanne, Switzerland

WILEY

Library of Congress Cataloging-in-Publication Data is available

A catalogue record for this book is available from the British Library.

ISBN 978-1-118-52737-5 (pbk) ISBN 978-1-118-78879-0 (ebk)

ISBN 978-1-118-78878-3 (ebk)

Set in 10/12 ITC New Baskerville Std by MPS Ltd, Chennai, India

Printed in Great Britain by TJ International Ltd, Padstow, Cornwall, UK

Dedication

To Joe DiStefano, who inspired and empowered our excitement for cross-cultural journeys. If we make a difference, it is in large part because you made a difference to us.

To all the friends who have helped me learn about their cultures, and my own.

Henry (Harry) W. Lane

To Julianna, Katie, Andrea and Hadley, to help them inspire the next generation.

Martha L. Maznevski

Contents

Acknowledgments

The seventh edition of this book has involved a major revision of material from previous editions.

With Professor DiStefano's retirement and absence from this edition, Professors Lane and Maznevski start by acknowledging his historical contribution to this book and to their careers. In 1975, Professor DiStefano interviewed Professor Lane who was a doctoral candidate at the Harvard Business School, and recruited him to Canada. He became a colleague, co-author, and friend. In 1974 at the Ivey Business School (at the time the Western Business School), Professor DiStefano started one of the first cross-cultural courses anywhere, which became the genesis of this book. He was also the Chair of Professor Maznevski's Ph.D. thesis committee. In January 2000, Professor DiStefano joined IMD in Lausanne, Switzerland, and recruited Professor Maznevski to IMD in 2001.

Another person at the University of Western Ontario who became a colleague, co-author, and friend, was Professor Don Simpson. He deserves special recognition for introducing Professor Lane to Africa and helping him begin his "voyage of discovery" into the reality of functioning in other cultures and doing business internationally.

Professors Lane and Maznevski have appreciated the support for their work on international business shown by their colleagues and research associates over the years at the Ivey Business School, Northeastern University, University of Virginia, and IMD.

Both of us owe a special debt to our professors, colleagues, and friends who shaped our interests and knowledge at Ivey. We are grateful to: Deans J. J. (Jack) Wettlaufer, C. B. (Bud) Johnston, Adrian Ryans, and Larry Tapp; Professors Jim Hatch, Terry Deutscher, and Ken Hardy; the directors of Research and Publications at the Ivey Business

School; and especially the donors of the Donald F. Hunter professorship (a Maclean Hunter endowment) and the Royal Bank professorship, which provided extra time for Professors Lane and DiStefano to undertake much of the initial work in developing this text. We all also recognize the special contribution and mentorship of the late Professor Al Mikalachki who taught us so much about change.

After the third edition Professor DiStefano moved to Hong Kong to launch the Ivey EMBA program there and acknowledges with thanks Ivey alumnus, Dr Henry Cheng, whose financial and personal support were so critical to the success of this effort and to the deepening of Professor DiStefano's understanding of Hong Kong and China.

In 1994, Professor Lane assumed responsibility for Ivey's Americas Program and that same year he began working with IPADE in Mexico and is very appreciative of the wonderful colleagues and friends he has made there over 20 years who have not only contributed to his education about Mexico and Latin America, but made it enjoyable to spend time there learning. In September 1999, Professor Lane moved to Northeastern University as the Darla and Frederick Brodsky Trustee Professor in Global Business. Professor Lane is grateful for their support and friendship.

In 1994, Professor Maznevski moved from Ivey to the McIntire School of Commerce at the University of Virginia. She thanks her colleagues there, in particular Dean Carl Zeithaml. The commitment of the school to making its programs global provided substantial support for her involvement in developing material for this book. Dean Zeithaml sponsored, both financially and with his enthusiasm, the first ION conferences and the genesis of a great network of colleagues.

In 2001, Professor Maznevski moved to IMD, and her learning and this book have been greatly influenced by her experiences there. She thanks her colleagues for their collaboration and learning adventures. As Program Director for large general management programs, of the full-time MBA, and of many programs for companies, she worked with senior executives from around the world, and accompanied them on their global development journeys.

To this list of acknowledgments we need to add a large number of people and institutions from around the world who have broadened and informed our experience: managers in both the public and private sectors; colleagues at other universities and institutes; companies who have provided access to their operations for the purpose of writing cases; and a number of former students and research assistants who worked with us to develop material for this and previous editions. Among the former research assistants, a special note of thanks is due to Professor Bill Blake of Queen's University and to Professor Lorna Wright of York University. We would also like to thank David Ager, Dan Campbell, Celia Chui, Karsten Jonsen, and David Wesley for their substantial contributions. Other previous doctoral students who contributed to the intellectual tradition in international business at Ivey and to our learning, included Paul Beamish, Neil Abramson, Shawna O'Grady, Terry Hildebrand, Professor Iris Berdrow of Bentley University, Sing Chee Ling, and Jonathan Calof.

The restructuring that has taken place in the publishing industry adds considerably to this list of acknowledgments. A series of acquisitions and reorganizations has led to our experience with six publishers and five editors during the writing of the six editions. Our sincere thanks go to Joerg Klauck who was at Methuen, Ric Kitowski who was at Nelson Canada, Rolf Janke who was at PWS-Kent and then Blackwell, and Catriona King at Blackwell. All were strong believers in, and advocates for, this book. Additionally, Rosemary Nixon who was at Blackwell has also been a strong supporter of our work in this and other books. When Wiley acquired Blackwell, Rosemary moved to Wiley and we are delighted to be continuing our relationship with her at Wiley. We also express our appreciation to colleagues who have provided the publishers, and us, with helpful critiques. To Nick Athanassiou, Bert Spector. Chris Robertson, and Jeanne McNett and Andy Savitz we say a special thanks for the reviews, suggestions, and editing which shaped this, and earlier editions.

Students and managers who have worked with our materials and colleagues who have adopted our book and have written to us with thanks and suggestions, have all helped us and others learn. To them we also add our gratitude. Professor Lane would acknowledge, in particular, Professors Nick Athanassiou, Sheila Puffer, Alexandra Roth, David Wesley and Tricia McConville who have used this book at Northeastern and the executives who have shared their experiences with us or have facilitated access to case situations: Ken Clark, Gail Ellement, Ted English, Charles Forsgard, Astrid Nielsen, Philipp Röh, and Ron Zitlow. Professor Maznevski thanks all the many executives on programs at IMD that have shared their stories and challenges.

We both warmly thank our friends and colleagues at ION, the International Organizations Network. This group has greatly facilitated and inspired our work, helped us make new friends and create new knowledge, and is always fun.

Last, but hardly least, we thank our families who have supported our learning and the publishing of what we have learned. This has meant time away from home, time spent alone writing, and time and energy devoted to the many visitors and friends from around the world who have shared our homes. All have been critical to our development. Our spouses, Anne and Brian have been more than patient; they have contributed significantly to our understanding and commitment, as have our children and grandchildren. We thank them all for their love and assistance. Notwithstanding this lengthy list of personal acknowledgments, we close with the usual caveat that we alone remain responsible for the contents of this book.

H. W. Lane
Boston, MA

M. L. Maznevski
Lausanne, Switzerland
May 2013

INTRODUCTION

The real voyage of discovery consists not in seeking new landscapes, but in having new eyes.

—*Marcel Proust*

This book is for managers like Lars, a senior German manager who has worked and lived in many countries and is now in charge of operations at a multinational technical firm, working with his teams to develop and implement global strategies; like Magdi, a senior Lebanese manager who has also worked and lived in many countries and is now in charge of an important, but challenging, country organization for a global multinational company; and like Amanda, an American senior manager with a great track record in new product development and marketing at many important Silicon Valley firms, now with direct responsibility for international operations.

The book is also for young managers like Rachna, an Indian now in Europe, globally sourcing service contracts for a US-based multinational; like Jonatas, a Brazilian now in the Middle East, optimizing supply chain for a Europe-based specialty chemicals firm selling its product to Asia; like Rich, a Canadian who returned to his home country after working abroad, to innovate new practices in the oil industry; and like Kathie, just starting her career, intrigued about international management and eager to learn what it entails.

It's also for people like Jemilah, Ed, Feena, Judy and Jim: senior leaders in global NGOs who are actively trying to help the world while simultaneously revolutionizing their industry to make aid more effective. And it is for Jesper, Mahoto, Ernest and Saskia, young managers creating innovative ways to combine aid, development, and entrepreneurship to help people help themselves in countries with developing economies.

The book is also for people like Josefine, Mads, Veronica, and other senior leaders in human resources responsible for attracting, assessing, developing, and enabling all the people who manage their organizations internationally.

This book is not just a book about global business. It is about *people who conduct business – and manage other types of organizations – in a global environment.* It discusses and explores typical situations that managers encounter: the problems and opportunities; the frustrations and rewards; the successes and failures; the decisions they must make and the actions they must take.

Global business is not an impersonal activity, and it should not be studied solely in an impersonal way. It is important to understand trade theories; to be able to weigh the pros and cons of exporting versus licensing; or to understand the advantages of a joint venture versus a wholly-owned subsidiary. But, eventually theory must give way to practice; strategizing and debating alternatives must give way to action. Working globally means interacting with colleagues, customers, and suppliers from other countries to achieve a specific outcome. We focus on these interactions, on getting things done with and through other people in an international context.

DEVELOPING INTERNATIONAL MANAGERS: RESEARCH-GROUNDED, PRAGMATICALLY-TESTED

We have developed, refined, and tested the perspectives in this book for over 40 years with undergraduates, graduate students, and practicing executives of all levels around the world. Combining conceptual knowledge and contextually based skill-building provides an effective learning package. In addition to drawing on the research of others, we have conducted our own research on the issues and skills relevant to international management, as well as how best to train global managers.

Management focus. We take a problem-solving approach to international business. International business activities are complex situations in which both business and cultural factors are often simultaneously embedded. The skills needed to cross boundaries cannot be isolated from business realities, and appreciating various and multiple influences on behavior can make a difference in outcome and performance.

Behavioral focus. The human element in managing effectively across cultures is just as important as, and sometimes more important than, the technical or functional elements. However, most managers have developed stronger technical or business skills than boundary-spanning interpersonal and cultural skills. They need to complement these strong technical backgrounds with the behavioral skills; if they don't, they may never get the opportunity to use the business or technical skills.

Process focus. Related to the behavioral orientation is a process orientation – behaving, interacting, learning, and moving forward to meet objectives. This perspective is an important contributor to success in a global market. In other words, leading well in an international setting is not just about having the right characteristics or competences, it's about the dynamics of knowing how to adapt quickly and effectively. Often, good international management is less about "finding a solution or making a decision" and more about "identifying and embarking on a process."

Intercultural focus.   The material in this text focuses primarily on the interaction between people of different cultures in work settings. This intercultural orientation is distinct from a comparative approach, in which management practices of individual countries or cultures are examined and compared. We will often report on cultural comparisons, but we will focus on what happens at the intersection. This is the interface that provides both the greatest challenges and the most interesting opportunities.

Culture-general focus.   This book is intended for a wide variety of managers and international staff who must function effectively in a global environment; therefore, we do not concentrate deeply on particular cultures, countries or regions. A culture-general perspective provides a framework within which country-specific learning can take place more rapidly as necessary. It helps to know what questions to ask and how to interpret the answers received when conducting business globally or helping others to do the same. It helps the learner become more effective at learning and adapting to other cultures. We do provide specific examples of cultures, countries and regions: not enough to take the place of in-depth culture-specific training for people who are assigned to a particular place, but enough to enhance the impact of that training.

OUTLINE OF THE BOOK: FOLLOWING THE CHALLENGES AND OPPORTUNITIES

The four parts of this book follow the main categories of challenges and opportunities we see international managers experiencing most frequently.

Part 1 is made up of Chapter 1, The Global Manager. This chapter explores the role of people who manage others in a global environment, and what makes it different from "regular" management. It introduces a global mindset, a global leadership competences model, and a set of principles for leading. These three elements set the organizing framework for the rest of the book.

Part 2 consists of three chapters that look at the individual and interpersonal sides of global management. Chapter 2 discusses culture and its effect on people and their behavior, Chapter 3 describes a model for interacting effectively across cultures, and Chapter 4 focuses on global teams and networks.

Part 3 moves the discussion from the individual to the organizational level. Chapter 5 focuses on strategy execution in a global context. Chapter 6 examines the challenge of complexity facing global managers and issues in recruiting and developing the people in this talent pool. Chapter 7 provides guidance on managing change in global organizations.

Part 4 has two chapters on competing with integrity in global business. Chapter 8 focuses on ethics at an individual level and Chapter 9 looks at corporate sustainability issues.

The chapters combine our own research and experience and that of many others. This is not a typical textbook in that we do not provide a review of all the research in the field. Other resources do that well. We focus here on the research that provides the most immediate practical guidance for managers, and present it in ways that have proven to be helpful for practice. We provide many examples throughout the book to help readers see how others have applied the lessons, and generate ideas for applying the ideas and behaviors themselves. Most of our examples come directly from the experience of managers we've worked closely with, and we've tried to capture the flavor, feeling, and tempo of these people and the places in which they live and work. They may not be as recognizable as leaders who capture headlines in the press, but we provide more behavioral and reflective insights. We find they provide great role models.

In this edition, we have not provided full-length teaching cases. If you are a professor using this book for a class or a consultant using it to develop others, please see our website www.wiley.com/go/lane7e for sample syllabi, annotated suggestions for teaching cases, and resources for teaching and developing global leaders.

Globalization means that one does not have to travel to another country to be exposed to situations of cultural diversity. For example, consider a manager in Boston who works for Genzyme which is one of the world's leading biotech companies. This company was founded in Boston in 1981 and was acquired by Sanofi SA from France in 2011. Now the American manager may be frequently travelling to France or interacting with French managers when they come to Boston. This same manager possibly interacts with a number of other local Boston companies that are also now foreign-owned. He or she may have an account with Citizens Bank (owned by the Royal Bank of Scotland Group plc) or Sovereign Bank (owned by Santander from Spain); purchase insurance from John Hancock (owned by Manulife Financial of Canada); and buy groceries from Stop & Shop (owned by Royal Ahold NV of the Netherlands). And managers from these companies are also likely to experience working with their Scottish, Canadian, Spanish and Dutch counterparts.

In countries with long histories of immigration, such as Canada, the United States, and Brazil, there is considerable diversity within the domestic workforce and many managers experience working with cultural diversity as part of their daily routine. Managers in all of these countries find the material in this book is also applicable in these situations and has been useful – without them ever having to leave their home base.

FOCUS ON THE VOYAGE

This book is based on the philosophy that learning is a life-long, continuous process. Rather than provide an illusion of mastery, we hope it stimulates and facilitates even more learning about other cultures and how to work effectively with others. For some readers, the material in this book may represent a first encounter with different cultures. Other readers may have been exposed to different cultures through previous courses or personal experience. For those with prior exposure to other people and places, the journey continues with a new level of insight. For those without prior experiences, welcome to an interesting journey!

Part 1

CHAPTER **1**

The Global Manager

It has become cliché to say that today's managers, wherever they are, must be internationally-minded. We have been saying it since the first edition of this book in 1988, and it seems to be more imperative with each year. In the twenty-first century, being a global leader is no longer a nice-to-have capability, it is a must-have for those who want to create value for their organizations. Recently we asked a group of executives from several countries, "How important is it for you to be a global leader – a leader who has expertise working effectively across countries?" Here are some typical responses:

Christine, head of a key product division in an industrial product firm's largest country market, Germany: "My customers are all in Germany and so is my team, so you would think my job is all in Germany. But our company is headquartered in Scandinavia and our plants are in several different locations around Europe. When we have challenges serving our customers, the people I need to work with are mostly outside of Germany and those are the interactions that make the biggest difference in my business. Maybe even more important, my new ideas come from outside of Germany. The German market is mature, saturated, we and the customers all know what to expect. It's when I work with people in the international arena that I learn how to build my business better within Germany."

Ho Yin, corporate director of human resources of a Singapore-based conglomerate's utility businesses: "You might expect that a business involved in generating, distributing and retailing electrical power is fundamentally local. But as we extend our reach to Australia, India, Southeast Asia and China, we need to identify and adopt the best practices in the industry worldwide. Regulators expect us to provide reliable service at competitive prices. To do this we need managers beyond our solid base of technical experts; people who are experienced at dealing with ideas and people from many countries and cultures, and who can lead in demanding circumstances in many different countries. Finding and developing such people is perhaps our biggest challenge."

Jesper, a Swedish social entrepreneur working in Kenya: "My not-for-profit provides solar-powered lamps to off-grid rural areas in Kenya to empower children to study.[1] My funders mostly come from the developed world, and I have close partnerships with colleagues in places like the US and Switzerland – individuals and companies – for this funding. The quality and price of the lamps is critical, so we ran an extensive global search and ended up with lamps sourced from China. The other part of my job is helping new investors come to Africa, both through investment funds I help to run, and providing advice for ethical business entry. My job is clearly global and I love that. The opportunities are enormous when you can bring the world together to address local challenges. It's clear to me that others are seeing those opportunities too."

Leading internationally is more complex today than it was a generation ago. At that time, "international managers" were a relatively small subset of managers, those who journeyed away from home as expatriates to do exciting things. They experienced hardship from (sometimes unexpected) foreign conditions, and rewards from generous expatriate compensation packages as well as fulfilling their need for growth and adventure.

With changes in arenas such as technology, finance, political systems, business models, air travel, and the media, most managers today work across national borders. Having a successful management career in any kind of business today requires effective international navigation. Moreover, international management today is rarely about just going from one culture to another. Typical international managers, like the executives quoted above, may travel to many different countries in any year, and frequently work with people from many different cultures at the same time. To be successful, they cannot simply learn about another culture and place, and adapt. The dynamics are much more complex.

In this chapter we discuss how the forces in the international environment are shaping the characteristics needed by global leaders. We explore what makes a leader's task more or less global, and we comment on the relationship between management and leadership. Then we review the characteristics, competences, knowledge, and skills that effective global managers need, highlighting the global mindset and competences. The last section of this chapter addresses how to become an effective global leader: how to develop the global mindset and competences, and some principles for navigating well in global complexity. We conclude by showing how the different sections of this book can help you on your personal development journey.

More and more, managers are dealing with different cultures. Companies are going global, and teams are spread across the globe. If you're head of engineering, you have to deal with divisions in Vietnam, India, China or Russia, and you have to work across cultures. You have to know how to motivate people who speak different languages, who have different cultural contexts, who have different sensitivities and habits. You have to get prepared to deal with teams who are multicultural, to work with people who do not all think the same way as you do.[2]

As we stand at the dawn of the 21st century, we must ask ourselves if we can truly manage ourselves cross-culturally. This is the principal question. A decade ago, culture was not a particular issue, but the more we advance, the more managing people of different cultures and beliefs becomes the benchmark of an efficient company. [3]

Carlos Ghosn, Chairman and CEO of Nissan Motor Company
and Chairman and CEO of Renault

GLOBALIZATION: THE SETTING FOR INTERNATIONAL MANAGEMENT BEHAVIOR

What is globalization? The Stanford Encyclopedia of Philosophy states that "the term 'globalization' has quickly become one of the most fashionable buzzwords of contemporary political and academic debate" and most often is nothing more than a synonym for the spread of classical liberal, "free market" economic policies; the spread and dominance of "Westernization," or even "Americanization" of political, economic, and cultural life; and the rise of new information technologies such as the Internet – all of which are bringing the world closer together.[4] And there is often an unarticulated assumption that globalization is good.

We should remember, however, that globalization is a process and not a destination. In *The Lexus and the Olive Tree*, Thomas Friedman pointed out that in addition to politics, economics, technology, and culture, globalization involves issues of the environment and national security. Terrorism and pollution also have "gone global" and there can be negative aspects of globalization as well as positive, the "good and bad globalization"; and globalization can spread evil as well as good.[5] On the negative side there are global criminal activities such as drugs and money laundering while on the positive there is the reduction of poverty and the increase of living standards. The Occupy movement focuses on the inequality associated with globalization, raising the voice of, in their words, "the other 99%" who are disenfranchised by globalization.[6] Therefore we must be specific when we discuss globalization – the "globalization of what?"[7]

There is also an implicit assumption that globalization and global organizations are new phenomena. By some accounts, globalization is as old as mankind and began when people started migrating out of Africa.[8] Globalization is an historical process: "Traveling short, then longer distances, migrants, merchants, and others have always taken their ideas, customs, and products into new lands. The melding, borrowing, and adaptation of outside influences can be found in many areas of human life."[9]

The basic feature of globalization is that people, countries, and organizations all around the world have become more interdependent. More activities affecting more people's lives have become more interdependent than ever before. In this book we focus primarily on the economic dimension of globalization and on companies that operate in many countries around the world and that attempt to integrate their global activities.

Recent Globalization: Transportation and Communications Connect Us

Modern globalization can be thought of as the erosion of national as well as company boundaries and the increase of economic interdependence. Trade liberalization has opened borders across which capital and products move easily. Airline travel and reliable, inexpensive communication have reduced distances and minimized the impact of physical boundaries so that corporations are able to manage far-flung operations. Alliances and networks blur the lines of organizational boundaries. The forces of deregulation, industry consolidation, and technology reshaped corporate and social landscapes. Both responding to and feeding the trend of boundary erosion, companies have been seeking to globalize.

In the early 1980s, Levitt, a pioneering observer of globalization, defined globalization as a "shift toward a more integrated and interdependent world economy . . . having two main components: the globalization of markets and the globalization of production."[10] Many academics and executives over-simplified the meaning of globalization and extrapolated it simply as "the production and distribution of products and services of a homogeneous type and quality on a worldwide basis."[11]

Most of the globalization descriptions refer to an increasing global reach but from narrow perspectives. These include the number of markets served; the global reach of the supply chain and sources of supplies; the locations in which parts of the company's value chain are located; and alliances or mergers and acquisitions to source intellectual capital (knowledge). However, such perspectives suggest that companies and executives are simply doing more of what they have always done, just in more places and with more technological sophistication. These perspectives are economic, market-oriented, and technology-oriented and although not incorrect, describe only a part of the reality of globalization.

The measures of globalization employed also tend to focus on measurable external factors such as a percentage of international sales to total sales. However, when we examine the processes of companies that globalize, the sterile statistics disappear and the people who create and manage the processes appear. The picture at the operational or "execution/make it happen" level is often much less rosy than the one provided by macro-level descriptions. The road to globalization has been littered with the debris of ill-considered mergers, acquisitions, and new market entry-attempts. Globalization is easy to talk about but difficult to do.

What exactly is a global company that operates in this new world of increased interdependence? Is it a company that has plants and subsidiaries in many countries? Or is it a company that sells its products and services around the world and derives more of its revenue from international sales than domestic sales, for example? There is no doubt that these are some of the characteristics.

However, just because a company operates in multiple locations around the world does not make it a global company. It simply means that it functions in a lot of countries. Global strategy is executed by, and global operations are managed by, people from one culture interacting with people from another country and culture. These are the managers who interface with the suppliers, alliance partners, and government officials. These also are the people who manage the plants and workforces around the world.

You don't globalize companies unless you globalize people. Think of a German company, for example, operating in many countries but whose top managers all have German passports. This is a German company operating in many countries – but not necessarily a company that has been truly globalized. Yes, a global company operates in many locations, and it also has developed a cadre of managers who have global mind-sets and understand how to operate in this world of economic, political, and cultural interdependence.

Sam Palmisano, former CEO of IBM, characterized the modern global company as a globally integrated enterprise (GIE) that "fashions its strategy, its management, and its operations in pursuit of a new goal: the integration of production and value delivery worldwide. State borders define less and less the boundaries of corporate thinking or practice."[12]

These GIEs use new technology and business models that allow them to combine functions and operations in multiple ways in "increasingly complex intercompany production networks" requiring new forms of collaboration and "high-value skills" that Palmisano said would allow managers to handle the "fluid and collaborative nature of work today."

Over two decades ago, C. K. Prahalad characterized the world of global business:

> A world where variety, complex interaction patterns among various subunits, host governments, and customers, pressures for change and stability, and the need to re-assert individual identity in a complex web of organizational relationships are the norm. This world is one beset with ambiguity and stress. Facts, emotions, anxieties, power and dependence, competition and collaboration, individual and team efforts are all present . . . Managers have to deal with these often conflicting demands simultaneously.[13]

Prahalad saw the outline of globalization and described it accurately. Although he did not use the term "complexity," he described this characteristic of globalization well. Rather than think about globalization as the proportion of trade conducted across national borders, or by some other economic or social measure, we argue that, as we talk about it in business, globalization is a manifestation of complexity and requires new ways of thinking and managing. Executives today have to be able to manage internal and external networks in a very complex environment.

Managing Globalization = Managing Complexity[14]

The last edition of this book was written just as the global economic crisis was unfolding. We fully expected that by the time we wrote this edition, the crisis would have been resolved and we would be describing the opportunities and lessons from recovery. Yet here we are in 2013 with a start-stop recession, a slow and uncertain (jobless?) US recovery, a Eurozone stuck in currency crises, and slowing growth in China. The final outcomes of the Arab Spring are not yet clear; sub-Saharan Africa's growth patterns are unsure; Latin America shows divergent patterns with different governments and challenges. Some observers, like Jean-François Rischard,[15] are pessimistic about our ability (and willingness) to resolve today's situation. Others, like Michael Spence,[16] are more optimistic that the converging rates of growth will create opportunities and can reduce inequalities. Few deny there is "new normal," and the term VUCA[17] - Volatile, Uncertain, Complex and Ambiguous, originally used by the US military to describe the post-cold war scene – has entered common usage.

Just over a decade ago we were trying to learn from managers what globalization meant to them. Economists tend to define globalization in terms of flow of goods or money or people across borders, compared to the flow within borders. But we sensed that managers experienced it a bit differently in their day-to-day operations. We spoke with managers who were working outside their home country or inside their home country, traveling a lot, or traveling little. When we asked them, "What is the effect of globalization on your management role?" the answer they shared was one that surprised us. They all responded: "It's exhausting."

When we probed further, we found that whatever level of cross-border transactions a single manager actually dealt with, the effect of a more globalized economy and society meant increased complexity in the management role. This increased complexity, in turn, meant that the traditional way of managing – often one learned in business school – was not adequate. Managers were working harder and harder to try and understand the complex forces, in order to plan and execute with any kind of predictability. The result was a feeling of being overwhelmed and yes, exhausted. Our experience with managers today suggests that this trend has continued unabated. This may be the "new normal," but most managers have not yet developed the habits or institutions to lead in it.

Interdependence: Increased Connections   How did this VUCA business environment arise? First, globalization of trade increased the *interdependence* between countries and people in those countries. We are all more connected to each other than we used to be. With the fall (or at least permeability) of barriers to cross-border flow of goods and money, events and decisions in one company or in one part of the world affect others who may be distant and seemingly unconnected with the initial event or decision. The recent financial crisis, for example, was triggered by the subprime mortgage crash in the United States and the derivatives based on it. It affected the ability of businesses as far away as South Africa to invest in improvements in manufacturing productivity. China's hunger for basic resources such as steel and wood affects the price of those commodities for all manufacturers, and affects environmental and social issues in South American countries with strong mining industries. With such high levels of interdependence, it is impossible for a manager to predict the impact of a specific action. This makes effective managerial decision-making extremely difficult.

Variety: Increased Variables and Options   Executives also face more *variety* than ever before. In many countries, the domestic workforce is becoming more diverse. For example, in Toronto, Canada, 46% of the population identifies a language other than English, French or Canadian Aboriginal as their mother tongue.[18] But workforce diversity is just one aspect of the increased variety that managers face today. With modern media and technology, both businesses and consumers have become more discerning customers, and companies must define customer segments much more carefully. Competitors, too, come with more variety in products and services. In the voice communications industry, companies like Nokia have found it difficult to respond to challenges from computer and consumer electronics firms like Apple and Samsung, and internet providers and services such as Skype, as consumers become more familiar with different ways of communicating with each other. Companies that operate in many countries face many different legal and economic environments. Developing consistent compensation policies worldwide for a company like Royal Dutch Shell, for example, is almost impossible. Making decisions and taking action as a manager are much more complicated when there are so many variables to consider.

Ambiguity: Decreased Clarity   Managers also face more *ambiguity*, or lack of clarity. First, interconnectedness and variety make it much more difficult to see cause-effect relations. What is cause and what is effect is not always clear. Why did the Euro lose a third of its value against the US dollar in the last decade?[19] Is it because of the debt crises in Greece and Portugal? The political crisis in Italy? The politicians in Germany and France not acting sooner to correct inequalities of productivity across the Eurozone? Did the falling Euro decrease consumer and investor confidence, decreasing the demand for Euros and exacerbating the problem? Or was it that the US economy just performed so much better (relatively) after the 2008 crisis? What is the effect of this relative change in positions? In theory, it should make Eurozone exports cheaper compared with their American competitors, but the factories are not seeing proportionately higher demand. Undoubtedly all of these factors are related, and there is plenty of blame to go around. However, simple cause and effect is difficult to establish.

Second, although we have more information available to us today than at any time in the past, the reliability of this information is not always clear, and we cannot always turn it into meaningful knowledge. Financial analysts give us ratings of particular companies – how do we know what information they've based those ratings on, and what should we do with the information? Customers complain to us through a website – how representative are they of all our customers? How much impact will their public complaints have on potential new customers? Again, decision-making and action are much more challenging when they are *ambiguous*, when we are not sure about the cause-effect relations or the clarity of our information.

The Multiplier Effect: Dynamic Complexity and Flux   Multiplicity x Interdependence x Ambiguity = Dynamic Complexity.[20] Tightly linked, complex global organizations operating in a tightly coupled global environment potentially become more vulnerable as

FIGURE 1.1   The complexity of globalization

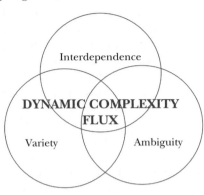

interdependence increases.[21] For example, a single email sent simultaneously to several locations in the world can not only be interpreted differently, but also forwarded to several other destinations, each generating varied interpretations and possibly actions. The increase in complexity leads to a decrease in buffers, slack resources, and autonomy of units. There also is less time to contemplate corrective action. Ambiguity makes problem diagnosis and action planning difficult. Problems appear and must be resolved. "Now" has become the primary unit of time in the world of global managers.

As if that weren't enough, the configuration of our complex environment is always shifting and changing. Even if you could take a snapshot today of the interdependence, variety, and information available and study it enough to understand and make clear decisions, tomorrow would be different. Decisions you made yesterday may not be ideal today or tomorrow. We refer to this as *flux* because it represents rapid unpredictable change in many directions, not predictable change in a few dimensions.

It is no wonder that managers feel overwhelmed by globalization, whether or not they are directly involved in cross-border transactions! This environmental complexity is depicted in Figure 1.1.

Managing Complexity: Hercules Meets Buddha

How do you manage this level of complexity in the environment? The way to manage the complexity of globalization is by using the capacity that is in people to manage it themselves. The most complex thing in any organization is people: human brains and the relationships among people. When managers simplify a few key control processes, such as the organizational structure, the company values, goals and strategy, and some key performance indicators, they can "let go" and empower people to manage complexity. We call the technique "Hercules meets Buddha."[22]

The Herculean mode in which the hero is pitted against external forces, originated in Greece, the cradle of Western rational thought. Hercules was given "stretch goals"; planned his forays; assembled resources; and used direct action, force and strength to overcome obstacles and accomplish his objectives. In modern terms it is similar to a control model of management that encourages the use of comparison, measurement, categorization, and analysis in understanding the world before taking action.[23] Such an analytic, strength-based, control mode of thinking and acting may not be sufficient to respond to globalization pressures since not everything is under our control.

Managers, especially those from the West, tend to have well-developed knowledge and skills about organization and control. The management of people in a complex setting like globalization presents much more of a challenge; however, as we have seen in our research on complexity, it is absolutely critical to the success of organizations today. The Eastern way of "seeing and understanding" as presented in Buddhism and Taoism seeks to achieve understanding of a world in which all things and events are interrelated and in which change is constant and natural. Understanding and using the natural processes that exist, a flow mode of operating, will make dealing with complexity more manageable. Global managers could benefit from understanding both Hercules and Buddha.

MANAGING PEOPLE ACROSS BORDERS: A JOB DESCRIPTION

In this section, we look at the role of a global (or international) manager (or leader): what makes it different from the job of someone doing the same things in a single country? We explore the context of globalization, the tasks an international manager is responsible for, and some basic definitions.

Not all Jobs are Equally Global

While it is clear that most managers' jobs have become more global, it is also true that some jobs are more global than others. The more global a job or mandate, the more it requires global leadership and the kinds of management competences and perspectives addressed in this book.

A leader's role is more global to the extent that it requires more:[24]

- Working with colleagues from other countries.
- Interacting with external clients from other countries.
- Interacting with internal clients from other countries.
- Speaking a language other than their mother tongue at work.
- Supervising employees who are of different nationalities.
- Developing a strategic business plan on a worldwide basis.

- Managing a budget on a worldwide basis.

- Negotiating in other countries or with people from other countries.

- Managing foreign suppliers or vendors.

- Managing risk on a worldwide basis.

Mendenhall and colleagues summarized these characteristics into three main dimensions, showing that a job and role is more global to the extent that it:

1   Takes place in a highly complex context. The more interdependence, variety, ambiguity, and flux a manager faces, the more global the position.

2   Includes a higher flow of boundary-spanning. The more a leader must interact with people across boundaries (especially cultural boundaries), with more types of information, and in more ways, the more global the position.

3   Requires spatio-temporal presence. The more a leader must be physically present in different cultural contexts, the more global the position.[25]

If we return to the managers who have appeared so far in this chapter, all of them are global leaders. That is, their role involves all three characteristics of a complex context, a high flow of boundary-spanning, and spatio-temporal presence across cultures, and they conduct many if not all of the list of global tasks. Carlos Ghosn, the Chairman and CEO of Renault and Nissan, has a highly global job. He conducts all ten of the global tasks regularly, and his job can be summarized as high on all three of the global dimensions. Jesper, the social entrepreneur living in Kenya, has a moderately high global job – his roles are high on all of the three global dimensions, and he conducts seven of the ten global tasks. Christine has a less global role – her role is moderately high on the first two dimensions above and lower on spatio-temporal presence, and she regularly engages in five of the ten global tasks. The global leadership competences and perspectives we will discuss are necessary for Carlos Ghosn and for Jesper; for Christine, they are less necessary, but they do create opportunities.

Glass Half Empty or Half Full?

While a great deal of research and writing about global business focuses on opportunities, most research and writing about global leadership focuses on challenges to overcome. Expanding strategy over borders provides opportunities for scale and scope that are not possible domestically, no matter how big your home market. Research on global strategy looks at which type of Foreign Direct Investment (FDI) is best for different situations, what is the optimum distribution of subsidiaries, managing supply chain and distributed operations to create the best value, and so on. The "why" of doing business internationally is easy, and global business strategy research attempts to answer questions about ideal configurations. But even the strategy literature admits that it is difficult to capture those opportunities. Implementing global strategies is easier said than done.

Leading across boundaries is more difficult than leading within boundaries, there is no question about that. Learning to overcome the challenges is the crux of global leadership. Most of the literature on global leadership addresses those challenges. But in addition to the opportunity to implement global strategies effectively and capture their benefits, there are many other positive sides of global leadership.[26] For example, not only are multicultural teams more creative than culturally homogeneous teams, but people are more satisfied working in multicultural teams than in culturally homogeneous teams.[27] People with a high need to learn and develop find the cross-cultural environment provides them with opportunities to question their assumptions and grow as individuals. Many managers find enormous joy in discovering that underneath the variety of cultural and institutional differences of people around the world, we share a basic humanity. These positive sides of international management are less tangible or rational than the challenges, but they are equally important.

Manager or Leader? International or Global?

In this book, we usually use these pairs of terms interchangeably.

The debate about management vs leadership is an important one conceptually, and when it was first raised by Zaleznik in 1977 it was helpful to identify the importance of taking responsibility, setting direction, and inspiring people (leadership) in addition to executing organizational mandates (management).[28] This debate generated an acknowledgement that those who lead businesses should include values, motivation, and other aspects of non-rational leadership in their agendas. Bennis and Nanus put it simply in 1985, "Managers do things right, leaders do the right things."[29] However, as Mintzberg pointed out 20 years later, we cannot lose sight of the fact that even leaders need to get things done, responsible leaders do it well, and this requires good management.[30] In reality, the *person* in the *role* of being responsible for mandates across borders must *both* lead and manage, more often than not at the same time. We therefore use the terms manager and leader interchangeably, and when it is important to specify which competences or perspectives are important for which aspects of the role, we do so carefully.

The distinction between global and international has also been the subject of much conceptual debate, both in the literature and in companies. In global strategy, it often differentiates an approach of having the same product or services everywhere (global) from one that is highly adapted to local conditions (multi-domestic or international).[31] This is often reflected in structures that are highly centralized or coordinated (global) versus ones that are more decentralized (international, multi-domestic).[32] And it is sometimes used as a way to raise awareness of potential opportunities in management discussions, like, "Yes, we operate in many countries, and that makes us international. But our managers don't yet see how they can learn from each other across those countries, and even serve clients who cross borders with new services that we develop from the synergies we see. That would make us truly global." For the purposes of our discussion, it is more important to define globalization as complexity, and identify different levels of "global" by the type of task and extent of global context, and it is less important to distinguish global from international. From the perspective of the *person* in the *role* of being responsible for mandates across borders, all of these situations involve working with people and getting things done across boundaries, and the focus of this book is those interpersonal and organizational dynamics. We therefore tend to use global and international interchangeably, and specify the nature of the boundaries and context involved and identify differences in approach as appropriate.

SUPERHERO OR ORDINARY HUMAN? WHAT DOES IT TAKE TO LEAD ACROSS BORDERS?

Because of its importance to business, research on global leadership has skyrocketed in recent years, and many studies have been published identifying the skills that global leaders need.[33] In fact, the lists are so long (up to 250 competences!), it seems that only a superhero can be a global leader. However, there are ways of sorting out the most important criteria, and we will share a framework here that we think best captures the most important capabilities. The Pyramid Model of Global Leadership developed by Bird and Osland summarizes the most important skills and knowledge, and illustrates how they build on each other.[34] In their view, global managerial expertise is a constellation of traits, attitudes and skills or what they call "global competencies." Their model of global competencies is shown in Figure 1.2. Each level presumes and builds on the level below, and the more global a job is, the more it requires sophisticated competences in the higher levels of the pyramid.

The foundational level is *Global Business Knowledge*. This is deep knowledge about the business a manager is in, and how that business creates value. It also includes knowledge about the political, economic, social, and technical environment. This foundational knowledge is necessary before any of the next steps.

The next level identifies *Threshold Traits*. Knowledge will lie dormant without the personal predisposition to use it. Among the myriad of personality traits associated with effectiveness, four stand out as differentiating people who are effective in global settings from those who are less effective: integrity, humility, curiosity, and resilience. Integrity is having a firm set of values associated with honesty and transparency, and being true to those values. Humility is recognizing that knowledge and skills are widely distributed, and that others know and can do things that you, yourself, may not. Humility opens one to accept differences and different ways of doing things. Curiosity is active motivation to know things one does not already know. While humility creates openness, curiosity drives action to learn more, and to experiment with different ways of creating value. Finally, resilience is the ability to persevere in the face of challenges and difficulties. This resides partly in the manager's own personality, and partly in the extent to which the manager has a support network of family, friends, and/or colleagues.

The next level of the pyramid is an important set of *Attitudes and Orientations* – ways of seeing the world and the task of international management. The basic traits suggest potential within an individual; attitudes and orientations guide that potential so the

FIGURE 1.2   Global competencies model

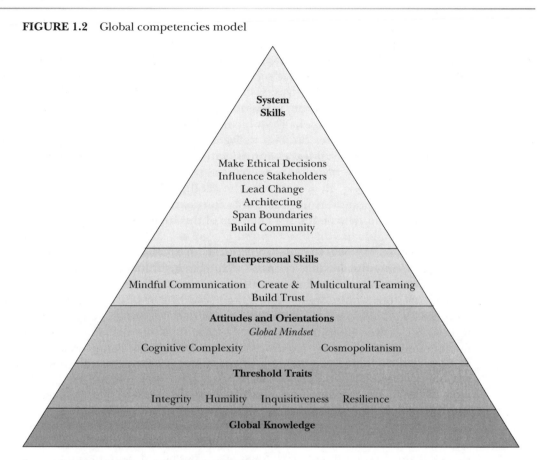

Source: Reproduced with permission of John Wiley & Sons

individual sees opportunities. The most important is a global mindset, or the tendency and ability to see and understand the world differently than one has been conditioned to see and understand it, in other words a view from outside of one's own borders. Two attitudes and orientations contribute to developing a global mindset. Cognitive complexity is the ability to see a situation from multiple perspectives, to see connections among the perspectives, and to build new connections with existing and new information. Cosmopolitanism is having a positive attitude towards people, things, and perspectives from other parts of the world. For example, people who are cosmopolitan are more likely to have close friends who are from countries other than their own. We address the global mindset in more detail later in the next section of this chapter.

Seeing opportunities in the business, the context, and other people only takes a leader so far. With skills, the leader can work with others to develop ideas further and implement them. The three most important *Interpersonal Skills* for global leaders are mindful communication, building trust, and multicultural teaming. Mindful communication is paying attention to how you communicate with others, especially those who are different, and adapting your communication as necessary in order to ensure that meaning is transmitted the way people intend. This includes both sending messages (speaking, writing and non-verbal acts) and receiving them (listening, reading and observing the behavior of others). Building trust is creating a relationship where both (or all) parties believe that the other(s) will act with good intentions for the relationship, and can make decisions on each other's behalf. Multicultural teaming is working effectively with people from different cultures on joint deliverables. Many other interpersonal skills are of course important to global leadership effectiveness, such as negotiation and conflict resolution. However, if a manager is adept at mindful communication, building trust, and multicultural teaming, then generally these other skills will follow. The reverse is not necessarily true – one can negotiate solutions and resolve conflicts without increasing trust, for example. The next three chapters of this book focus on interpersonal skills.

Finally, a set of six *Systems Skills* are critical for global leaders: spanning boundaries, building community, leading change, architecting, influencing stakeholders, and ethical decision-making. Boundary-spanning is working effectively across countries, organizations, divisions within organizations, and so on. It involves using all of the skills and attitudes identified in lower parts of the model to create insights and synergies across different perspectives. Building community is creating a sense of identity and joint commitment among a group of people distributed across different countries and units. Leading change effectively is about helping an organization through different ways of doing things, while creating capabilities for adapting to further change. Architecting is designing and implementing organizational structures and systems that facilitate the organization. Influencing stakeholders is an important part of any leadership role, more complex in a global role, because there is more variety of stakeholders with different interests and different contexts. Ethical decision-making is about making and implementing decisions that take into account the long-term benefit of individuals and society.

We believe these systems skills are the most important part of global leadership, recognizing that they rest on the levels below. But international managers find much less guidance for these systems skills than for the levels below. We take a systems approach throughout this book, and the third and fourth sections address them specifically. Table 1.1 presents a summary of the global competences.

Global Managing Starts with a Global Mindset

In this book, we assume that the reader has a certain level of global business knowledge and is developing more knowledge and skill. We also assume that the basic traits are given. We focus on the upper levels of the pyramid, starting here with the global mindset.

As implied by the higher-level competences, international managers must learn how to function as effectively in other contexts as they do in their own country, and to build bridges across the world by leveraging both similarities and differences. In the broadest

TABLE 1.1   Global leadership competencies descriptions

Level	Competency	Description
Threshold Traits	Integrity	Adherence to moral and ethical principles; soundness of moral character; honesty
	Humility	A willingness to learn from others and not assume that one has all the answers
	Inquisitiveness	An interest in learning; questioning; curious about other people and cultures
	Resilience	Capable of surviving under unfavorable conditions; resistance to stress; emotionally resilient
Attitudes & Orientations: Global Mindset	Cognitive complexity	Ability to balance contradictions and ambiguities; ability to view a situation from many ways and with many connections
	Cosmopolitanism	External orientation; free from local, provincial, or national ideas or prejudices; at home everywhere
Interpersonal Skills	Mindful communication	Culturally appropriate and skillful communication
	Create and build trust	Ability to inspire confidence in the certainty of future actions
	Multicultural teaming	Ability to lead and work effectively in multicultural teams, including geographically distributed teams
System Skills	Build community	Ability to bring the members of heterogeneous groups together to act in concert
	Span boundaries	Creating and maintaining linkages that integrate and coordinate across organizational boundaries
	Architect	Build organizational structures and processes that facilitate effective global interactions
	Lead change	Lead individuals, teams and organizations to new ways of doing things, build capacity to learn and adapt.
	Influence stakeholders	Consider multiple, often conflicting stakeholder needs; make decisions taking them into account; influence them towards alignment
	Making ethical decisions	Adhere to accepted standards of behavior; Identify a clear and strong set of values and act according to them.

terms, this means reorganizing the way they think as a manager. As one executive put it, "to think globally really requires an alteration of our mind-set." Thinking globally means extending concepts and models from one-to-one relationships (we to them) to holding multiple realities and relationships in mind simultaneously, and then acting skillfully on this more complex reality.

At the heart of the global mindset is the ability to see and understand the world differently than one has been conditioned to see and understand it. It is a meta-capability that permits an individual to function successfully in new and unknown situations and to integrate this new understanding with other existing skills and knowledge bases.

A global mindset enables a person to adapt to the changing needs of global business. It is a way of organizing a set of attitudes and skills for developing and acting on knowledge in a dynamic world. A global mindset incorporates knowledge and openness about working across cultures, and about implementing business across strategic complexity.[35] We define a global mindset like this:

> A global mindset is the capacity to analyze situations and develop criteria for personal and business performance that are independent from the assumptions of a single country, culture or context; and to implement those criteria appropriately in different countries, cultures and contexts.

For example, one company was implementing self-managed teams throughout the organization for its new modular-based production facilities. In its dynamic and interdependent environment, the company believed it was important to have decision-making authority with the people who had the most immediate information to make the decisions, and who had to implement the decisions. The company developed a model of how self-managed teams should work; pilot-tested it in their home country; then rolled out the new structure around the world. However, it met with resistance. In many parts of the world, the idea of teams managing themselves, without a specific boss to lead them, is completely unheard of. Some plant managers pushed through the self-managed teams program to greater and greater dissatisfaction; others gave up and just kept the more rigid and hierarchical teams.

Some managers, however, did something a bit different. They looked at the two most important criteria for identifying who should make a decision in this new manufacturing context: the people who have the information, and the people who have to implement it. They also realized that manufacturing would not achieve its potential unless there was more interdependence among the various parts of the process. Then they questioned whether the only way to accomplish this was the self-managed team model that headquarters dictated. They met with their managers and teams, and developed a way to achieve the required working relationships and decision processes that fitted with the local teams' preferences and context. In some cases this had more hierarchy, in others it had fewer specific roles and more fluidity, and still others had more individual responsibility. In all cases, it achieved the performance goals.

These last managers were working with a global mindset. They were able to separate performance criteria, like "people with the information make the decisions," from culturally influenced contextual preferences, like "self-managed teams." Then they found a way to achieve the performance criteria in different contexts.

Components and Domains of a Global Mindset   The crux of developing a global mindset is achieving self-awareness and other-awareness, and awareness of the relationship between context and characteristics of the self and others. How much of my behavior is "me" and how much of it is influenced by my context? Or, more appropriately, *when* and *how* is my behavior more or less influenced by my context? When and how is this the case

TABLE 1.2 Domains of a global mindset

	Individual	*Organizational*
Self	**Type 1: Myself** Understand myself and how who I am is associated with the context I am in.	**Type 3: Own organizations** Understand my own organizations and how their characteristics and effectiveness are associated with the context we are in.
Other	**Type 2: Others** Understand how characteristics of people from other countries and cultures are associated with the contexts they are in.	**Type 4: Other organizations** Understand how characteristics and effectiveness of organizations from other countries and cultures are associated with the contexts they are in.

for others? In business, we need this understanding both about ourselves and others as individuals, and ourselves and others in social groups, especially organizations.

As identified above, two orientations that characterize a global mindset are cognitive complexity and cosmopolitanism.[36] These orientations help to develop four types of knowledge in the domains in which a global mindset operates, shown in Table 1.2.

Type 1: Knowledge about Self. A global mindset incorporates a concept of self, both as an individual and as part of an organization. We need to acknowledge and understand what it is about our mindset that has been shaped by our own context.

A critical part of context that influences self is culture, and a global mindset should include sophisticated knowledge about culture. Culture is an implicit agreement among a group of people concerning what people's actions mean. It is their list of shoulds and oughts for life or, as Hofstede described it, the collective programming of the mind that distinguishes one group from another.[37] As Brannen has pointed out, we should not use "nation as a cognate for culture."[38] Gender, age, religion, or region of a country, for example, can be considered cultures, and a person can be a member of many cultures simultaneously. Culture is often hidden from members of the culture: we rarely examine our own values or context in the normal course of doing things – it is there, taken for granted as the foundation. To paraphrase Edward T. Hall, culture is like air to us, all around and necessary for survival but usually not noticed. Hall observed:

> [Culture] is a mold in which we are all cast, and it controls our daily lives in many unsuspected ways . . . Culture hides much more than it reveals, and strangely enough what it hides, it hides most effectively from its own participants. Years of study have convinced me that the real job is not to understand foreign culture but to understand our own.[39]

Becoming aware of the influence of culture on one's self can be both uncomfortable and difficult. But the ability to "see" it and to examine it is critical to developing an effective global mindset.

Type 2: Knowledge about Others. Of course, different contexts create different assumptions and value systems. This is the more obvious part about cultural differences. It is easy to see people from different cultures perceive the same situation differently; interpret what they notice differently; evaluate the situation differently; and take different actions. A global mindset means going beyond these superficial observations and understanding the deeper nature and impact of these differences.

Type 3: Knowledge about Own Organization. Similarly, a global mindset requires understanding how the organizations of which we are a part (families, peer groups, institutions, companies) are influenced by their context. Most companies have a particular administrative heritage that has evolved within the culture of their home countries. This means that a potential cultural bias may exist in their strategy, systems and practices – "the way things are done in the headquarters' home country."

Hofstede reminded us that "theories reflect the cultural environment in which they were written."[40] Management concepts and practices are explained by theories regarding organization, motivation, and leadership. Therefore, theories of management systems and management practices may work well in the culture that developed them because they are based on local cultural assumptions and paradigms about the right way to manage.

Type 4: Knowledge about Other Organizations. Knowledge about other organizations and the relationship with their context allow a manager to adapt continually to business and contextual contingencies. This is what helps the manager identify criteria for performance that can be universally applied, and then adapt them to different contexts. For example, a human resource system that provides collective performance bonuses in Mexico and individual performance bonuses in the United States might fit with cultural preferences in those countries and encourage high performance today. However, a human resource system dedicated to "motivating all employees to perform well, whatever their background or preferences" will always be subject to adaptation and will encourage high performance into the future.[41]

Developing Global Mindsets in Theory and Practice   A global mindset is not something innate, it can be learned. However, it cannot be developed by simply reading a book on an airplane or by being lectured about in a classroom. It has to be shaped or developed, which implies changes have to take place.

A global mindset is a specific type of mental framework, or cognitive schema, for organizing information, in other words, a worldview. Schemas influence what we notice and what meaning we attribute to perceptions and guide the actions in the world around us.[42] Schemas are simple at first and become more complex with greater experience.[43] This development of more complex schemas allows a person to process enormous amounts of information and to see patterns without getting lost in the detail. There is a difference in the way that expert and novice global managers think, as shown by Osland and Bird:

When entering into a new situation [experts] notice more and different types of cues, they interpret those cues differently, they choose from a different, wider range of appropriate actions than do novices, and then they execute/implement their chosen course of action at higher levels than do novices. In the case of global managers, these differences between novices and experts are magnified . . .

[As] they become more competent, they recognize complexity and a larger set of cues. They are able to discern which cues are the most important and are able to move beyond strict adherence to rules and to think in terms of trade-offs. On attaining the expert stage, they can read situations without rational thought – they diagnose the situation unconsciously and respond intuitively because over the years they have developed the holistic recognition or mental maps that allow for effortless framing and reframing of strategies and quick adaptation.[44]

Once a schema, or mindset, exists, it changes through one of two processes – assimilation or accommodation.[45] In assimilation, new information is seen to be consistent with the schema and is incorporated readily, perhaps refining the details of the schema. In accommodation, new information contradicts the schema to the extent that the schema itself is changed. In organizational learning, these processes have been referred to as single-loop and double-loop learning[46] and evolutionary and revolutionary change.[47] Good learning maximizes both processes.

Assimilation is the easier of these two processes. When perceptions are consistent with assumptions, people don't need to question assumptions, they can simply "bolt on" new knowledge. For example, Jack, a US manager in a consumer products firm, learned that people are motivated by individual monetary incentives such as bonus schemes and commissions. He implemented incentives to influence his salespeople's focus on specific products in the portfolio – one shampoo brand this season, a shower gel product next season. The results were immediate, sales in the right categories went up, and his knowledge was reinforced through assimilation.

Accommodation is a much more difficult and uncomfortable process. When people encounter something that contradicts existing assumptions, they experience "cognitive dissonance," a feeling of imbalance. People try to reduce the imbalance to achieve consistency again by either changing perceptions of the evidence to match the assumptions (call into question the other), or by changing assumptions to match the evidence (call into question ourselves). People are more inclined to invoke the first method than the second; it requires a great deal less energy, is reinforced by others who hold the same assumptions, and is less confusing. The other option, altering one's own assumptions, unfortunately is usually a less chosen alternative.

After several years of success, Jack moved to his company's Norwegian subsidiary. But when he implemented his trusted incentive schemes and bonuses, he did not see corresponding increases in sales of the desired products. Why not?

At first I thought there was something wrong with the salespeople. I knew the incentive schemes and bonuses always work, so it must have been the local salespeople that created the problem. I started to think about how to fix that – maybe I had the wrong staff? Then I started to wonder maybe, just maybe, they motivated salespeople differently here. I began asking my Norwegian colleagues how they influenced salespeople to change their focus in their portfolios. The sales managers told me that they just talk with them, ask them questions, and then sales change to the right things. This sounded crazy to me, but they were getting results, so I started sitting in on the discussions to see what was going on. I saw what I thought was a very complex process of managers discussing the market with each salesperson, and combining the salesperson's advice with the manager's own expertise, to kind of emerge to an agreement about what to sell. It seemed that the Norwegian salespeople – in our company at least – were more motivated to change by having their expertise valued, than by financial incentives. It took me a while, but I learned to work with my salespeople in this way, and then I began to wonder if this approach would also work back in the US. I'll sure try combining it with traditional methods when I go back.

Jack's response is an accommodation response – questioning your assumptions and adjusting the schema itself.

To learn through accommodation, the manager must be able to articulate her current schema accurately. She must realize that a current schema exists to shape information processing; only with this knowledge can she identify its limits and address them with a new structure. Feedback is critical for learning through accommodation. A learner best judges the appropriateness of his or her schema if the impact of the schema is clearly seen.[48] This is why experiential learning is generally so much more effective than passive knowledge acquisition: the experience usually provides immediate feedback.[49]

Developing your Own Global Mindset   First, it requires active learning. You have to engage problems where you must assess the situation, see options, make decisions, implement actions, and experience feedback. Second, it requires mindfulness, or paying close attention to your own reactions and to what is happening in the environment.

You will become aware of how your assumptions and frameworks shape perceptions, values and behavior only as you confront different sets of assumptions guiding the views and practices of others. If you are exposed to new experiences under the right circumstances, part of your response may include an examination of your own guiding values and theories of management – the beginning of developing a global mindset. You may find that your existing frameworks are incomplete or are disconfirmed because you did not see the whole picture or could only see it from a narrow point of view. The use of case studies, experiential exercises and the facilitation of personal experiences in group settings are useful tools and techniques. The educational experience is also richer and can have a greater impact if it also includes a diverse set of participants.

As you go through the material in this book, focus both on building awareness of yourself in your own context, as well as learning about others in their contexts. Question your assumptions and those of others, and test the application of your knowledge in different contexts. Ask people you work with questions – questions you may not have thought of before. Pay attention to surprises, both as you read the book and as you ask questions and engage with others. Surprise is an indicator that you had hidden assumptions, it is an opportunity to identify them. These actions will help you build a global mindset. They will extend your repertoire of behaviors and enrich your personal experience of the world.

Opportunities for Global Managers

Poul, a Danish senior executive in charge of integrating a Chinese acquisition into his company, told us:

> Global leadership isn't just about overcoming the challenges. There are lots of those of course. More importantly it's about the opportunities. The global environment creates more opportunities than a domestic one – opportunities for growth, innovation, learning. My motivation for becoming a better global leader is to be able to find and take advantage of those opportunities.

Poul's company is facing a shortage of engineers in its European operations. He believes that the acquisition in China might open the door to a new source of talent – engineers from China coming to Europe. But he is not sure his organization is ready for that yet, and he is working on developing ways to increase his company's global leadership even in its home country.

In this chapter, we have acknowledged that today's business environment is highly complex, and the trends creating the complexity are accelerating. Global leadership is about leading across countries, and it is also about leading for opportunities related to globalization within a single country. Success in such an environment means leading people to achieve results. Global leaders must have a global mindset – a way of organizing knowledge to create openness to new ways of thinking and acting about personal and business effectiveness. Global leaders must also have a set of competencies, including interpersonal and systems skills. The remaining chapters of this book help to develop these global mindset and leadership skills.

Notes

1   GiveWatts, www.givewatts.org

2   Ghosn, C. Quoted in Stahl, G. K. and Brannen, M. Y., "Building Cross-Cultural Leadership Competence: An Interview With Carlos Ghosn," *Academy of Management Learning and Education*, 2013.

3   Ghosn, C., Khazanah Global Lecture Series, 21 March 2007. Published by Khazanah Nasional (Malaysia), *Khazanah Merdeka Series: A Year in Pictures 2007–2008*, 102.

4   Scheuerman, W., "Globalization," *The Stanford Encyclopedia of Philosophy (Summer 2010 Edition)*, Edward N. Zalta (ed.), http://plato.stanford.edu/archives/sum2010/entries/globalization/.

5   Temu, P. E., *The Unspoken Truth About Globalization: Eight Essays* (Lincoln, NE: iUniverse, 2005) 5, 7.

6   http://www.occupytogether.org/. Accessed May 3, 2013.

7   Temu, P. E., *op. cit.*, at 5.

8   Chanda, N., *Bound Together: How Traders, Preachers, Adventurers, and Warriors Shaped Globalization* (New Haven CN: Yale University Press, 2007).

9   http://yaleglobal.yale.edu/about/history.jsp. Accessed March 15, 2013.

10 Hill, C., *International Business: Competing in the Global Marketplace,* 3rd edn. (Irwin McGraw-Hill, 2000) 5.

11 Rugman, A. M. and Hodgetts, R. M., *International Business: A Strategic Management Approach,* 2nd edn. (Financial Times Prentice Hall, 2000) 438.

12 Palmisano, S., "The Globally Integrated Enterprise," *Foreign Affairs,* 85(3) (May/June 2006) 127–136. See also "A Bigger World: A special report on globalization," *The Economist,* September 20, 2008, 12.

13 Prahalad, C. K., "Globalization: The intellectual and managerial challenges," *Human Resource Management,* 29(1) (1990) 30.

14 This section relies greatly on perspectives originally published by Lane, H. W., Maznevski, M. L., and Mendenhall, M, "Globalization: Hercules meets Buddha," in Lane, H. W., Maznevski, M. L., Mendenhall, M. and McNett, J. M. (eds.), *Blackwell Handbook of Global Management: A Guide to Managing Complexity* (Blackwell Publishers, 2004).

15 Rischard, J-F., *High Noon: Twenty Global Problems, Twenty Years to Solve Them* (Basic Books, 2003).

16 Spence, M., *The Next Convergence: The Future of Economic Growth in a Multispeed World* (New York: Farrar, Straus and Giroux, 2011).

17 ASTD, "Developing leaders in a VUCA environment," February 19, 2013. http://www.astd.org/Publications/Blogs/ASTD-Blog/2013/02/Developing-Leaders-in-a-VUCA-Environment. Accessed April 26, 2013.

18 Statistics Canada, 2011 Census Information, released January 2013. http://www12.statcan.gc.ca/census-recensement/2011/geo/map-carte/ref/thematic-thematiques-index-eng.cfm?TABID=1#tabs1_3, accessed April 15, 2013.

19 Average of USD 1.09 per Euro, January 1 2000 to January 1 2003. Average of USD 0.75 per Euro January 1 2010 to January 1 2013. http://www.oanda.com/currency/historical-rates/.

20 Senge, P., *The Fifth Discipline* (Doubleday, 1990).

21 Weick, K. E. and Van Orden, P., "Organizing on a Global Scale: A Research and Teaching Agenda," *Human Resource Management,* 29(1) (Spring 1990) 49–61.

22 For a more in-depth discussion of this see "Globalization: Hercules Meets Buddha," in Lane, H. W., Maznevski, M. L., Mendenhall, M. and McNett, J. M. (eds.), *Blackwell Handbook of Global Management: A Guide to Managing Global Complexity,* n. 14 above.

23 Capra, F., *The Tao of Physics* (Bantam Books, 1984).

24 Caligiuri, P. M., "Developing global leaders," *Human Resource Management Review,* 16 (2006) 219–228. Caligiuri, P. and Tarique, I., "Predicting effectiveness in global leadership activities," *Journal of World Business,* 44 (2009) 336–346.

25 Mendenhall, M. E., Reiche, B. S., Bird, A., and Osland, J. S., "Defining the 'global' in global leadership," *Journal of World Business,* 47(4) (2012).

26 Stahl, G., Mäkelä, K., Zander, L., and Maznevski, M., "A look at the bright side of multicultural team diversity," *Scandinavian Journal of Management,* 26(4) (2010) 439–447.

27 Stahl, G. K., Maznevski, M. L., Voigt, A., and Jonsen, K., "Unraveling the effects of cultural diversity in teams: A meta-analysis of research on multicultural work groups," *Journal of International Business Studies*, 41 (2010) 690–709.

28 Zaleznik, A., "Managers and leaders: Are they different?" *Harvard Business Review* (1977), reprinted in January 2004 (74–81) in the "Best of HBR" series.

29 Bennis, W. and Nanus, B., *Leaders: The Strategies for Taking Charge* (New York: Harper and Row, 1985).

30 Mintzberg, H., *Managers not MBAs: A Hard Look at the Soft Practice of Managing and Management Development* (San Francisco: Berrett-Koehler Publishers 2005).

31 Bartlett, C. A. and Ghoshal, S., *Managing Across Borders: The Transnational Solution* (Harvard Business Press, 2002).

32 Bartlett and Ghoshal, *op. cit.*

33 Mendenhall, M. E., Osland, J. S., Bird, A., Oddou, G. R., Maznevski, M. L., Stevens, M. J., and Stahl, G. K, *Global Leadership*, 2nd edn. (Routledge, 2013). This book has the most extensive and comprehensive review published of global leadership literature.

34 Bird, A., and Osland, J., "Global Competencies," in Lane, H. W., Maznevski, M. L., Mendenhall, M. and McNett, J. M. (eds.), *Blackwell Handbook of Global Management: A Guide to Managing Complexity* (Blackwell Publishers, 2004). Updated in Osland, J., "An overview of the global leadership literature," in Mendenhall et al., *Global Leadership*, 2nd edn. (Routledge, 2013) Chapter 3.

35 Levy, O., Beechler, S., Taylor, S., and Boyacigiller, N., "What do we talk about when we talk about 'global mindset': Managerial cognition in multinational corporations," *Journal of International Business Studies*, 38 (2007) 231–258.

36 Ibid. See also "The Crucial Yet Illusive Global Mindset," Levy, O., Beechler, S., Taylor, S., and Boyacigiller, N., *Blackwell Handbook of Global Management: A Guide to Managing* Complexity (Blackwell Publishers, 2004).

37 Hofstede, G., *Culture's Consequences* (Thousand Oaks, CA: Sage, 1980).

38 Brannen, M. Y., "The Many Faces of Cultural Data," AIB Newsletter, First Quarter 1999. See also Tung, R. L., "The cross-cultural research imperative: the need to balance cross-national and intra-national diversity," *Journal of International Business Studies*, 39 (2008) 41–46.

39 Hall, E. T., *The Silent Language* (Garden City, NY: Doubleday and Company, 1959) (Anchor Books, paperback edition, 1973).

40 Geert Hofstede, "Motivation, Leadership, and Organization: Do American Theories Apply Abroad?" *Organizational Dynamics*, 8(2) (1980) Summer: 50.

41 Lane, H. W., DiStefano, J. J. and Maznevski, M. L., *International Management Behavior*, 5th edn. (Oxford, UK: Blackwell, 2006).

42 Lord, R. G., and Foti, R. J., "Schema theories, information processing, and organizational behaviour," in H. P. Sims Jr. and D. A. Gioia, *The Thinking Organization* (San Francisco: Jossey-Bass Publishers, 1986) 20–48. See also Rhinesmith, S. H., "Global mindsets for global managers," *Training and Development*, 46(10) (1992) 63–69.

43 Lord and Foti, *op. cit.*, See also Salancik, G. R., and Porac, J. F., "Distilled ideologies: Values derived from causal reasoning in complex environments," in H. P. Sims Jr. and D. A. Gioia, *The Thinking Organization*, (San Francisco: Jossey-Bass Publishers, 1986) 75–101.

44 *The Blackwell Handbook of Global Management: A Guide to Managing Complexity*, *op. cit.*, 58.

45 Furth, H. G., *Piaget for Teachers* (Englewood Cliffs, NJ: Prentice Hall, 1970).

46 Argyris, C. and Schon, D. A., *Organizational Learning: A Theory of Action Perspective* (Reading, MA: Addison-Wesley, 1978).

47 Gersick, C. J. G., "Revolutionary change theories: A multi-level exploration of the punctuated equilibrium paradigm," *Academy of Management Review,* 16(1) (1991) 10–36.

48 Argyris, C. and Schon, *op. cit.,* See also Woolfolk, A. E., *Educational Psychology,* 7th edn. (Boston: Allyn and Bacon, 1998).

49 Kolb, D. A., *Experiential Learning: Experience as the Source of Learning and Development* (NJ: Prentice Hall, 1983).

PART 2

CHAPTER **2**

Understanding Culture: Through the Looking Glass

International management, as we discussed in Chapter 1, is about leading people and implementing mandates with people across cultural borders. The starting point for effective international management behavior, therefore, must be a deep understanding of culture. It is easy to see cultural differences in how people dress, speak, eat and behave. In Japan, business cards are given and received with two hands. European countries categorize themselves based on the number of kisses used in greetings among friends. In the US, handshakes should be strong and firm. It is important to know these differences, and most businesspeople have funny (or not-so-funny) stories about making mistakes with these behaviors. The British bank, HSBC, has leveraged these surface levels of cultures in a very insightful series of advertisements about the importance of local knowledge.[1] But in fact it is much more important to see what is behind these surface-level behaviors. Just like Alice in Wonderland,[2] when we go through the looking glass we see the underlying assumptions of culture. It is these assumptions that provide both the barriers to communication and the opportunities for synergy.

Consider this interchange between two technology developers in Dubai: Jan, a Dutch expatriate, who had lived in many countries with a strong record of effectiveness before coming to Dubai, and Ahmed, an Emirati. They were talking about a deal that Ahmed and his team had been working on with a potential foreign partner:

> Ahmed: I couldn't believe how rude that guy was. He refused my coffee, he handed papers to me with his left hand, he showed the sole of his shoe. He was completely ignorant of our culture. I can tell you, we won't be doing business with him!

> Jan: (laughing) Yeah, I've seen a lot of that. It's amazing how oblivious some people are. But tell me, Ahmed, really. You're a smart businessman. Is that really

why you wouldn't do a deal with him? Just because he handed papers to you the wrong way?

Ahmed: (thoughtfully) Well, no, now that you mention it. Those were just the tip of the iceberg. What was really frustrating was that he didn't seem to care about us. He didn't want to tell us anything about why doing business with us was important to him. He wasn't interested in why we developed our technology, or the history of our company. He treated my boss like he was an assistant. And when we tried to show him our way, he just ignored us. It's easy to laugh at how stupid he was with some of our customs. But it was these other things that told us we couldn't develop trust with him.

The potential partner in this situation missed the deeper importance of relationships and hierarchy in the Emirati culture. This created barriers with Ahmed and his team, and also prevented the possibility of, for example, long-term technological development that could combine different perspectives.

In this chapter we will go through the looking glass and into an "alternative world" to examine the world of culture. We'll look at what culture is, how it influences perceptions and behavior, why it raises barriers, and how it provides opportunities. There are two basic categories of knowledge about culture. *General* cultural knowledge is an understanding of how culture works and how to observe and gain insights about the effect of culture in different settings. *Specific* cultural knowledge is the set of facts and information about a particular culture, such as China or Nigeria or the Southwest US. In the first part of this chapter we examine culture in general, and in the second part we introduce a framework for mapping, or describing, characteristics of specific cultures.

CULTURE: EASIER TO IDENTIFY THAN DEFINE

Think about the following examples of cultures: Nigerian, Japanese, Québécois, soccer (football) fans, golfers, snowboarders, wine connoisseurs, Generation Y, engineers, artists, Nestlé Corporation and Toyota. What other examples have you come across? What do they have in common? What makes each a culture?

Culture is the set of assumptions and values that are shared by a group of people and that guide that group of people's interaction with each other. It is a commonly held body of general beliefs and values that define the "shoulds" and the "oughts" of life.[3] These beliefs and values are taught to us so early and so unobtrusively that we are usually unaware of their influence. Hofstede refers to culture as "the collective programming of the mind which distinguishes one group or category of people from another."[4]

As shown in the example above, culture is most readily seen in norms and practices, such as language, clothing, and behavior; however, its meaning and important influence are much deeper than these surface manifestations. Speaking French and eating *poutine* do not make one automatically Québécois; watching the World Cup and wearing a football jersey do not make one automatically part of the football (soccer) culture. A new employee at either Nestlé or Toyota becomes part of the culture slowly.

The assumptions and values that define culture – the ones that are held by members of the culture – are those that identify what is successful and what isn't, what is to be prioritized, and how people should behave in the world and towards each other. These assumptions and values are learned by passing them on from one generation to the next in both formal ways, such as school or orientation programs, and informal ways, such as story telling and social reinforcement.

All Groups Have Cultures

Culture serves two important functions for groups. First, it makes action more simple and efficient. When people know what to prioritize and how to interact with each other, business and social interactions take place quickly and easily. There is no need to question each action. Members of the Japanese culture can produce and interpret each level of bowing without conscious thought; engineers can easily proceed together using standardized work methods and mathematics.

Think about the last time you were in a new culture, working or as a tourist. How did you feel at the end of the first day? Some people say excited or exhilarated, some say frustrated, but most people say they were exhausted. This exhaustion comes from spending the day wondering what is meaningful and what is not. Should I tip the driver? How much? The receptionist didn't smile at me. Is that normal or was I rude? Or was the receptionist rude? Which side of the sidewalk should I walk on? What are others doing? Oops I just used my left hand – is that impolite here, or is it okay? Or should I have used both hands? Even if you have read all the guide books, questions like these arise. When you are interacting across cultures, you lose the efficiency that comes from shared meaning and values within a culture.

Second, culture provides an important source of social identity for its members. Humans have a basic need to belong to social groups. Belonging to a culture – as demonstrated by acting in accordance with the norms and values – brings safety and security from the group, and separates the group from outsiders who are different and perhaps even threatening. Interestingly, most people feel this identity even more strongly when they are outside their own culture than when they are in it. Foreign students or expatriates from the same country often choose to socialize more closely than the same individuals might when in their own country.

Culture and individuals interact in many ways. Culture is a characteristic of groups, and is defined in terms of what group members share. However, individuals within the culture are all different and subscribe to the culture's assumptions and values to a greater or lesser degree. We are all members of many cultures – cultures related to our national, regional, professional, organizational, age, gender, hobby, and other identities.[5] The culture we identify with most closely in a given situation influences which set of assumptions and values we prioritize in that situation. When a Nigerian oil engineer is working at the company's Norwegian headquarters office as an internal consultant, she may

identify most closely with her professional and corporate cultures and act with the priorities and assumptions of a corporate engineer. When she is working in her home country on the oil rig supervising local employees, she may identify more with her national
culture and interpret events and act according to Nigerian cultural assumptions.[6]

Culture is an important context for people's behavior together. We often use Edward
Hall's analogy that says culture is to people like water is to fish. Water is all around the
fish and is critical to a fish's survival, but the fish does not notice it or know what water
is. It is simply the context in which the fish lives. However, a fish out of water could not
function normally. Most people are unaware of their own culture; it is simply a set of
unquestioned assumptions that create a context for their interactions together. People
become much more aware of their own cultures when they visit other cultures. This
awareness, however it is gained, is critical to leading effectively in an international context and overcoming the "fish out of water" syndrome.

Is Culture Becoming Less Important?

A basic premise of this book is that working across cultures is one of the two fundamental characteristics that distinguish international management from "normal" domestic
management (strategic complexity is the other). It is worth taking a moment here to
reflect on this assumption, since many people argue that this perspective is misleading.
They assert that cultures around the world are converging, that business is business everywhere, and that people are basically the same all over. Of course, there is some truth
to all these statements, and when we present them to groups of managers, they provide quick examples to support the case. People around the world wear jeans and carry
European bags and pens, eat at McDonald's, talk on Samsung phones, work on iPads,
and play games and DVDs on their Nintendo or Sony devices. Currencies are traded
globally every moment, and there are global infrastructures and norms for conducting
business. Accounting standards are becoming more and more global. Everyone has the
same basic physiological and psychological needs.

However, as we argued above, leading effectively in the complexity of globalization means
empowering people to make decisions and implement them in ways that are consistent
with the important priorities for the company. This means understanding the relationship
between people and organizations, on the one hand, and their context on the other. This
is an underlying component of the global mindset. And one of the most important elements of the context – especially for understanding people and their behavior – is culture.

Take another look at the converging cultures examples. We think McDonald's is an
interesting example to analyze. Yes, the golden arches and basic format are recognizable
everywhere, as are some of the menu items. Kids all over the world love the Happy Meal,
and in fact, McDonald's is the world's single largest toy distributor. The Big Mac is such
a universal item that the magazine *The Economist* has selected it as the best example of a
world consumer commodity, and bases its purchasing power parity (PPP) index on the
price of a Big Mac in different countries.[7]

However, look a bit deeper. McDonald's has different menu items in different countries. Beer is served in Germany and some other countries, a McArabia is on the menu in the Middle East, and there is no beef in Indian McDonald's. Corn is an alternative to fries in many Asian countries, and it is very hard to find a VeggieMac in Italy. A few years ago, Consumer Reports found McDonald's premium coffee in the US to taste better than Starbucks,[8] but this would come as no surprise to Australians who have long had McCafé shops in almost all McDonald's outlets, complete with a whole menu of specialty coffee drinks and high-end cakes and pastries.

Look a bit deeper still: watch the people, learn to see the norms about McDonald's. In North America, a large proportion of revenue comes from drive-through. This proportion is increasing in other locations, but nowhere else does it reach the same level as in North America. What might this indicate about North American culture? The importance of efficiency, of being on the go, of moving from one place to another? The unimportance of eating as a social event, where people sit down for a meal together? In Delhi, India, outside the expatriate areas, McDonald's is frequented by small, wealthy families. It is more of a luxury family experience than a commodity eating experience. In downtown Cairo, Egypt, many McDonald's customers are businesspeople holding meetings, and the restaurant layout caters to this with bright lighting, photos of dynamic places in the city, and tables far enough apart to encourage conversation. McDonald's is a symbol of progressive capitalism while encouraging socialization and business discussions around meals. In Saudi Arabia, McDonald's has two sections which are completely separated from the front door to the service to the eating areas: one for singles (men), the other for families (women or mixed groups). In the family section, the booths can be closed with a curtain so women can eat in privacy and remove their veils if they choose. In southern Norway, McDonald's is the place families go on rainy Sunday afternoons. Why? It has the only indoor playground in town, and both family time and activity are important in Norwegian culture. In Malaysia and some other predominantly Muslim countries, McDonald's has an all-you-can-eat event during Ramadan. Ramadan is the traditional month of fasting in the Islamic calendar, and adherents must fast during the day but may eat in the evening. More and more people in Kuala Lumpur take advantage of McDonald's one price evening ticket. This creates some controversy in the city, with some appreciating McDonald's adaptation to their culture, and others decrying a degeneration of Ramadan that focuses on consumerism rather than discipline. This is an ongoing debate in Malaysia and other countries, and it is played out even at McDonald's.

In short, McDonald's, one of the icons of globalization, represents the complexities of culture and the debate on cultural convergence and divergence. Cultures are both converging and diverging. The convergence allows us to do business together. It allows mergers and acquisitions to be negotiated, money and goods to be traded, and employees to stay briefly in foreign countries without too much trouble. It allows us to work together, at least on the surface. However, deeper level differences become apparent when people have to interact more intensively with each other on a day-to-day basis. As a Chinese student said to her American peers, "To say that we're becoming westernized because McDonald's does well in Shanghai, is like saying that the US is becoming easternized because there are a lot of Chinese restaurants." Naïve assumptions about convergence can cause problems or disappointments such as when the synergy anticipated from a merger or acquisition is more elusive than expected or when goods purchased don't arrive on time or are not as expected.

Incidentally, the McDonald's story also shows the opportunities of cultural understanding and globalization. For example, when McDonald's entered Europe, most countries, and France in particular, protested at the low nutritional value. As a response, McDonald's developed a wide range of healthy food (salads, sandwiches, drinks, alternatives for Happy Meals, etc.) for Europe, much more extensive than the range in the US. When US consumers started decreasing their McDonald's intake due to health concerns, McDonald's was ready, and they took their learning from Europe back to the US. Australian McCafé shops sprung up in Europe and the US in McDonald's response to Starbucks. This kind of synergy from understanding cultural differences is one of the sources of opportunity from international management.

In short, managers must understand the context of the people they are working with in order to lead them well, and one of the most important elements of context is culture. As long as people live and work in groups, managers will need to work effectively across cultures.

Why Focus on Country Cultures?

Although we defined culture above as the set of values and assumptions shared by any group of people, in international management we tend to focus on the role of country cultures. There is a good reason for this. The institutions that carry culture tend to be very powerful and consistent within a country. For example, most countries have one official language that is the language of most families, is taught in all state schools, is the language of regional- and country-level government, and is the language of official and most unofficial media. Most countries have a single basic legal system (e.g., constitutional or civil or Islamic law), a system of government that is relatively consistent across regions (e.g., representative democracy in different states or cantons, or a monarchy that reigns throughout the country), a single relationship between church and state (e.g., there is a strong relationship or there is officially no relationship). These practices and relationships are often different from those in the country next door. The beliefs and values associated with these institutions are taught to people early and implicitly through family norms and institutional practices, so that most people are unaware of their influence.

There are some important exceptions, such as Canada, Belgium, Switzerland, and India, which have two or more official languages and cultures. However, the generalization is true for most countries. Country is therefore a very important type of culture to account for in international business. For most of this chapter, and indeed the book, we will focus, therefore, on country-based cultures. However, towards the end of the chapter we turn to some important caveats around this notion, and throughout the book we will acknowledge the important influence of other cultures.

CULTURE INFLUENCES HOW WE SEE THE WORLD

To understand culture's influence, we need to understand first the basic role of assumptions and perceptions in influencing our own thoughts and actions. This allows us to see our own culture's influence on us, and why cross-cultural encounters are both so difficult to understand and so interesting.[9]

An assumption is an unquestioned, taken-for-granted belief about the world and how it works. Assumptions help create our worldview, or the cognitive environment in which we operate. They come in many different varieties. Some are so deeply ingrained and unquestioned that it is difficult ever to surface them, and even when surfaced, they are not testable. For example, assumptions about the basic nature of humans are normally surfaced and questioned only by philosophers and religious leaders, and even they cannot test them in an unambiguous way. Culture incorporates many of these deep assumptions, and we will elaborate on more of them presently.

Other assumptions are learned at various stages of our lives, and once learned, are taken for granted without further questioning. A child comes into the world with no knowledge of it, yet in the first few years learns to take so much for granted: day and night follow each other; manipulating switches makes things work or turns them off; things that move are either alive or powered by something; living things need nourishment; and, when in doubt, Google it. As we develop through life, we learn more and more, and each lesson becomes a basic building block for adding new skills and competencies. A financial analyst valuing companies takes for granted certain assumptions about efficient markets and develops analyses that affect the companies' ability to obtain resources. An advertising account manager takes for granted certain assumptions about human motivations and produces advertising campaigns that play to those motivations and invoke them.

Assumptions influence the process of perception, or what we notice and how we interpret events and behaviors. Assumptions influence our perceptions themselves, our interpretations of events and behaviors or the meaning that the events and behaviors have for us. The expression "we see what we want to see and hear what we want to hear" is a reflection of how our assumptions affect our perceptions. Karl Weick, a social psychologist, suggests "I'll see it when I believe it" is more accurate than proclaiming "I'll believe it when I see it."[10]

The financial analyst focuses on financial ratios, earnings growth or dividends but may not notice programs with long lead times that may enhance the company's reputation for social responsibility. If she did notice this information, she may interpret it as something admirable but nothing that should influence stock price or ability to borrow money today. The boundary conditions for such financial assumptions became abundantly clear in 2008 when they failed to hold, and banks around the world collapsed. The advertising account manager may notice only product features that fit into his framework of assumptions about motivation for the target audience and miss other implications of those features. The first marketing campaigns for cellular phones focused exclusively on the business audience. The next generation of campaigns realized that the same features were equally important for families involved in multiple activities and attractive to teenagers wanting to stay in touch with their friends. If marketers' assumptions had not focused exclusively on business, they might have tapped this broader consumer market much earlier. Today's telecommunications industry includes a wide variety of competitors, from Internet providers to handset manufacturers to content developers, all vying to create the next set of assumptions.

Assumptions are necessary. Without assumptions, we would be paralyzed by the constant need to inquire about the meaning of events and the motives of others. The more others share our assumptions, the more easily we can interact and communicate effectively with each other. It is not surprising that our assumptions are generally effective when we operate within our own culture.

Clearer Vision With D-I-E

A simple way to remember this process of social perception is captured by the acronym D-I-E, which stands for Describe, Interpret, and Evaluate. We observe something and take note of its characteristics, or describe it. In describing something we stay with the objective facts. What we are inclined to notice is influenced in part by our assumptions of what is important. We then interpret those facts, or give them meaning, again based on our assumptions. Finally, we evaluate the facts and take action based upon our evaluation.

When selecting a potential supplier for specialty chemicals, a purchasing agent may notice that different companies offer different prices for the same grade of chemical. The purchasing agent will build a table comparing the different suppliers, describing their price ranges. The purchasing agent may not notice that the suppliers offer different types of technical assistance or compound customization, because his assumptions about priorities do not include this. Although price is sometimes an indicator of quality, the purchasing agent may interpret the chemical grade as the quality information. As long as prices are identified for the same chemical grade, the purchasing agent interprets that he is comparing them on an equal basis. Finally, the purchasing agent evaluates the lowest price compound as good for the company. He takes action and buys this compound.

Just like the purchasing agent, we all act based on the world we perceive, the world we see through the Describe, Interpret, Evaluate sequence. Since the sequence builds so heavily on our assumptions of the world and how it works, those assumptions end up influencing our own actions and what we think of others' actions. Therefore, when we cross cultural boundaries we need to be especially careful in our tendency to interpret and evaluate from our own perspective. Our "rule of thumb" regarding the D-I-E model is to spend more time on description, treat interpretations as hypotheses and defer evaluation until we have explored multiple possible interpretations.

Culture Influences our Lenses

Figure 2.1 shows the influence pattern of culture on assumptions, perceptions, and management behavior, and demonstrates why culture and assumptions play such a large role in cross-cultural encounters.

A good way to identify someone's cultural assumptions is to ask a series of "why" questions. For example, consider the following conversation:

> Colleague: We should adjust our incentive scheme for salespeople so they have more commission.
>
> You: Why?
>
> Colleague: That way they'll be more motivated to sell the products.
>
> You: Why will it work?
>
> Colleague: Because they'll see that if they sell more products, they'll get more money.
>
> You: Why will they change their behavior?
>
> Colleague (getting frustrated with you): Because everyone wants more money!
>
> You: Why?
>
> Colleague (not believing he is part of this conversation): Just because!

FIGURE 2.1   Culture's influence on individual behavior

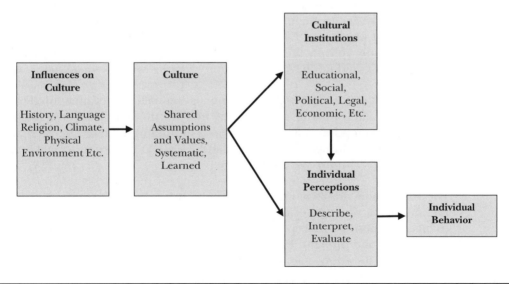

When you get to this response – "just because" – you have reached the level of assumptions. These assumptions are often provided by the person's culture. You can also identify assumptions by giving people examples of situations that involve the assumption and asking them how they would respond. For example, people may not be conscious enough about their basic belief about human nature to articulate it. However, ask someone "What do you expect someone to do if she found a large amount of money in an unidentified package on the street?" and "What type of system should be put in place to prevent dishonest employees from stealing money?" Your respondent would probably be able to reply easily, and this will give you clues about his assumptions regarding human nature. In general, people are more consciously aware of how they ought to behave in situations that are specific and concrete; but people are not usually aware of where those "oughts" originate. Often, they come from culture.

When Cultures Meet – Question the Other or Question Ourselves?

If culture is a set of shared deep-level assumptions and values, and these assumptions and values influence thoughts and behavior, what happens when people from two or more different cultures meet or work together? Their assumptions and value systems (cultures) may direct them to perceive the same situation differently, interpret what they notice differently, evaluate the situation differently, and take different actions. Consider this short exchange:

> Susan (British): Pablo, the company has decided to transfer you to the regional headquarters in Sao Paulo.
>
> Pablo (Chilean): That will be very difficult. I think I'll stay here.

There is an awkward pause. What are both thinking? The same situation – transferring Pablo from Santiago to Sao Paulo – is interpreted and evaluated differently by each of them. Susan is probably wondering whether Pablo is really interested in developing his career: "A transfer to regional headquarters is an important promotion. Very strange he would not want that." Pablo may wonder why Susan or the company would transfer him: "My family and my life are here. Why would I want to go to Brazil? I don't speak Portuguese; I could not have a life there."

Cross-cultural interactions like this set up a potential conflict situation. From "my" point of view, "you" are thinking and behaving in a way doesn't fit with my assumptions about the world (assumptions I am not conscious of holding). As we discussed in Chapter 1, I experience this conflict as dissonance and I want to reduce it, to make the interpretation consistent with my assumptions.

The easiest and most common way for me to reduce dissonance is to revise my perception of the situation – learning through assimilation (see Chapter 1). Susan could change her positive perception of Pablo's career potential, and "realize" he is not as ambitious as she thought; Pablo could change his positive perception of the company, and "realize" they don't care about him.

With this interpretation, both people make assumptions about the other's motivations and values, based on their own assumption set. Even worse, because we make interpretations from our own assumption set, we are prone to ethnocentric error. Ethnocentrism is essentially seeing "us" as better and "them" as worse. We have a strong tendency to use our own group's assumptions as the benchmark when viewing other groups, placing our group at the top of a hierarchy, and ranking all others as lower.[11] Susan's thoughts may continue with, "No wonder the Chilean economy is still struggling." Pablo might think, "This is just another example of Anglo values colonizing the rest of the world." Our advice at the end of the DIE model section above was to defer evaluation and explore multiple interpretations; this is important advice for avoiding misunderstanding and ethnocentrism, and for moving to the second way of reducing dissonance.

The other way to reduce dissonance is to change assumptions. This is the accommodation response we discussed in Chapter 1. It is harder, and requires more awareness and energy. Susan could wonder whether managers have different typical career paths in Latin America than in the UK and develop a broader understanding of human motivation and leadership development in different contexts. Pablo could wonder whether UK firms look after employees differently, and develop a broader understanding of human capital in multinational firms.

The dynamics of what happens when cultures meet are shown in Figure 2.2. The same perceptual process occurs as described earlier and shown in Figure 2.1, but in this case two different people are acting based on two different sets of cultural assumptions. The resulting different decisions or behaviors set up the conditions for conflict – or synergy, as discussed below.

We tend to become aware of how our assumptions shape perceptions, values and behavior only as we confront a different set of assumptions guiding the views and practices of other people. If we are exposed to new experiences under the right circumstances (including the person's own motivation), part of our response will include an examination of their own guiding values. The next stage of Susan and Pablo's hypothetical conversation could easily have been one of open dialogue about reasons for moving or not, and how those were related to different values. Both could be enriched by the conversation.

Culture Creates Efficiency and Identity

In the above section, we focused mostly on the cognitive aspect of culture: our shared values and assumptions influence how we perceive the world and the people in it, how we make choices, and how we act. For the mechanics of doing business, this cognitive aspect is important. Furthermore, it is the aspect of culture that managers misinterpret most, leading to conflict more often than synergy in intercultural interactions.

It is equally important to respect the identity that culture provides. Managers have a tendency to downplay cultural identity: "We are all part of a global business culture." But remember that identity becomes more important to the extent that it is threatened.

FIGURE 2.2   Cross-cultural encounters

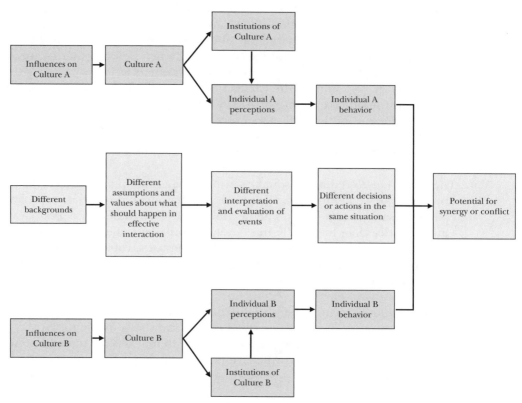

If you disrespect someone's identity – for example by behaving in a way that is considered rude in his culture, by serving food that is unacceptable in her country, by not accommodating requirements of their culture – you set up a situation in which the other person becomes more locked into his or her cultural identity in order to defend it. This makes conflict even more likely, and makes it even more difficult to achieve synergies.

MAPPING CULTURES

In the first part of this chapter we looked at culture-general knowledge to develop an understanding of how cultures work. Now we address culture-specific knowledge: information about a particular culture. It is outside the scope of this book to provide such specific information about any one culture; we suggest readers turn to any of a myriad of guides for tourists, traveling businesspeople, or expatriates in various countries and cultures. Instead, we provide a tool for mapping specific cultures – for comparing cultures with each other, and for developing expectations about how to work with people from different cultures. This kind of tool is invaluable for managers who work across multiple cultures, especially when the cultures are also complex and changing.

We use the metaphor of mapping quite deliberately. A map is a tool for navigating in a new territory. The map is useful to the extent that it is accurate, provides just the right level of detail and scale, and shows reference points. It should help you develop a guess about how to get from one place to another. A "you are here" point makes a map even more practical.

Maps of social features are less common than maps of geographical ones, and mapping social features of groups is difficult because it is hard to verify the data against an objective, unchanging reality. However, social maps that are carefully constructed help people enter new cultural territories as much as geographical maps help people enter new physical territories.

Just as a geographer uses different types of maps for different purposes, an international manager has access to several cultural maps. Each map shows different dimensions of culture, and allows different types of cultural comparisons. For example, Edward T. Hall has written several books and articles describing elements of culture that are relevant to business. In his classic article, *"The Silent Language in Overseas Business,"* he describes cultural differences and their impact on international behavior, relating to the five dimensions of Time, Space, Things, Friendships, and Agreements.[12]

Geert Hofstede has developed the most extensively researched framework or cultural map.[13] By examining the satisfaction surveys of employees in a multinational company, he identified four basic value patterns of cultures around the world: Individualism, Power Distance, Uncertainty Avoidance, and Masculinity. He also linked these dimensions to management theories and practice. Later, with colleague Michael Bond, he identified a fifth value of Confucian Dynamism, or Long-term Orientation.[14] Hofstede's framework was recently validated across multiple organizations and countries and updated by Robert J. House and colleagues in the GLOBE project.[15]

Following Hofstede, but incorporating more dimensions developed in sociology and anthropology, Trompenaars developed a map of seven dimensions: Universalism versus Particularism, Collectivism versus Individualism, Affective versus Neutral Relationships, Specificity versus Diffusiveness, Achievement versus Ascription, Orientation towards Time, Internal versus External.[16] He assesses a country's positioning on these dimensions by asking managers to respond to a series of short, often amusing, dilemmas and summarizing patterns among responses.

Schwartz developed a framework of values, specifically focusing on the values that are related to an individual's interaction with society.[17] Schwartz found that cultures differ in terms of valuing mastery over versus harmony with the environment, embedded versus autonomous relations, and hierarchical versus egalitarian control.

All of these mapping tools have different strengths. Hofstede's, for example, provided the earliest comprehensive set of data and has been used extensively to guide interactions since its publication in 1980. Trompenaars's vignettes provide vivid and interesting applications of cultural maps, and his focus on bipolar (either/or) dimensions supports his process of resolving cultural dilemmas. Schwartz's dimensions allow a translation from country- to individual-level values.

When we map cultures, we prefer when possible to draw from one of the longest-established frameworks in anthropology, the Cultural Orientations Framework of Kluckhohn and Strodtbeck.[18] We find it has the most comprehensive set of dimensions that are relevant for comparing cultures, even today. It allows us to examine variations within cultures by measuring individual values and cultural values, and so create maps that reflect more closely the complexity of the real world of intercultural interactions. As a result of our own research using this framework over the past 20 years, we have adapted the description here from the original to reflect the dimensions and comparisons most relevant to management.[19]

The Cultural Orientations Framework and International Management

Kluckhohn and Strodtbeck found that there are common themes in the issues or problems that different societies have faced throughout time, and these universal issues provide a way of viewing culture objectively. Kluckhohn and Strodtbeck produced their Cultural Orientations Framework by analyzing hundreds of ethnographic descriptions of cultures from around the world, conducted by researchers from many different backgrounds. They identified six problems or challenges that all societies throughout recorded history have faced. Different societies have developed and continue to develop different ways of coping with these challenges, but there tends to be a basic pattern of response configurations. The six issues are referred to as *cultural orientations*, and the different responses to each issue are called *variations*. The six issues are:

1 Relation to the environment.

2 Relationships among people.

3 Mode of normal activity.

4 Orientation to time.

5 Belief about basic human nature.

6 Use of space.

For all of these orientations, there is no possible "proof" that one variation is better or worse. In fact, all variations exist because they are useful in particular situations that are relevant to the group. What is important is that members of a culture agree on a set of values and priorities related to one or more of the variations, then behave as if that is the best way of believing and doing things. This agreement brings the efficiency and identity we discussed earlier. The different types of agreement give us different cultures.

Our research suggests that the first four of these issues are most related to the cultural differences important for business, so we will focus only on these.

We measure individuals' variations of the Cultural Orientations Framework using the Cultural Perspectives Questionnaire (CPQ), which we developed. The discussion in this chapter is based on our analysis of responses to our previous and current versions of the survey. The graphs which follow are based on our analysis of over 20,000 respondents from more than 200 countries. *Almost all of our respondents are business students and people working mostly in business organizations, and may not be representative of the general population.* About one-third of our respondents are business students, mostly MBA and some undergraduate. The other two-thirds are practicing managers with an average age of about 40, and with an average of 15 years of full-time work experience.

To create the country comparisons, we only included data from respondents who represent the culture. They were born in the country, have lived there longer than living anywhere else, and identify most closely with that country's culture. For example, someone who was born in Japan, lived most of his life in Japan, and specified his cultural identity as "Japan," was included in the sample for Japan. A person born in Japan who lived half her life in the United States and France, and identified her culture as "global," was not included in the sample for Japan.

The number of respondents for each country sample is included after the country's name in the graph. Remember that smaller sample sizes are less generalizable to the businesspeople of that culture. To be mindful of this, we only included sample sizes smaller than 100 if the sample had relatively low variance among individual respondents, and if the respondents came from different companies and regions of the country.

When you are looking at the graphs, a good rule of thumb to keep in mind is that a difference of 0.2 is almost always both statistically significant and meaningful. In other words, a difference between two countries' scores that is 0.2 or greater is enough to be reflected in quite different patterns in members' expectations of how to respond to challenges related to that dimension.

How do we Engage the World Around Us?

The issue of people's **relationship to the environment** reflects how people in a society orient themselves to the world around them and to the supernatural. What do people direct their attention to, and what do they see as their role in the environment? There are three main variations of responses.

Harmony. Harmony is a belief that we are not separated from the world – that we and the "world around us" are all part of the same system. The system has a natural balance, and we must keep in balance for things to go well, for life to progress and grow. In cultures with a high orientation towards harmony, people believe that our role as humans is to keep this system in balance and, when things are out of balance, we should nudge the system to realign it. Most Aboriginal cultures are strongly harmony-oriented. Native Americans, for example, are traditionally hunters as well as gatherers, and their traditions for hunting incorporate strong norms of studying the ecosystem to ensure that no more game is hunted than the system can tolerate without becoming unbalanced, and utilizing every single part of the hunted animal without any waste. Their social traditions also encourage harmony within the tribe. Today's Chinese cultures tend to have a strong emphasis on harmony. In these cultures, managers prefer look at all aspects of a business system and engage in small actions to affect various parts of the system and bring it into alignment. They also tend to encourage harmony among people in the social system. This can be frustrating for members of other cultures who would like to see direct action on a particular issue, but it has enabled China to develop a powerful economy and social force.

Mastery.   Mastery is a belief that humans are separated from the world around us, and that our role is to influence and control our environment. Mastery is reflected historically in pioneering and colonizing movements, taking over land and controlling it. Mastery cultures believe that if enough time, money, and brains are applied to a goal, nearly anything is achievable. If we control things well enough, we will have the right outcome; when things go wrong, it's because we did not control well enough. Western cultures, especially Anglo and Northern European ones, tend to be highest on mastery orientation. This is reflected in the Anglo business emphasis on direct consequences for individual managers who do or do not achieve their goals. It is commonplace to pay top managers seemingly exorbitant packages for (short-term) company success, and to change the CEO when a company is not doing well. The underlying assumption is that the CEO has a direct influence on such results. Today, people are questioning such rewards and consequences; a tacit questioning of the mastery assumption which has guided these cultures for generations.

Subjugation.   Subjugation is a belief that the environment is dominated by something other than humans, typically God, fate, or a supernatural force. Life in this context is viewed as predetermined or preordained, or, less often, an exercise in chance. One should not try to alter the inevitable, for such actions will be futile at best and blasphemous at worst. To a devout Muslim, the expression "Insh'allah," which means "Allah willing," reflects a worldview that plans can be made, but will only take place according to the will of God. Although Islam is a religion and not a country-culture, many countries have Islam as their official faith, and the religion strongly influences business practices.

People who do not come from societies with an appreciation for subjugation often view it as a variant of fatalism: why bother working hard, for example, if everything is preordained anyway? This quotation from a Muslim friend helps explain subjugation as active submission:

> Through meditation and prayer, I am to understand what it is that Allah has planned for me – what role I am to play in His plan. Then it is my own responsibility to fulfill that role as well as I can. If I understand my role well and work hard to be effective in it, then if something happens to prevent me from doing it well, I know that act was meant to happen and is part of Allah's larger plan. If I do not understand my role – which may be because I have not communicated well with Allah – and something happens to prevent me from doing it well, that act might be predetermined to help me understand my role better. If I do understand my role but I am lazy and don't work well towards it, and something happens to prevent me from fulfilling my role, that act may be my own responsibility. So it's a lot more complicated than "God determines everything," meaning every detail.

Country Comparisons.   The three orientations of harmony, mastery, and subjugation exist in all cultures all the time. This is important enough to restate: there is no such thing as a culture with no harmony, no mastery, or no subjugation. Cultures differ only in the extent to which they prefer one variation or another – or some combination – across situations. Figure 2.3 shows our research for mastery and harmony. The graph was created by subtracting a country's harmony score from its mastery score, so countries above the zero line prefer mastery over harmony, while those below the line prefer harmony over mastery. Those hovering around the zero line score the same on both, suggesting they differentiate between situations and maximize harmony in some and mastery in others.

Figure 2.3 mostly confirms the pattern we described above, with Anglo and Northern European cultures on the left (more mastery-oriented) and Chinese and other Asian cultures on the right (more harmony-oriented). Japan may appear to be an anomaly, with a slightly higher mastery than harmony score. Many people expect Japan to be further to the right with its focus on *wa*, or harmony. This is seen, for example, in Japanese gardens and scripted social relationships, and the popular Japanese saying that "the nail that sticks up gets hammered down." However, a closer look at Japanese culture shows that such harmony is achieved through strong mastery. The Japanese garden must be tended every day, and would never achieve such a state naturally. Japanese companies are much more likely than those from other parts of Asia to send their own managers to control operations abroad, rather than promote local managers. Even the Japanese nail is "hammered" down. This example illustrates the importance of mapping with data whenever possible, rather than relying on stereotypical descriptions of cultures. Managers from other cultures will be more able to avoid conflicts and create synergies with Japanese companies if they recognize the importance of mastery in addition to harmony in that culture.

We have found that in all countries we've measured, mastery and harmony are both higher than subjugation. Some groups certainly have a stronger belief in subjugation than others: managers in our research from Thailand, Philippines, Malaysia, and Saudi Arabia, for example, have subjugation scores on average much higher than managers from Australia, New Zealand, Mexico and Brazil. However, even the countries with higher subjugation scores do not prefer it over mastery or harmony. Managers moving from a very low subjugation culture, such as Australia, to a higher subjugation culture, such as Thailand, may notice the subjugation simply because of the difference. But placing too much emphasis on this may lead to misleading conclusions. An Australian manager from a shipping company assumed, for example, that managers in Thailand were unlikely to take charge of situations or take initiative to influence them. He learned his mistake three years after arriving in Thailand, when he decided to try a pilot test with empowerment practices. To his surprise, the Thai managers responded very well and service improved dramatically. The Australian manager wished he had questioned his assumptions earlier.

Environment dilemmas in real life.   A global chemicals company had quality control units at different sites around the globe. According to the Cultural Perspectives

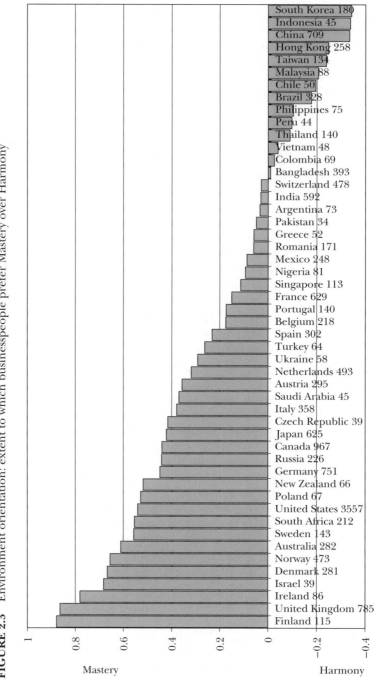

FIGURE 2.3 Environment orientation: extent to which businesspeople prefer Mastery over Harmony

South Korea 180
Indonesia 45
China 709
Hong Kong 258
Taiwan 134
Malaysia 88
Chile 50
Brazil 328
Philippines 75
Peru 44
Thailand 140
Vietnam 48
Colombia 69
Bangladesh 393
Switzerland 478
India 592
Argentina 73
Pakistan 34
Greece 52
Romania 171
Mexico 248
Nigeria 81
Singapore 113
France 629
Portugal 140
Belgium 218
Spain 302
Turkey 64
Ukraine 58
Netherlands 493
Austria 295
Saudi Arabia 45
Italy 358
Czech Republic 39
Japan 625
Canada 967
Russia 226
Germany 751
New Zealand 66
Poland 67
United States 3557
South Africa 212
Sweden 143
Australia 282
Norway 473
Denmark 281
Israel 39
Ireland 86
United Kingdom 785
Finland 115

1   0.8   0.6   0.4   0.2   0   -0.2   -0.4

Mastery   Harmony

Questionnaire, employees at the quality control sites in the US and Canada shared a strong mastery orientation, while those at the sites in Europe shared a strong harmony orientation. At one point there was a quality problem at a site outside these two continents, which had no established quality control unit. The plant was still producing, but the quality was lower and the output would have to be sold at a lower price. Members from Europe and the US were sent to this other site to address the problem. Serious conflict erupted immediately! The Europeans wanted to understand the entire system – upstream, downstream, all possible causes in technology systems, and so on – before proposing a solution. They wanted to ensure that anything they did would not cause other problems, and in fact would prevent other problems that might be waiting to happen. The Americans wanted to pinpoint the one place where the problem was happening and fix that. Days went by while the team argued about which approach was correct, each group blaming the other for lack of progress. Of course, from the company's perspective, both approaches were valuable. The mastery approach would have resolved the immediate issue, while the harmony approach would have prevented it from occurring again and perhaps improved quality overall. However, this time the company stumbled to a mediocre solution.

After the crisis was over, the different quality control units decided to map their cultural differences, to see if they could understand what had gone wrong. They discovered their profound split in terms of mastery and harmony, and realized that this was the cause of their inability to work together. They discussed the importance of each, and agreed to use each other's strengths in the future. Shortly afterwards, the company built a new plant in yet another location. The team that had failed in the improvement operation was given a chance to redeem themselves by planning for and implementing the quality control systems at the new plant. That plant set a record for the company, operating at its target quality and production levels well ahead of time and under budget, in large part due to the teamwork of the quality control group who this time combined the harmony systems approach with the mastery control approach.

Differences in expectations about relationship to the environment are evident in many other spheres of organizational life. For example, goal-setting is a cornerstone of most business management. But managers in mastery-oriented cultures tend to set goals to identify specific achievements, while managers in harmony-oriented cultures tend to set goals related to entire systems, and to link goals to each other. Budgeting is another managerial activity affected by relation to the environment. In stronger mastery-oriented cultures, the budget is assumed to be a tool that influences people to control its different aspects. In more harmony-oriented cultures, the budgeting exercise is often seen as a way of analyzing the entire business system and the relationships among the parts, and the process of creating a common language for this system is more important than accountability for specific results.[20]

Summary.   While assumptions about mastery over, harmony with, and subjugation to the environment are present in all cultures, most cultures prefer one over the others in most situations. People are expected to act according to that preference, and actions are interpreted from that perspective. All of these variations offer important value, and none of them is "correct" across all situations. Managers who can interpret others' perspectives according to this mapping dimension are more likely to be able to combine them for synergies.

Who has Power? Who is Responsible?

The orientation to **relations among people** answers questions about power and responsibility. What responsibility do people have for the welfare of others? Who has power over us, and over whom do we have power?

Collectivism. In a culture that is collective, the group is dominant. Members of the group look after each other, and subordinate their own wishes to those of the group. This does not mean complete conformity; it simply means that on issues that are related to maintaining the group, the group has power over its members. The southern African philosophy of *ubuntu* (Zulu) translates as "I am because you are," a powerful way of summarizing collectivism. Archbishop Emeritus Desmond Tutu explained *ubuntu* this way:

> We believe that a person is a person through another person, that my humanity is caught up, bound up, inextricably, with yours. When I dehumanize you, I inexorably dehumanize myself. The solitary human is a contradiction in terms and therefore you seek to work for the common good because your humanity comes into its own in belonging.[21]

An important corollary in collective cultures is the notion of in-group and out-group. The rules and privileges of the group apply only to members of the group, and there is no obligation to help or care for people outside the group (they are assumed to have their own groups). This complexity of collectivism can give rise to many misunderstandings. They are exemplified by the apocryphal story of an American who assisted a pedestrian brushed by a passing car in a busy street in an Asian city. Appalled by the lack of attention to the injured stranger, the American yelled at a nearby police officer, provided first aid, and insisted on hailing and paying for a taxi to take the person to a hospital. Afterward, the American muttered about the inhumanity of the local population. Meanwhile, the police officer's family listened, horrified, as the officer told about the American who treated a stranger like a family member, then was so indifferent as to send the person off in a taxi, rather than accompany the injured to the hospital personally and to attend to the victim properly afterwards.

A related question that is critical to ask in collective cultures is: "What is the group?" The dominant group could be based on extended family, on companies, on communities, on society as a whole, or any other collectivity. As we will see later when we compare countries, cultures that are equally collective may prioritize different types of groups.

Individualism. Whose welfare is primary? This variation's answer is the "individual." Individualism is a belief that if people look after themselves and if no one has absolute power over anyone else then we will all be better off. Individuals should make their own decisions, and live with the consequences of them. In individualistic cultures status is usually based on personal achievements, and these cultures also tend to be egalitarian.

In our research we have found very few cultures who prefer to prioritize the individual over the group. Rather, while some cultures have a high preference for collectivism over individualism, other cultures prefer collectivism and individualism more or less equally. One country that has a slight but consistent preference for individualism over collectivism is Switzerland. The Swiss system of democracy is one of the few in the world that is almost truly representative at the individual level. Many important decisions are made at the level of small villages, and many federal proposals – including laws about immigration, smoking, animal rights, and mandatory vacation – become laws (or not) by means of whole-population referenda. Immigrants to Switzerland are often surprised that neighbors of 10 years or more may not even know each other. On the other hand, the sense of individual accountability and responsibility for self – for example, for safety – is very strong in Switzerland.

Hierarchy. In hierarchical cultures, relationships of power and responsibility are arranged such that those higher in the hierarchy have power over those lower in the hierarchy. In return, they are expected to look after and provide for those lower in the hierarchy. All cultures have hierarchies; however, those with a lower hierarchical value tend to have fewer layers whose boundaries are more flexible. In strongly hierarchical cultures the hierarchy tends to be stable over time, such that most people remain in the same general level throughout their lives. Preference for hierarchy is usually associated with patterns in information-sharing. While low hierarchy cultures share information broadly – sometimes attaching a price to it, but making it accessible to many – hierarchical cultures tend to share information freely only up and down the vertical lines.

In a small Malaysian services organization, all 30 members of headquarters (four departments) sit in the same large room, and eat lunch together in groups that are unrelated to departments. However, members of the staff discuss work only with their bosses and direct reports (sometimes not even openly within the same department), and blame their managers when they do not know what is going on in other departments. After attending a management course, the president saw the need for cross-fertilization and interdependence below the management level, so she tried to encourage and facilitate cross-department communication. Her attempts failed miserably; people simply could not understand what she was getting at. Finally, she used her hierarchical authority to insist that each department post an information board describing all the activities they were currently working on, the involvement of different department members, and progress towards goals, and she insisted that the boards be updated once a week. The boards were posted in heavy traffic areas so everyone would walk by them. Through this action, departments slowly started noticing each other's board and activities, and over time, information became shared across hierarchical levels without losing the comfort of the hierarchy.

Country Comparisons. All cultures have all three types of power and responsibility patterns: collectivism, individualism, and hierarchy; cultures simply differ in their prioritization. Figure 2.4 shows the relative preference for collectivism and individualism (the individualism score subtracted from the collectivism score) for the countries in our research. The further a country is to the left, the more strongly it prefers collectivism

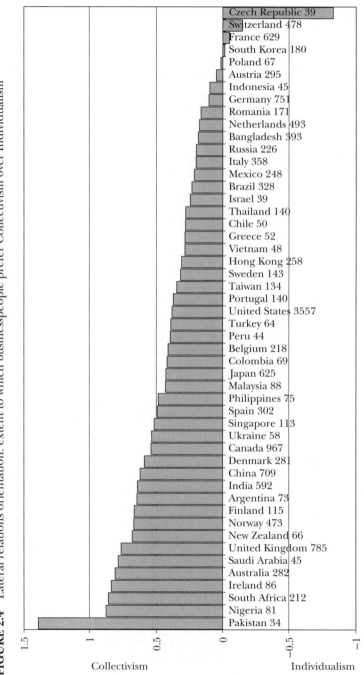

FIGURE 2.4 Lateral relations orientation: extent to which businesspeople prefer Collectivism over Individualism

over individualism. The first thing to notice in Figure 2.4 is that no country in our sample strongly prefers individualism over collectivism – the most extremely "individualistic" cultures prioritize individualism and collectivism about the same.

Most people expect that the United States would be far to the right, rather than in the middle. This is because previous research and popular culture highlights the stereotype of individualistic Americans, including the "lone cowboy." However, the US shows strong collectivism within communities, churches, teams (particularly team sports), and in patriotism for the country as a whole. There is less collectivism among extended families or the workplace than in other countries, which is partly why expatriates from those other countries may not notice the collectivism in the US. Moreover, with the multicultural nature of the US, many people come from countries or cultures that do have high collectivism around the family. This pattern of collectivism is evident in our research in all regions of the US, although it is possible that different regions focus on different groups. Managers from other countries going to the US should remember how important these groups are to Americans. We have worked with many managers from other parts of the world who were confused in the first years in the US – pleased (even if overwhelmed) with the warm welcome given to strangers, but sometimes offended when the welcome didn't translate to deep friendship. For most of them, the cultural breakthrough came from joining and being active in a church community and/or a team sport, especially with their children. By integrating into the collective, expatriates created a place for themselves in the group, and their management became more productive afterwards.

The relative preference for hierarchy is shown in Figure 2.5, where the higher a score is above 0.0, the higher the culture's preference for hierarchy. The cultures on the left – high hierarchy – are Asian and African, but South Africa has a low preference for hierarchy. The high negative score for Sweden is interesting. In Sweden, a boss who tells others what to do is a bad boss. What does a Swedish boss do, then? Most Swedes say that the role of a boss is to facilitate the performance of others – to guide subordinates to develop their own way of doing things. This works very well for commitment and innovation, and Swedes were instrumental in developing such high-performance work practices as self-managed teams. But there is a "dark side" as well, as we explored with a number of senior Swedish executives recently. Such negative hierarchy is extremely inefficient, and this inefficiency can be costly or even deadly in a crisis. After some chagrin, this group of highly successful executives admitted to each other that in crises they had learned to manage in an "un-Swedish" way, deliberately stepping out of character, then apologizing later. Swedish managers who work abroad often have a difficult time being taken seriously by their new direct reports, until they learn to adapt and step into a more hierarchical role, at least sometimes. This situation is explored further in Chapter 3.

Relations among people dilemmas in real life.   It is a common misconception that collective cultures engage in more teamwork than individualistic cultures do. In fact, all cultures work in teams; they just do it differently.[22] The less collective a culture is, the more team members prefer to have specific roles and responsibilities and the ability to identify individual team contributions. Their commitment is to the task, rather

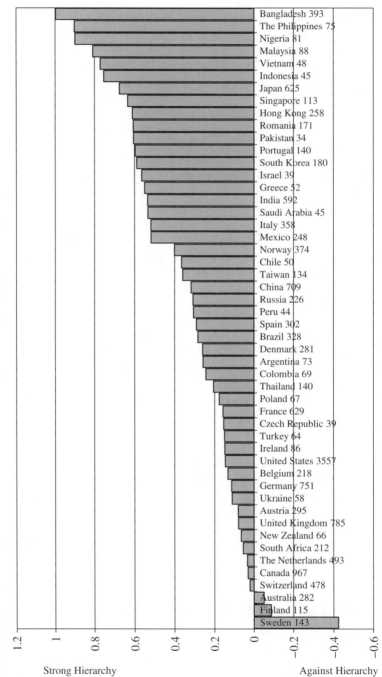

FIGURE 2.5 Vertical relations orientation: extent to which businesspeople prefer Hierarchy

than to the team. The leadership role may change depending on which part of the task needs to be emphasized, and membership may change frequently depending on the needs of the task or of the individuals on the team with respect to other tasks. In highly collective cultures, roles are more fluid, and commitment is to the team itself. Each person is responsible for his or her own contribution, but also for the success of the team itself. Membership is less likely to change. As a Malaysian manager told us, "In Asia, 'we' means something different in a team than 'we' does in less collective cultures. For us, 'we' means 'we are really all one' and 'team' and 'we' is the same. In other places I've worked, 'we' in the team means 'we are, each one of us, acting according to the team, as long as we, each one of us, agree with the team.'" In hierarchical cultures, team members have specific levels and roles in the hierarchy, and the team is directed clearly by the leader. People contribute to meetings and discussions in accordance with their place in the hierarchy.

What happens when all these cultures get together in the same team? Lijong, a Global Account Director from a global computer firm, was in charge of one of the largest accounts in the company – a global financial services firm headquartered in the Netherlands. The global account team consisted of a small core of three regional representatives, each of whom liaised with up to 40 local representatives in the customer's different markets. All members of the team had strong relationships with customers. Because of the different cultures involved, managing relationships in the team presented difficulties. Local account managers from some countries responded better to global coordination if Lijong played a strong hierarchical role and dictated the orders, others responded better if he made suggestions and listened to their responses, letting them decide. Some identified more closely with the customer than they did with their own company (defined the group as local relations), while others had fierce loyalty to the company at the expense of the customer (defined the group as the company). Some preferred clear roles within the team (more individualistic), others expected flexible roles (more collective). Lijong came from a Chinese family of immigrants in Latin America, and had moved to the Netherlands as a young adult. He had developed a high level of global leadership competences through practice and careful reflection on his experiences. He found that to be successful with this team, he was constantly shifting roles and behaviors. He got to know team members from their own perspectives, and appreciated how each contributed something important to the customer experience. He led the team towards the common goal of serving the global customer, learning from each other and developing best practices. Lijong's ability to read (map) the cultural differences and adjust his behavior according to them, created great synergies in the team. It also made it easier for the team to face its greatest challenge – merging with another team when the client acquired another one of the company's customers.

Summary. All cultures are collective, individualistic, and hierarchical, but they emphasize the different types of relationships to different degrees. High-performing teams and organizations in fact incorporate all three sets of relationships, depending on the situation. Multicultural organizations, therefore, have an opportunity for higher performance, if they can capture these synergies.

How do we Coordinate Collective Action?

The **activity orientation** does not refer to a state of activity or passivity, but rather, the desirable focus of activity. There are two variations of activity found across business cultures: doing and thinking.

Doing.   Doing is akin to the story of Prometheus from Greek mythology. Prometheus stole fire from Olympus and gave it to humans to use. As punishment, he was chained to a rock and tormented by vultures. Throughout eternity, he strained to break free of his chains, but new chains constantly reappeared when he was successful. The relentless striving to achieve and compulsive attempts to accomplish are the core of the doing variation. This is often associated with the Protestant work ethic, which dictates that hard work is pure, and it is seen in many western European and Anglo cultures. Marxism, too, argues that work is part of humans' identity, and goes so far as to say that the problem with capitalism is a separation of the identity of work from the person through management ownership.

In doing cultures, "when in doubt, take action." This action may be to fix or resolve an issue, as tends to be the case in pragmatic Finland, or it may be to do something to get feedback – to learn more – as in process-oriented Japan.

Thinking.   Thinking is closer to the Apollonian mode, in which the senses are moderated by thought, and mind and body are balanced. Thinking-oriented cultures place a high value on being rational and carefully thinking everything through before taking action. In thinking cultures, "when in doubt, get more information and plan more." These cultures also place priority on reflecting, for example analyzing past performance to learn from it. At the extreme, they may value the beauty of an elegant argument at least as much as the results it creates. Most academic and research institutions have thinking-oriented cultures, and countries with a strong focus on careful engineering often have thinking-oriented cultures.

Country Comparisons.   Figure 2.6 shows the results for our respondents with respect to doing and thinking in the Activity orientation. The graph was created by subtracting the doing score from the thinking score. Countries with scores below the zero line and to the left prefer doing over thinking, whereas countries with scores above the zero line and to the right prefer thinking over doing.

People from other countries are often surprised to see the Nordic countries on the left of this graph. In the words of an Italian manager in a Norwegian multinational, "those Scandinavians talk and talk forever before getting anything done! How can you say they're doing oriented?" Once again though, the data helps us examine underlying assumptions and question them. Managers in the Scandinavian countries of Denmark, Sweden and Norway do engage in long discussions with each other before making decisions (in the fourth Nordic country of Finland, the long "conversations" happen at least as much with signals and non-verbal language as with talking). However, from a Nordic

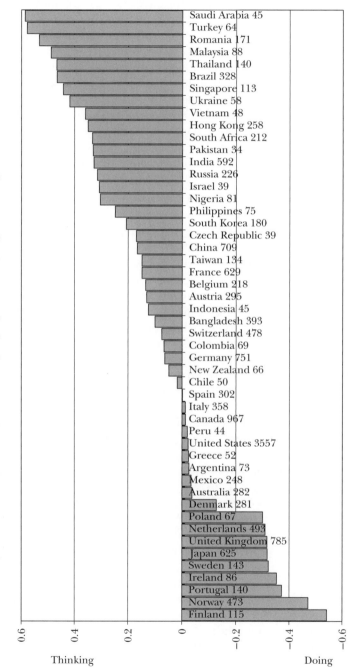

FIGURE 2.6 Activity orientation: extent to which businesspeople prefer Thinking over Doing

Saudi Arabia 45
Turkey 64
Romania 171
Malaysia 88
Thailand 140
Brazil 328
Singapore 113
Ukraine 58
Vietnam 48
Hong Kong 258
South Africa 212
Pakistan 34
India 592
Russia 226
Israel 39
Nigeria 81
Philippines 75
South Korea 180
Czech Republic 39
China 709
Taiwan 134
France 629
Belgium 218
Austria 295
Indonesia 45
Bangladesh 393
Switzerland 478
Colombia 69
Germany 751
New Zealand 66
Chile 50
Spain 302
Italy 358
Canada 967
Peru 44
United States 3557
Greece 52
Argentina 73
Mexico 248
Australia 282
Denmark 281
Poland 67
Netherlands 493
United Kingdom 785
Japan 625
Sweden 143
Ireland 86
Portugal 140
Norway 473
Finland 115

0.6   0.4   0.2   0   −0.2   −0.4   −0.6

Thinking   Doing

point of view this is not so much *planning* as it is *aligning*. Remember that the Nordic countries are moderately collective and relatively (or very) low on hierarchy. To make a decision, management teams need to discuss an issue to ensure that everyone is committed and aligned before going ahead. To outsiders, these discussions look like planning. But to Nordics there is a crucial difference. Once agreement is made, it is not agreement to a particular plan (a process or sequence), but commitment to a set of ideas and roles. In fact, Nordic managers assume that once commitment is made, the individuals or team involved will figure out how to implement it – in other words, the plan has not been made. Non-Nordic managers, especially those from thinking-oriented cultures, are often left confused once the decision has been made and the Nordic members of the team just start implementing, without discussing specific plans. Managers from other countries going to the Nordic countries or working in a Nordic firm should understand this distinction. In the "pre-decision" phase, they can learn to focus on aligning roles and commitment, rather than making specific plans that may be futile later. The implications of this dynamic are explored further in Chapter 3.

Activity dilemmas in real life.

An Austrian firm that makes precision components for manufacturing processes, such as those used in the making of clothing and sporting goods, was working with a large US customer. The manager for new products, Tomas, was developing a new version of the components that had potential to decrease manufacturing costs dramatically, but it was not yet ready for use. He described all the features and the testing process so far enthusiastically (thinking) to his counterpart at the US customer, with the intention of getting the customer excited about future possibilities. However, the US customer was so impressed he wanted it now (doing) for his factories in China. When Tomas said it wouldn't be ready for at least another year, the American replied, "you guys always over-engineer everything [are so thinking-oriented], I'm sure it's good enough to go and make a difference to us [we are doing-oriented]." Tomas finally agreed to try. But the implementation had to be done through the Singapore office of the Austrian company, which was its Asian headquarters. The Singapore office was even more reluctant than Tomas, because the component wasn't ready (Singapore is even more strongly thinking-oriented). "What if they put it in place, and it creates more problems than it solves? Besides, we still haven't got the extra functionality worked out. It needs more development before we let it out." The customer reiterated, "We don't want that extra functionality. If it has these basic functions, that's great for now." Problems also arose around the contract. The US customer wanted a contract based on cost-savings achieved, but the Austrian firm was used to charging prices based on features and technical standards, plus a maintenance contract. In the end, the customer waited for the product but was frustrated enough to negotiate much more difficult contracts afterwards. Tomas was frustrated and knew he had missed something, but wasn't sure what he could have done to convince the customer. If both had realized the nature of the cultural difference – the US doing and the Austrian and Singaporean thinking – then they might have been able to arrange something beneficial for everyone. For example, the US company could have been heavily involved in beta tests of the technology, paying for a technician from the Austrian company to be on-site at the factories, rather than paying for the technology itself.

In doing-oriented cultures, decisions tend to be made with pragmatic criteria, reward systems are results-based, and there is a compulsive concern for achieving tangible performance measures. These are the cultures that invented "to do" lists and extensive personal calendars that allow people to track their activities and accomplishments. In work and team settings, meetings are used to make decisions, and they close with everyone committing to action points. In cultures with a dominant thinking orientation, decisions are more likely to be made based on rational criteria, rewards are distributed logically with complex formulae, and output is measured against balanced objectives such as long- and short-term profitability, quality as well as quantity of production, and so on. While companies from all cultures use Balanced Scorecards to assess performance, companies with thinking-oriented cultures excel at them. They spend more time designing the process to identify what goes into the scorecard, tracking indicators with detailed measures, assessing the extent to which indicators relate to other dimensions of performance, and designing reward systems that fit the performance shown by the indicators.

Summary. Doing and thinking orientations are strong in all cultures, at least in the business and management aspects of the cultures. Things are planned, and actions are taken. However, different cultures tend to prioritize the doing or the thinking mode in their coordinated action. They agree that in most situations it is better either to act more, or to plan more. Since business situations themselves are complex, international organizations that encompass both types of culture have opportunities to leverage these differences.

What is our Timeframe?

There are two basic ways to think about time. The first involves a general orientation toward time; the second is about how people think about or use specific units of time.[23] Our research does not measure people's perspectives towards time so we cannot provide country data, but we provide examples here to help you interpret your own experiences.

A culture's general orientation to time reflects the time-related criteria used to make decisions, interpret events, or prioritize actions. For example, in a *past*-oriented culture, people respond to a new challenge by looking to tradition and wondering: "How have others dealt with this kind of problem before?" If people primarily consider the immediate effects of an action, then the dominant orientation is more likely to be *present*-oriented. If the chief concern is "What are the long-term consequences of this choice?" then the dominant orientation can be described as *future*-oriented.

Our research suggests that this general time orientation is more related to company cultures than to country cultures. In this way, country cultures are shifting. Although it used to be the case that Japanese companies, for example, were very long-term focused, with lifetime employment and long planning horizons (such as Konsuke Matsushita's famous 250-year corporate plan[24]), today they are shifting, and many companies are losing these traditions in the interests of efficiency. On the other hand, it used to be the case that American companies were focused only on tomorrow's returns. While most US-based companies still look first to the current quarter's results, the assumption that this is the best indicator of performance is being questioned. Within a given country, some companies are much more focused on longer planning horizons and reward systems, which tends to be associated with a combination of past and future orientations; while others are focused on short planning horizons and reward systems, more associated with a present orientation.

Another aspect of time orientation that strongly influences behavior asks the questions: What are the most important units of time, and how does time flow? In some cultures, time is broken up into small, specific, equal units, and it is assumed to flow in a linear fashion. These cultures are called *monochronic* cultures. In these cultures, such as most Anglo cultures, time is a valuable commodity. People save, spend, and waste time. People live by their schedules, and punctuality is valued. In Switzerland, the famous Swiss railway system apologizes publicly if a train is more than one minute late, which is a very rare occurrence; in Japan there is no need to apologize – the trains are always exactly on time! Punctuality is defined by the most natural division of time. Pay attention to when people start to explain why they are late, or offer an apology for their tardiness, and you will have a clue to what is the natural division of time for that society.

In *polychronic* cultures, time is seen as elastic. Units may be small or large, depending on what is being done or experienced at the time. Several timelines flow in parallel, and people believe it is natural to be doing many things at the same time. Arab and Latin cultures are typical polychronic cultures. In these cultures, time schedules are less critical. It might be 45 minutes to an hour before an apology or explanation for being late is expected, and among friends no explanation is ever needed. In polychronic cultures, individuals who are driven to meet schedules and deadlines are seen as lacking patience, tact, or perseverance. Polychronic cultures are often also collective, and they use the parallel modes as a way to build relationships. Someone from a monochronic, less collective culture may want to "get down to business" quickly, which prevents taking the time to develop relationships. Many Americans and western Europeans have stories of how they have destroyed opportunities to conduct business or negotiate contracts by underestimating the combination of collectivism and polychronic time orientation!

Monochronic and polychronic time is related to country-cultures, but it is in the midst of a transition related to globalization. The increase in global interdependence we discussed in Chapter 1 has led to an increase in coordination, and coordination requires both a monochronic base for planning and a polychronic approach for dealing with inevitable changes. So although countries tend to prefer a monochronic or polychronic approach, global businesspeople have developed an appreciation for the necessity of both. Moreover, the formal global business culture is probably shifting more towards monochronic. However, if one is doing business with people from another culture beyond basic transactions, then one will encounter the monochronic-polychronic difference in the rest of the culture. Managers will be able to perform more effectively if they can navigate this dimension well, regardless of what happens on the surface.

One of us recently went on a trip to Saudi Arabia as a guest of a large multinational there. She received a four-day agenda two weeks in advance, and it was meticulously planned to the 15-minute interval. The agenda included many non-company meetings and locations in order to help the author learn to understand the complexity of the culture. The company had planned according to monochronic time, and the author greatly appreciated this planning. Once she arrived in Saudi Arabia, about half of the agenda happened in ways other than what was planned, with often quite dramatic changes in events, timings, or people involved. The implementation of the event was more polychronic, and this she also appreciated since the guides took advantage of whatever would work best at the time. In this way, the author was able to see much more of the culture and appreciate the people who have created success there.

A summary of the Cultural Orientations dimensions reviewed here is shown in Table 2.1.

TABLE 2.1 Summary of the cultural orientations framework

Orientation	Variations		
Relation to the Environment How do we relate to the world around us? This includes the physical, economic and social worlds.	*Harmony* The environment is a complex system of which we are one part. Our actions should keep the system in balance, then everything will work well.		*Mastery* The environment is separate from us, and something to be managed. Our actions should influence and control the environment to get things to work well.
Relations among People How do we think about relationships of power and responsibility among people?	*Collective* People in the group should be responsible for each other, and everyone is responsible to fulfill the group's needs. The group may be the extended family, the community, or any other large group.	*Individual* Each of us should be responsible for him- or herself alone, and perhaps the immediate family if necessary. Society works better if everyone looks after him- or herself.	*Hierarchy* Power and responsibility are arranged such that those above have power over those below, and responsibility for them. Those below should obey the wishes of those above.
Mode of Activity What is the basic sequence of activity we agree to use together?	*Doing* We agree it is important to jump into action. When in doubt, do something.		*Thinking* We agree it is important to plan carefully, before taking action. When in doubt, plan and analyze.
Time How do we measure and use time in an ongoing way?	*Monochronic* We measure time in linear, equal units. We prefer to do one thing at a time, then move to the next. Punctuality is important.		*Polychronic* We think of time as flexible, and we do many things at a time. Punctuality is less important than doing things in their time.

Note: Although these are presented in rows, there is no correspondence or correlation. For example, a culture that is harmony-oriented is not necessarily also collective-oriented. Every combination is possible.

TABLE 2.2   Potential cultural contributions to multicultural teamwork

Cultural Variable		Contribution to Task	Contribution to Process
Environment	Mastery	Focus on the immediate problem	Drive to solution
	Harmony	Understand the problem from a holistic view	Don't come to closure too quickly
Relations	High Collectivism	See the problem from different stakeholders' perspectives	Help the group converge and commit
	Low Collectivism	See the problem from different individuals' perspectives	Help the group value minority contributions
	High Hierarchy	Anticipate implementation challenges	Efficient communication, not endless communication
	Low Hierarchy	Openly approach information sources	Encourage ideas regardless of source
Collective Activity	Doing	Suggest actions	Pilot test, try it out
	Thinking	Conduct in-depth analysis	Team reflection, careful prototype

Cultural Contributions in Multicultural Teams

As we have implied several times above, the members of a multicultural team will bring different perspectives to the team, not just about the task itself, but about how to engage with the team and in the task. These different perspectives are likely to create conflict if team members are unaware. However, with knowledge and effective communication (see Chapter 3) they can also be leveraged in a constructive way to perform even better. Table 2.2 provides some highlights of these potential contributions.

The Discipline of Cartography: Cultural Mixes, Changes, and other Complexities

Being able to map involves more than the knowledge of the framework. It requires *using* the framework to understand, explain and predict others' attitudes and behavior. Mapping creates awareness and appreciation of differences and their implications in a structured and consistent way. It begins a conversation about similarities and differences using a common language and framework, and allows the conversation to move quickly and constructively to individual and situational differences. Like cartographers, managers need to combine various sources of information to create their own dynamic maps and use them to navigate complex territories. Just like any other skill, managers can practice mapping and improve their ability to map.

FIGURE 2.7   Distribution of mastery scores for USA and Taiwan

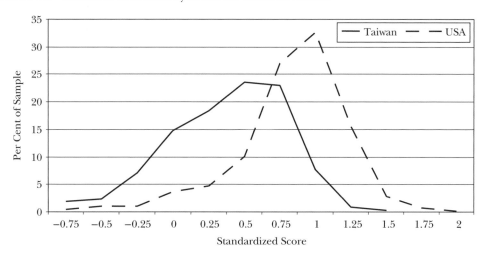

The Limits of Maps   Mapping is a good first step to cross-cultural understanding, but it is important to recognize its limits. We describe the four most important ones here.

The first is that *individuals do not always conform to their cultures*. Variety and unpredictability are both the beauty and the complexity of human nature. We are all different, and we do not always behave as predicted! Within cultures, some people hold more strongly to the cultural norms than others. Personality and environmental factors influence individual behavior. Even people who are strong proponents of their culture's values do not always behave in a way that is consistent with those values. [25] This limitation is called the *ecological fallacy*: by knowing the culture (ecological level) you cannot always predict individuals; by knowing an individual, you cannot automatically predict the culture. Figure 2.7 illustrates this principle with data from our research, showing distributions of mastery scores in the US and Taiwan. In this figure you can see that in both countries there are individuals who cluster around the norm, and others that are *atypical* of their country. There are differences between the two cultural groups: on average, Americans score higher on mastery than Taiwanese; but there are overlaps, too. Some individuals in each cultural group are more like those in the *other cultural group*! On the Cultural Perspectives Questionnaire, most people are close to their country's norm on most variations, and quite different on at least some variations. However, most people perceive themselves as atypical of their culture. Think about yourself; are you more or less typical of the cultural group you identify yourself with?

Not surprisingly, some countries are more culturally diverse than others. Our survey data showed some interesting results when we looked at within-country homogeneity or diversity, as shown in Table 2.3. Countries like Brazil and Canada are diverse due to

TABLE 2.3 Countries categorized by within-culture variance

High Cultural Homogeneity	Mod. Cultural Homogeneity	Mixed	Mod. Cultural Diversity	High Cultural Diversity
Belgium	Austria	Australia	Greece	Brazil
Japan	Finland	Denmark	India	Canada
South Korea	France	Hong Kong	Ireland	China
Saudi Arabia	Germany	Italy	Switzerland	Philippines
Singapore		Malaysia	UK	Romania
Taiwan		Mexico	USA	Russia
Thailand		Netherlands		South Africa
		New Zealand		
		Nigeria		
		Norway		
		Spain		
		Sweden		

patterns of immigration, while China, Russia are diverse due to ideological shifts in the country. Kluckhohn and Strodtbeck held that within-culture diversity is important for cultural change and adaptation. Japan's cultural homogeneity was seen as a key factor for creating initial growth through efficiency in alignment, but may now be associated with less growth from innovation.[26]

Second, *all individuals belong to multiple cultures, and types of cultures, simultaneously*. Jemilah, for example, considers herself part of the Malaysian, Malay, Chinese, medical doctor, Muslim, female, mother, humanitarian aid, and global business cultures, and she articulates clearly what it means to be part of each of those cultures. Which culture she draws upon to guide her perceptions and behaviors depends on her context. She is always guided by her religious culture, covering her hair with a scarf in public, observing prayers and other disciplines, and reflecting in her behavior the lessons of the Prophet and the Koran. She is proud of her Malaysian culture and a strong advocate of Malaysians worldwide. She also celebrates Chinese holidays and traditions, and has close ties with her Chinese family. When delivering babies at the hospital, she behaves according to the norms and values of the medical doctor culture. When providing medical aid in an emergency situation, such as after natural disasters in Indonesia or Myanmar or as a result of conflict in Iraq or Gaza, she disregards some of the procedures typical of the hospital culture and behaves according to the emergency (for example, doing surgery outside her area of specialization), consistent with the humanitarian aid culture. When negotiating for resources with corporate sponsors for her humanitarian organization, Mercy Malaysia,[27] or when gaining access to emergency situations, she acts according to the global business culture, and she is well-respected as a tough player. She does not always choose to act according to a single culture, because she carries all these cultures in her, and often uses several at the same time to guide her behavior. For example, when trying to get emergency supplies to a conflict site, she uses both the humanitarian aid and the global business culture, and leverages her identity and expertise as a doctor to establish her credibility.

Jemilah's set of cultural identities is more complex than many people's. She is one of a growing minority of people in the world who are considered bicultural by having two (or more) ethnic cultures. Research on biculturalism shows that people who grow up with two or more cultures, such as children of immigrants or children whose parents come from two cultures, face unique challenges in developing their identity but also can develop advantages such as flexibility and cognitive complexity.[28] They manage these identities in different ways, for example they may prioritize one identity over another, they may separate them and draw on each in different situations, or they may combine them in various ways. Although Jemilah is an extreme example, it is important to remember that the pattern is common to everyone, and we all identify with multiple cultures.[29]

Third, cultures are much more **complex** than can be described simply by these orientations with their aggregate variations. The configuration of preferences themselves leads to complex differences. Mastery combined with doing, for example, looks different from mastery combined with thinking. Mastery-doing is associated with obsessive task activity for accomplishment; mastery-thinking is associated with more depth in analysis before controlling. More importantly, the dimensions cannot ever capture the richness of cultures. We have provided examples to illustrate some of the principles, but the art, music, literature, traditions, practices, and beliefs of cultures go far beyond these dimensions. As we discussed earlier, multiple cultures exist in the same social "space" simultaneously. The existence of subcultures and complementary cultures also adds to the complexity of culture.

Finally, cultures are **dynamic**, always changing. In fact, Kluckhohn and Strodtbeck argued that cultures must change or they will stagnate and die, and that change is made possible by the variation of individuals within cultures and the existence of subcultures.[30] Usually change is quite slow, but sometimes external and internal events combine to create fast change. For example, our data show that in some emerging markets – notably China, India and Russia – the preference for collectivism over individualism is much less pronounced now than it was four years ago. This suggests the possibility that economic growth is somehow associated (cause or effect?) with a shift away from strong collectivism. However, we see the same shift towards lower relative preference for collectivism in France and Greece, where growth has slowed or even reversed. What are the causes and effects there? We will leave it to others to speculate. Our point here is that maps show a misleadingly static picture. Those who use maps must remember that cultures shift.

For example, when we look at our data on some cultures in transition, we see differences between businesspeople aged 35 and younger versus businesspeople aged 36 and older. In all of the BRICs, the older generation has a higher preference for collectivism over individualism than the younger generation does. In China, the two generations are the furthest apart, with the older generation having higher preferences for mastery over harmony, and for hierarchy as well. But it is not only the emerging markets who experience generation differences. In both France and Spain, for example, the younger generation shows a much lower preference for both collectivism and hierarchy. Generational differences can be seen as creating both conflicts and social movements within the countries, and it will be interesting to see the dynamics in another generation.

The Map is Not the Territory   Maps are critical tools for navigation, but it is important to remember that the map is not the territory. In its most basic form, mapping is sophisticated stereotyping. Sophisticated stereotyping is describing cultures using objective, non-evaluative data to predict thinking and behavior patterns of the culture's members.[31] As we illustrated above, sophisticated stereotyping is extremely helpful when we enter new situations or try to understand unexpected events. People who go into new countries and cultures without sophisticated stereotypes, saying "I have no expectations, I have an open mind," are really assuming "I think they will be like me." This is due to the basic human processes related to the assumptions and perceptions described earlier in this chapter. When people go into a new situation with a map of expectations concerning how the others are likely to be different from oneself – sophisticated stereotypes – they are more prepared for differences in thinking and behavior, and they manage those differences much better.[32] We often hear students say "I will go into [the new country] having an open mind," really meaning they are not going to conduct any pre-departure investigation of the culture. One of the best rejoinders to that came from another student who said, "Remember, having an open mind is different from having an empty mind!"

CULTURE IS AT THE CORE OF INTERNATIONAL MANAGEMENT

Knowledge about culture is one of the most important foundations of the global mindset and global leadership competences. Culture is the context in which international management is conducted. Culture provides guidance for how to decide and behave, and provides an important source of identity for its members. In this chapter, we discussed culture-general knowledge in depth: knowledge about how culture influences its members. We also provided a framework for developing and applying culture-specific knowledge that managers should find useful for organizing their interpretations of cultures with which they operate.

It is possible to ignore cultural difference for a short time or for basic transactions – that is, to operate without a global mindset – especially if you have power or other resources. However, it is impossible to create high performance or sustain performance over time in a multinational business world without a sophisticated understanding of culture, and an ability to draw on the strengths of different cultures in different situations. Moreover, all international managers we know agree that cultural differences create the most interesting, dynamic, and ever-enjoyable canvas possible on which to paint a management career.

Notes

1   www.hsbc.com , accessed April 25, 2013.

2   Carroll, L., *Through the Looking Glass and What Alice Found There* (London: Macmillan, 1871).

3   Kluckhohn, F. and Strodtbeck, F., *Variations in Value Orientations* (New York: Row, Peterson and Company, 1961).

4   Hofstede, G., *Cultures and Organizations: Software of the Mind* (Maidenhead, Berkshire, England: McGraw-Hill Book Company Europe, 1991).

5   For an elegant and powerful work on identity, see Amin Maalouf, *In the Name of Identity* (New York: Penguin Books, 2000).

6   Gibson, C. B., Maznevski, M. and Kirkman, B. L., "When Does Culture Matter?" in R. S. Bhagat and R. M. Steers (eds.), *Handbook of Culture, Organizations, and Work* (Cambridge, UK: Cambridge University Press, 2009).

7   http://www.economist.com/blogs/graphicdetail/2013/01/daily-chart-18. Accessed April 25, 2013.

8   http://www.consumerreports.org/cro/food/beverages/coffee-tea/coffee-taste-test-3-07/overview/0307_coffee_ov_1.htm. Accessed November 1, 2008.

9   Erez, M. and Earley, P.C., *Culture, Self-Identity, and Work* (Oxford: Oxford University Press, 1993).

10 Weick, K., *The Social Psychology of Organizing* (Reading MA: Addison-Wesley Publishing Co.: 1979).

11 Berry, J. W., Poortinga, Y. H., and Breugelmans, S. M., *Cross Cultural Psychology: Research and Applications* (Cambridge, UK: Cambridge University Press, 1992) 8.

12 Hall, E. T., "The silent language in overseas business," *Harvard Business Review*, 38(3) (1960) 87–96.

13 Hofstede, G., *Culture's Consequences: International Differences in Work Related Values* (La Jolla, CA: Sage Publications, 1980). Also "Motivation, leadership and organization: Do American theories apply abroad?" *Organizational Dynamics*, 9(1) (1980) 42–63. Geert Hofstede, *Culture's Consequences: Comparing Values, Behaviors, Institutions, and Organizations Across Nations,* 2nd edn. (Thousand Oaks, Calif.: Sage Publications, 2001).

14 Chinese Culture Connection, "Chinese values and the search for culture-free dimensions of culture," *Journal of Cross-Cultural Psychology*, 18(2) (1987) 143–164. Hofstede, G. H., *Cultures and Organizations: Software of the Mind*, revised edn. (New York: McGraw-Hill, 1997).

15 House R. J., Hanges, P. J., Javidan, M., Dorfman, P. and Gupta, V. (eds.), *GLOBE, Cultures, Leadership, and Organizations: GLOBE Study of 62 Societies* (Newbury Park, CA: Sage Publications, 2003).

16 Hampden-Turner, C. and Trompenaars, F., *The Seven Cultures of Capitalism.* (New York: Currency Doubleday, 1993). Also Hampden-Turner, C. and Trompenaars, F., *Riding the Waves of Culture: Understanding Cultural Diversity in Global Business,* 2nd edn. (New York: Irwin Professional Publications, 1998).

17 Schwartz, S. H., "Beyond individualism/collectivism: New cultural dimensions of values," in U. Kim, H. C. Triandis, C. Kagitcibasi, S. Choi and G. Yoon (eds.), *Individualism and Collectivism: Theory, Method, and Applications* (Thousand Oaks, CA.: Sage, 1994) 85–119. Schwartz, S. H., "A theory of cultural values and some implications for work," *Applied Psychology – an International Review – Psychologie Appliquee – Revue Internationale*, 48(1) (1999) 23–47. Sagiv, L. and Schwartz, S. H., "A new look at national culture: Illustrative applications to role stress and managerial behavior," in N. M. Ashkenasy, C. P. M. Wilderom and M. F. Peterson (eds.), *The Handbook of Organizational Culture and Climate* (Newbury Park, CA.: Sage, 2000) 417–435.

18 Kluckhohn, F. R. and Strodtbeck, F. L., 1961. *op. cit.*

19 Maznevski, M. L., Distefano, J. J., Gomez, C. B., Noorderhaven, N. G., and Wu, P-C., "Cultural Dimensions at the Individual Level of Analysis: The Cultural Orientations Framework," *International Journal of Cross-Cultural Management*, 2(3) (2002) 275–295.

20   Perret, M. S., *The Impact of Cultural Differences on Budgeting* (unpublished doctoral dissertation, London, Canada: The University of Western Ontario, 1982).

21   Tutu Foundation UK. http://www.tutufoundationuk.org/ubuntu.php. Accessed April 25, 2013.

22   Gibson, C. B. and Zellmer-Bruhn, M., "Metaphor and Meaning: An Intercultural Analysis of the Concept of Teamwork," *Administrative Science Quarterly*, 46 (2001) 274–303.

23   Hall, E. T., *The Silent Language* (New York: Doubleday and Co, 1959).

24   Lightfoot, R. W. and Bartlett, C. A., "Phillips and Matsushita: A portrait of two evolving companies," in Bartlett, C. A., Ghoshal, S. and Richard, D. (eds.), *Transnational Management: Text, Cases and Readings in Cross-border Management*, (Homewood, IL: Irwin, 1992).

25   Gibson, C. B., Maznevski, M. and Kirkman, B. L., "When Does Culture Matter?" in R. S. Bhagat and R. M. Steers (eds.), *Handbook of Culture, Organizations, and Work* (Cambridge, UK: Cambridge University Press, 2009).

26   Maznevski, M. L. and Chui, C. 2012. "Following our own nation's path," conference paper presented at the Academy of Management Annual Meeting, Boston.

27   Dr. Jemilah Mahmoud, President of Mercy Malaysia, personal communications. www.mercy.org.my

28   Fitzsimmons, S. R., "Multicultural employees: A framework for understanding how they contribute to organizations," *Academy of Management Review*, (2013). "Biculturalism pays," David C. Thomas, *National Post*, November 11, 2008, Toronto, Canada. Fitzsimmons, S. R., *Multiple Modes of Biculturalism: Antecedents and Outcomes* (unpublished PhD dissertation, Canada: Simon Fraser University, 2009). Brannen, M., Thomas, D., Roth, K., Cheng, C., Locke, G., Garcia, D., Lee, F. and Fitzsimmons S., "Biculturalism in the global marketplace: Integrating research and practice," Symposium presented at the Academy of Management Meetings, Anaheim, CA, 2008. Cheng, C., Lee, F. and Benet-Martinez, V., "Assimilation and Contrast Effects in Cultural Frame Switching (CFS): Bicultural Identity Integration (BII) and Valence of Cultural Cues," *Journal of Cross Cultural Psychology*, 37(6) (2006) 1–19. Brannen, M. Y. and Salk, J., "Partnering across borders: Negotiating organizational culture in a German-Japanese joint venture," *Human Relations*, 53(4) (2000) 451–487. Leu, J., Benet-Martinez, V. and Lee, F., "Bicultural identities: Dynamics, individual differences, and socio-cognitive correlates," *International Journal of Psychology*, 35 (2000). Brannen, M. Y., "Organizational Culture in a Bi-national Context: A Model of Negotiated Culture," *Anthropology of Work Review*, 13(2) (1992).

29   Boyacigiller, N. A., Kleinberg, M. J., Phillips, M. E. and Sackmann, S. A., "Conceptualizing culture: Elucidating the streams of research in international cross-cultural research," in Punnett, B. J. and Shenkar, O. (eds.), *Handbook of International Management Research*, 2nd edn. (Ann Arbor: University of Michigan Press, 2004).

30   Kluckhohn and Strodtbeck, *op. cit.*

31   Adler, N. J., *International Dimensions of Organizational Behavior*, 5th edn. (Kentucky: Thomsom South-Western, 2008).Bird, A. and Osland, J., "Beyond sophisticated stereotyping: Cultural sense-making in context," *Academy of Management Executive*, 14 (2000) 65–79.

32   Ratiu, I., "Thinking internationally: A comparison of how international executives learn," *International Studies of Management and Organization*, 13(1–2) (1983) 139–150.

CHAPTER 3

Interpersonal Skills for International Management: The MBI Model for High Performance

Which performs better – a diverse team or a homogeneous team? It's a trick question of course, and the answer is the same as the answer to any management question: "It depends." Let's take a closer look.

First, it depends on what we mean by *diverse*. There is, of course, no such thing as a completely homogeneous team. Everyone on a team is different from each other. But some teams are more diverse than others. For example, a team of six people who are men and women from different countries and ethnic cultures, professions, and organizations, is more diverse than a team of six men or women from the same country and culture, profession, and organization. In most of today's organizations, teams are more diverse than they were in the past. With increased workforce diversity, more organizational structures with units that reach across professional and country borders, and with more alliances across organizations, teams inevitably are composed of people from more diverse backgrounds. As we discussed in the previous chapter, cultural differences, and in particular, country-based cultural differences, are an important source of difference in perspectives and values.

Second, it depends on what we mean by *performance*. A diverse team brings many different perspectives to a task. This diversity increases divergent processes in teams – processes related to creativity and questioning of assumptions to develop new ideas.[1] If the task is a routine, structured task, such as calculating the best combination of production runs, then this diversity may not bring any advantages, and in fact the group may have difficulty becoming aligned around a solution. But if the task is an unstructured, ambiguous task, such as developing a strategy for a new market, then the diversity may bring helpful perspectives. Furthermore, because diverse groups tend to have broader sets of networks than homogeneous groups do, diverse groups can be better set up to implement change effectively.[2]

Third, and most importantly, it depends on how you *manage the interactions in the team.* Some teams use their diversity effectively, combining ideas and building on them to create new and better ways of doing business. We call these teams "creators." Other teams we refer to as "destroyers"; they let the differences lead to destructive conflict and personal disputes, ending up with poor solutions. Most teams do something safer – they suppress differences and pretend the differences don't exist. These "equalizer" teams focus on similarities among team members.[3] This is usually done for noble reasons ("it's what we have in common that matters"), but the equalizer approach has two problems. The obvious shortfall is that it does not realize the potential of the team. It leaves unused resources on the table, and sub-optimizes decision quality and implementation. "Okay," some managers respond, "it's not worth the effort or the risk of conflict. For us, it is a good rational decision not to invest in the diversity." Maybe, in the short term.

But the second problem with the equalizer approach is both more subtle and more damaging. Have you ever worked on a team where you felt like you couldn't be yourself? Where you had to work, for a sustained period of time, in a way that was not comfortable for you? When someone's perspectives and ways of working are suppressed over time, he acts through a filter. He's constantly spending energy thinking about *how* to present his ideas and *how* to participate, rather than on creating and presenting ideas and reflecting on others' ideas in the first place. Most people in this situation eventually become frustrated and disengaged. They may even initiate serious conflicts or, more likely, simply leave the team.

Joan (her English name), a Hong Kong immigrant to Scotland, was frustrated with her performance reviews and career potential. She was working as a senior staff accountant at a large audit firm. She finished her university education in the UK, and became a chartered accountant in the minimum possible time in Scotland. She knew that she had a good reputation for reliability, that people saw her work as extremely accurate, and that her clients found her to be helpful, polite, and constructive when working together. She also knew that she was shouldering more work on audits than any of her teammates. Yet still, when it came to performance review time, her reviews were average, while others got higher reviews. They were also more likely to get their choice of assignments than Joan.

Joan was used to a culture of high hierarchy, preference for harmony over mastery, and preference for thinking over doing. Scotland was essentially the opposite on all three of these dimensions. Joan's Scottish peers and bosses were not "seeing" her performance. So Joan decided to start acting like her Scottish peers. She was more vocal in teams, sometimes even disagreeing with her boss when he overlooked something. She took control more, volunteering for assignments before others, and making recommendations for the client to change their business. Her peers and bosses started paying more attention to her, and complimented her for adapting so well. However, after several months, Joan's accuracy level began to drop, and she found herself showing frustration to her peers and clients. Her boss wondered what was wrong, and what he could do to fix the situation (a mastery and doing approach).

The equalizer approach of Joan's boss and team, while seeming to increase performance in the short-term, affected Joan's level of motivation and energy and eventually her performance. The team lost out on the additional perspectives Joan could have brought with her attention to planning and systems, and later they also lost out on getting Joan's best individual performance on the audits.

The "equalizer" approach reduces the challenges of diversity in the short term, but over time it ends up sliding into the "destroyer" approach.

Diverse teams can perform better than homogeneous teams, and multicultural teams can perform particularly well, if they manage the diversity constructively.[4] Our research shows that performance in diverse teams, especially multicultural ones, derives from a basic set of interactions we call Map-Bridge-Integrate, or MBI.[5]

MBI processes are so fundamental that they are necessary not only for teams to perform well, but for effective and constructive interaction among people who have different backgrounds and related perspectives and values, whether they are leader-subordinate, co-workers, partners in a customer-supplier alliance, or managers adapting business practices from one place to another.

In this chapter we focus on the interpersonal MBI processes themselves, and in the next, we add other layers of complexity associated with global teams.

"Mapping" is about understanding cultural and other differences among each other. "Bridging" is communicating effectively, taking those differences into account. "Integrating" is bringing the different perspectives together and building on them. When these three skills are executed well, interactions between individuals or among team members result in high performance. The basic model is shown in Figure 3.1. Integrating leads directly to effectiveness, but Bridging accounts for more than

FIGURE 3.1   MBI in brief

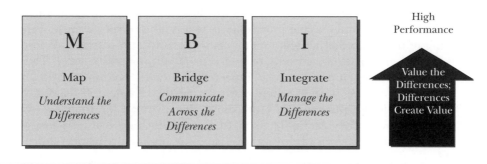

two-thirds of the variance in Integrating. In other words, if Bridging is done well, Integrating follows almost naturally; if Bridging is not done well, there is likely to be no Integrating. Moreover, Bridging cannot be done without good Mapping, no matter how skilled or well-intentioned the people involved. Below, we discuss and illustrate each of these skills.

MAPPING TO UNDERSTAND AND DESCRIBE DIFFERENCES

In Chapter 2, "Understanding culture," we introduced the metaphor of mapping culture. Mapping is systematically and objectively describing characteristics of people and identifying similarities and differences that can be used to help each other perform. The most useful Mapping uses data and summaries of facts, organized with frameworks that help compare the data and facts across groups and individuals. In Chapter 2 we described the results of our research with the Cultural Perspectives Questionnaire, which maps culture. It is possible – and often desirable – to map other characteristics such as personality, profession, or gender.

Most people are afraid of Mapping because they worry it will lead to stereotyping. They resist being put into a box as an unthinking representative of a group, and do not want to categorize others that way. This is a healthy fear and resistance, and we encourage it. Like any tool, Mapping can be misused. However, Mapping is such a powerful tool that it is worth using. Maps are objective descriptions of characteristics that are relevant to an interaction. They help people respect each others' values and perspectives, and give people suggestions about how to use each other's ideas better. Maps are revised whenever new data are available, and are constantly tested as hypotheses rather than taken for granted as truths. Maps should be seen as windows to the complex territory of human beings, ways of entering the different perspectives and really seeing the person inside.

Stereotypes, on the other hand, are subjective descriptions of groups of people that are usually used to judge those people, often in a negative way. Stereotypes are assumed to be true and are neither tested nor changed with new information. They usually lead people to close doors – making assumptions about how people will behave – rather than open windows. The differences between Mapping and stereotyping are subtle, but important.[6] Mapping leads to healthy dynamics among individuals, with people casting aside the maps as they develop more insight into the territory.

Above we described "equalizer" teams, those that focus only on similarities. Research shows that without explicit intervention, teams tend to spend most of their time discussing information that all team members share, and only a small portion of the time discussing information that only one or a few team members have.[7] This dynamic is not conducive to high performance, especially if the task is complex and multidimensional. Explicit Mapping is an excellent way to avoid this dynamic. If team members are aware of the different perspectives – the different points on the map – and of the potential contributions, they are more likely to bring them into team discussions and to create better solutions. Among individuals, such as between a leader and a subordinate or

FIGURE 3.2   MBI – Focus on Mapping

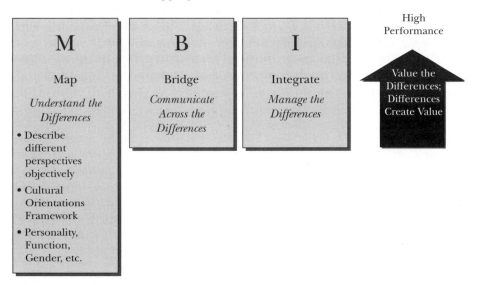

between a customer and a supplier, Mapping helps prevent conflict and aids in seeing opportunities. The more the people involved understand the nature of each other's different perspectives, the more they can use those differences to achieve high performance. Mapping is summarized in Figure 3.2.

Mapping in Action – A New Team

How important is it to sit down and create detailed maps, with survey data about individuals involved, or can you just know the general patterns and map from there? There is a trade-off between investment and results. Explicit Mapping takes time, but it pays off in more ideas coming into the group, more comprehensive examination and analysis of the ideas, and more possibility of building on ideas in innovative ways. The more important the task and/or the more diverse the people involved, the more critical Mapping is.

In our experience, it is best for a group to go into detailed Mapping on at least two dimensions that are important to the group's work, such as culture and personality or gender, then use those discussions to access Mapping on any other relevant dimensions. The use of an outside facilitator to help with Mapping is not necessary, but some managers prefer it, for example if the leader would prefer to be a neutral participant rather than lead the process. Some maps, such as many personality surveys, must be administered and facilitated by a certified professional, so if you want to use these maps an outside facilitator may be necessary.

Reinhard was appointed to lead the global marketing group for a new, highly innovative medical product. The product was based on a combination of robotic, bionic, wireless, and biologic technologies, and had the potential to revolutionize the treatment of debilitating diseases. It had the potential to be the "next big thing" for the company, and everyone involved was excited about the impact. Reinhard knew he needed a diverse team of professionals to tap into different ideas and different aspects of the task and the market, so he deliberately recruited his ten direct reports to reflect a scope of organizational veterans and newcomers, medical professionals, engineers and social scientists, young and experienced people, and people from multiple country-cultures and with different personality types.

Shortly after the team launched, Reinhard brought the team together for a Mapping exercise. Given the importance of the product launch, the sensitivity of the product, and the diversity of the team, he decided to work with an outside facilitator although he remained very active in the Mapping process and often took the lead. He first used an exercise called Trialogue, which uses a short survey and a specific process to get people to explore the different team roles they prefer to contribute and the implications for the team. Trialogue creates a positive environment for discussions about diversity, opening people up to Mapping and the entire MBI process.[8]

Reinhard had the team map personality and culture, the former using the Myers-Briggs Type Indicator (MBTI),[9] the latter using the Cultural Perspectives Questionnaire. For each of these maps, the team discussed patterns associated with different dimensions, such as the examples we described for culture in Chapter 2, and identified each individual's position on the Map. Who prefers extraversion and who prefers introversion as a personality dimension? Who prefers mastery and who prefers harmony as a cultural dimension? In this Mapping discussion, people identified specific potential contributions of individual team members. For example, the mastery-oriented members will help us remember to take charge of the market, and identify what we can control; the harmony-oriented members will help us remember to keep in mind the whole medical system and all the different players, and how we can work through the system.

After these discussions, the team created a large grid on the wall, with team members' names down the left as rows and dimensions of diversity across the top as columns. The grid with some of the team members is shown in Table 3.1. By the end of the process, team members were even more excited about working together, learning from each other, and using the different perspectives and some newly-discovered commonalities to create a great product launch.

The team succeeded beyond the company's expectations in terms of creating new markets and value for both customers and the company. This initial Mapping set them up well, and as a team they took their interaction seriously, engaging in reflection and development frequently. Three years later the five most senior members of the team (including Reinhard) had been promoted to lead other big opportunities across the globe, and one of the more junior members of the team was successfully leading the team to innovate and perform even more. Reinhard is clear that good Mapping started the team in the right direction, and continues to use the process with all his new teams.

TABLE 3.1   MBI - Example of a team's map

	Culture	Trialogue	Personality (MBTI)	Gender	Country Location	Organizational function, (education)	Hobbies
Reinhard	Low Hierarchy Mastery Thinking	Blue (red, green)	ENTJ	Male	Switzerland	Director (Sciences)	Family, sports, outdoors
Rachna	Collective High Hierarchy Harmony Thinking	Red (blue)	ESTP	Female	Belgium	Purchasing and logistics (Engineering)	Family, arts
Alejandro	Collective High Hierarchy Mastery	Red (green)	INFP	Male	South Korea	Business development (Engineering)	Music, sports
Takashi	High Hierarchy Mastery Doing	Blue	ESTJ	Male	Japan	Marketing & advertising (Business)	Movies, sports
John	Individualistic Low Hierarchy Mastery Doing	Green	ENTP	Male	USA	Technology, sales (Business)	Technology, travel
Marije	Against hierarchy Harmony Doing	Green (red)	ENFJ	Female	Switzerland	Post-sales technical management (Medicine)	Outdoors, travel
Claire	Collective Mod Hierarchy Thinking	Blue (green)	ISTJ	Female	Dubai	Finance (Economics)	Theatre, classical music

BRIDGING DIFFERENCES THROUGH COMMUNICATION

Mapping to understand the lens through which others see the world is an enormous aid to intercultural effectiveness. But this understanding provides little benefit as long as it remains latent. It must be put into use to help the flow of ideas among people in a conversation, a team, or an organization. The goal of these interpersonal flows is effective communication, or the transfer of meaning from one person to another as it was intended by the first person. Most managers recognize that effective communication within one's own culture is difficult enough. Interactions with people from different cultures are even more difficult. The challenge is to interpret correctly what a person from a different culture means by his or her words and actions. Even if interaction is aided by slowing speech, speaking more distinctly, listening more carefully, or asking more questions, there still remains the problem of interpreting the message. When your

Japanese direct report says "yes," what does he mean? That he agrees, that he will undertake the action, that he accepts the importance of your input? It can make a big difference in implementing strategy!

Resolving miscommunication depends, in large part, on a manager's willingness to explain the problem rather than to blame the other person. The quality of the explanation depends, in large part, on the manager's ability to map the other person's culture or background with respect to his or her own.

Although language is an important part of communication, communication is not simply a matter of understanding and speaking a language. Communication is broader than language alone. Someone who is able to speak five different languages still may not be able to understand the issues from the viewpoint of those from another culture. Or, put more eloquently by an Eastern European manager to the Australians in an English-speaking group, "I can speak to you in your language, but I can't always tell you what I am thinking in my own language."

There are three skills important to effective communication in a cross-cultural setting: preparing, decentering, and recentering.[10] These three skills help improve all communication anywhere. In interactions within a single culture, people generally operate under the same set of background assumptions, so the steps can be conducted implicitly, often without people even being aware they are doing them. The more culturally diverse the setting, the more difficult it is to accomplish these steps, and the more explicit they should be. But they also result in bigger payoffs. This Bridging component of the MBI model is summarized in Figure 3.3.

Prepare to be Open, Optimistic and Active

Preparing is about setting the ground for communication. The most important place to set the ground is in one's own mind. Two attitudes are especially predictive of effective communication: motivation and confidence. Motivation is having the will to communicate across a cultural boundary both to be understood and to understand others. We are usually very good at the former, but not as good at the latter. The confidence part is believing it is possible to overcome any barriers and communicate effectively. Ironically, people with little cross-cultural experience and those who have never tried to understand others from their own perspective tend to have high confidence, but that confidence disappears quickly with initial experiences and the realization of how difficult cross-cultural communication is. However, with practice and even small successes, confidence increases rapidly. This later confidence has a much more realistic foundation.

These attitudes may sound simple, but actually acting this way is difficult in the rush and pressure of making decisions and getting things done. We have a tendency to assume that others are like us, and to forget the importance of deliberately seeing things differently.[11] There are some simple things we can do to help ourselves, aside from just trying

FIGURE 3.3   MBI – Focus on Bridge

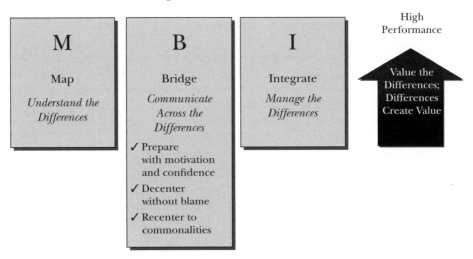

to remember to be motivated and confident. For example, learning even some of the others' language signals motivation and optimism, and opens doors into how the others think and what they value. Learning the language creates a positive, reinforcing cycle in cross-cultural communication, even if you do not approach fluency. Reading and studying about other countries' cultures, meeting people from the culture and asking them to help you immerse in the culture, watching their movies, are other ways of increasing your confidence in your cross-cultural communication ability. Mastering a cultural framework or "map," you have the motivation and confidence to ask questions that will be especially helpful in preparing yourself for future understanding.

Decenter to Transfer Meaning

Decentering is actively pushing yourself away from your own "center." It involves moving into the minds of the other people to send messages in a way they will understand, and to listen in a way that allows you to understand the others from their own point of view. The fundamental idea of decentering is empathy: feeling and understanding as another person does. But decentering requires going beyond just having empathy, to using one's empathy in hearing and speaking. A child sees two cookies on the table and is about to take both. The mother says, "Now, if you take both cookies, how will your sister feel?" The child knows her sister will feel terrible (strong empathy), but goes ahead and takes both cookies anyway (not decentering). This interaction happens all the time in cross-cultural situations. The Canadian manager says, "I know that as a Chinese it's hard for you to disagree openly with your boss, but I want you to know it's okay to do that with me. I don't mind when you disagree with me, in fact I expect you to." Or the Brazilian manager, "I know that in your [Scandinavian] culture it's not good to be open about feelings, but I am Brazilian and in my culture it's fine. So when I express my anger, don't worry, it's okay." We all know people who understand exactly how we feel, but nevertheless go ahead and say or do something awkward or hurtful anyway. This is practicing empathy without decentering.

There are two main elements to decentering. The first is perspective taking, which is the skill of being able to see things from the other person's point of view to the extent that you can speak and listen that way. The second is explaining without blame. When problems in communication do occur, and they inevitably will, it is critical that no one blames the other in a personal way, but that all parties seek an explanation in the situation: the differences in initial starting assumptions.

> People who withhold blame and search for situation-based explanations of miscommunication interact more effectively. In our research this emerged as the single best predictor of effective cross-cultural interaction.

Does this mean that all you have to do is explain without blame? No. But look at the sequence of events initiated when blame is suspended. This simple act leads a group into a positive cycle of decentering, exploring alternatives to build a shared reality, developing trust and common rules, and building confidence in the group's ability to use different perspectives productively. This process not only resolves the present miscommunication, but also prevents some further ones and provides ideas for creative synergy.

Good decentering is largely dependent on good Mapping. The map warns you that surprises and problems may have different explanations, and also provides you with some alternatives to explore. The Describe-Interpret-Evaluate framework identified in Chapter 2 is also very helpful here. When differences are encountered, the people involved should try to come to a point where they can agree on a description: what are the tangible, concrete facts we are talking about? Next they should explore their different interpretations: what do those facts mean to each person, and why? This is where the map provides a common language for sharing the analysis of interpretations. Finally, they should try to understand the different evaluations of the facts: why do some people see something as an opportunity and others as a threat? In cross-cultural situations, the greater the tendency to judge events, the greater the probability of making errors. Resisting the interpretive and evaluative modes while maintaining a descriptive posture for as long as possible is the best protection against cultural gaffes.

Decentering in Action – Scandinavian Managers Abroad

During our culture research studies, we developed a dialogue called "the Dark Side of Scandinavian Management." Scandinavian (the collective name that usually encompasses Norway, Sweden and Denmark, sometimes Iceland, but not Finland, which is Nordic but not Scandinavian) management has often been described as unique, and several groups of Scandinavian managers asked us to help them understand the challenges they were facing when they worked with people from other cultures.[12] Based on our Cultural Perspectives Questionnaire study and work done by Smith and colleagues,[13] we developed a data-based picture of the generic Scandinavian management style (Mapping). Although all organizations and all leaders are different, and the Scandinavian country cultures differ from each other, Scandinavian managers and those from other cultures who work with Scandinavians, agreed that the picture was generally accurate. We mapped Scandinavian management style as (see Chapter 2 for more details):

- **Strongly collective** – especially with respect to co-workers and society in general; the group is important, it is critical to get everyone aligned and on board, opinions of co-workers and subordinates are very important.

- **Strongly anti-hierarchical** – power and influence come not from your position but from your ideas and values and contributions to the group; considering your co-workers' and subordinates' ideas is often more important than considering your boss's ideas.

- **Action-oriented and pragmatic** – take control of situations, influence them, get things done, task focus, change actions as necessary to achieve the goals.

- **Not necessarily slow** – the stereotype of Scandinavian management style is that things move very slowly; however, the bias towards action is strong, and once the decision is made from group alignment, action is quick.

Based on this Mapping exercise, we created a typical conversation between a Scandinavian manager and his or her non-Scandinavian subordinates, outside Scandinavia. This hypothetical conversation brought tears of laughter to Scandinavian executives who recognized themselves in the middle of it.

This conversation shows what happens when decentering is *not* practiced by *anyone* involved. Notice the evolution to blaming that comes from not understanding each other's starting point: Scandinavian managers assuming the others are unenlightened, the others assuming Scandinavian managers are weak. Scandinavian managers who are effective in other cultures say that they adapt this process through decentering in several ways. They report they believe that in most situations getting ideas from subordinates and developing alignment is the best way to make decisions and implement change. However, when they first go to a new culture where hierarchy is stronger, they are more likely to use their position as boss to manage explicitly a process of getting ideas from others. They "command" people to take part and contribute their own ideas directly, and they use the hierarchy to dictate each part of the process. Effective Scandinavian managers abroad are also more likely to incorporate specific planning into the early discussions, recognizing others' need to make firm plans.

On the other hand, the executives in these workshops volunteered that the real "dark side of Scandinavian management" emerges in crises. Precious time can be lost getting alignment and assuming people will act in a unified way, when what is really important

1. Scandinavian manager . . . Asks subordinates and co-workers for their opinions, tries to negotiate alignment.

2. The others . . . Don't understand why the Scandinavian boss can't just decide. May want to make decision quickly so planning phase can begin.

3. Scandinavian manager . . . Responds to the requests and anxiety for decisions by asking more questions to get ideas and create alignment.

4. The others . . . Become even more frustrated with the lack of decision-making, complain that decision-making is SLOW, we'll never get to planning.

5. Scandinavian manager . . . Becomes paralyzed by not wanting to act in an authoritarian way. Not sure what to do.

6. The others . . . Become convinced that the process is SLOW, lose respect for the business capability of the Scandinavians.

7. Scandinavian manager . . . Finally, in frustration, makes and announces a decision.

8. The others . . . Relieved, voice agreement with the boss.

9. Scandinavian manager . . . Assumes agreement = alignment and signals readiness for action, moves onto considering other things.

10. The others . . . Either wait for further directions for action, or act in unaligned ways.

11. Scandinavian manager . . . Becomes frustrated by lack of action or unaligned action, waits for it to improve.

12. The others . . . Continue to wait or to act in many different directions.

13. Scandinavian manager . . . Becomes frustrated with unenlightened subsidiaries.

14. The others . . . Under-perform according to standards or expectations.

15. Scandinavian manager . . .
"Knows" (assumes) that everyone will contribute to their potential for the group, and will self-correct performance. Does nothing.

16. The others . . . "Know" (assume) everything is fine because the boss has not said anything. Nothing changes.

17. Scandinavian manager . . . Waits patiently for performance to self-correct; perhaps manages the environment to make it easier for people to self-correct.

18. The others . . . Start to recognize performance problem but see that boss doesn't "care" about it. Nothing changes.

19. Scandinavian manager . . . Becomes frustrated with unenlightened, unempowered subsidiaries.

20. The others . . . Become convinced that Scandinavians avoid conflict and are weak managers.

is taking a single decision and clarifying a set of actions for everyone to follow together. These executives admitted that they had learned to manage in an "un-Scandinavian way" when crises arose, even within Scandinavia.

Recenter to Align and Agree

The final step to effective communication is recentering, or establishing a common reality and agreeing on common rules. Like the other elements, establishing a common reality is easier said than done. For example, the implicit definition and purpose of "a meeting" varies from one culture to the next, with some cultures using meetings to discuss perspectives and come to a joint decision, and other cultures using meetings to publicly formalize decisions that were discussed informally among smaller subgroups of a team. A multicultural team that has not addressed even this basic definition is bound to find at least some members very frustrated with the first meeting. Again, good mapping helps to find a common definition and give the team a point of leverage.

Members of a multi-site global R&D team differed enormously on Relationships and Environment orientations, but virtually all preferred thinking strongly over doing for

Activity. They were able to use their common ground of the preference to plan and be rational to discuss their differences and work together. A team managing a strategic alliance in a manufacturing technology firm consisted of members from all over Europe, North America, and Asia. Like the team of R&D scientists, they had strong differences on many cultural orientations. Coincidentally, though, all were engineers for at least some part of their career, and they shared the same mastery orientation to the environment. Their common reality was based on what had to be done (changed and controlled), and they used this point to launch discussions about how to divide the work and what task processes to use.

Common norms for interacting must be established. It is less important to agree on a single set of norms for everyone, and more important to agree on a range of acceptable norms, with acceptance for some degrees of freedom for individual team members. As we showed in the opening of this chapter, it is futile to expect someone to behave in a way that is uncomfortable to them, yet still expect them to participate to their full potential. Asking someone who prefers a thinking orientation to jump in and "do" because that is the dominant mode and "you'll just have to adapt," is like asking that person not to bother contributing his best ideas to the group.

The most effective groups find ways of allowing different members to work with the group differently. Finding these norms is a creative process. It takes time and relies on strong relationships and trust within the group. But, like good preparing and decentering, the effort is well worth it. When the processes are not explored or discussed to find common ground, serious misunderstandings can occur, even when the cultures are not dramatically different.

For this example we look at the subtle differences among Nordic cultures, rather than Scandinavian management as a generic whole. The following exchange took place between the Finnish operating head and a senior Swedish executive of a software company grown by a series of acquisitions across the Nordic countries.

The Finn was explaining the decision-making process in the company:

> We reach our decisions by informal consultation "feeling out" positions, evolving into a common view of what should be done – what is possible, what alterations to each others' views are necessary, etc. This all occurs during the "feeling-out" process. Then when I think everything is clear I put the issue on the agenda of a meeting that ratifies the result of this process.

His Swedish colleague, who had been working as part of the senior executive team for nearly two years, interrupted and exclaimed heatedly:

> This is exactly the problem with you Finns! It [annoys me very much] when I don't have the opportunity to contribute . . . or even worse, I come to the meeting expecting it to be the first of a series of discussions and after I talk, you Finns give a PowerPoint presentation with the decision already included!! Don't insult me by pretending to ask for my involvement and opinion when you've already made up your mind!!

When he calmed down he explained more mildly:

> We Swedes expect a series of meetings, each an opportunity for extensive discussion among the participants with all involved, until a consensus is achieved or an explicit decision is taken. Since Finns occupy many of the senior posts at headquarters, we often find ourselves really annoyed by the process. Now I know why!!

Recentering in Action – A Multicultural Team   We captured a classic example of cross-cultural communication when we videotaped a group of executives discussing the possibility of their company acquiring another firm. The group consisted of five senior managers from: the United States (two members), United Kingdom, Japan, and Uruguay, and we videotaped them at their request to help them develop their Bridging skills. After studying various aspects of the potential deal, they had come together to make a recommendation.

The discussion was dominated by the American and the British managers, who were concerned about the lack of compatible strategies and financial problems in the nego-tiations. In the first hour, two key incidents happened which showed the need for recen-tering. First, the Uruguayan manager tried three times to introduce the issue of who would constitute the top executive team should the deal be struck. Would the buying company or the acquired organization supply the key executives for the merged entity? But each time he tried to raise the issue, the three others brushed his comments aside. Soon their dominance in the discussion extinguished the Latin American's view of what was important. Second, after 40 minutes of discussion, the British manager stood up in the room and went to the flip chart and wrote: "Do Nothing!" He punctuated his writing by saying, "I don't usually entertain this option, which is always raised as a 'straw man' by business school professors, but I really think in this situation it is our best choice. The deal is far from being ready to make for a whole host of reasons." There was a moment of silence, then the Japanese manager cleared his throat and quietly said, "Wait." The others thought that he was asking for a chance to discuss the "Do Nothing" option, but only a silence ensued. After a barely discernible pause, the British manager crossed out "Do Nothing" and wrote next to it, "Wait," and then he proceeded with his next point.

After one hour of discussion, the group stopped and looked at the video before continuing on. They analyzed the two incidents above. Regarding the Uruguayan's concerns, the group learned that, for him, relationships were fundamental and in fact, were related to the financial and strategic analysis of the deal. If certain members of the acquired organization were maintained, the price could be lower and returns could be more certain than if those individuals were not part of the deal. The Anglo-American managers were more focused on quantitative and product-market issues and missed the potential link. Through this discussion, the group recentered around a new com-mon objective. Their original goal was simply to evaluate the deal, but they realized they were all using different criteria to evaluate, so this was not as common as it seemed. Their new goal was to identify combinations of factors that could create a positive investment outcome, then to analyze the extent to which it was possible to create those combinations of factors. This was a more complex goal, but one that the group mem-bers all agreed to and that eventually led to better value creation for the company.

The group then explored the British "Do Nothing" vs. the Japanese suggestion to "Wait." The British executive literally meant "don't do anything more; proceed to look for other deals unless the other party indicates a change in the conditions." In contrast, the Japanese executive's "Wait" was filled with subtle actions including continuing to get to know the other parties, extending attempts to get more information about their business, and so on. Both wanted action, but in the British manager's mind, "waiting" was a passive mode and to be avoided. It was better to do nothing on this deal, and move on with other things. In the Japanese manager's mind, "waiting" was a very active mode and would help create the conditions for a good deal. The group members realized that the two actions could be complementary and recentered around a more comprehensive strategy of concerted dialogue and extended research, including into alternative deals.

Finally, the group discussed some of the norms they saw, such as the dominance of three of the members. They realized after watching the video that the Uruguayan had posed his ideas in the form of questions ("Don't you think we should explore from which company the top officers will be drawn?"). The Anglo-Americans were much more definite and assertive in their phrasing ("That's irrelevant until we get the financials and strategy agreed to!"). The Uruguayan was not really asking questions, he was using the phrasing of questions to demonstrate his respect for the collegial relationships in the group. But in the Anglo-American cultures phrasing something as a question signals uncertainty. In their mind, this was not a time for uncertainty in the analysis; it was time to be assertive. The team learned to recenter on norms by picking up the Uruguayan's cues about his opinions and learned to listen and take him seriously, even when he phrased his ideas as questions. It was also quite evident from the video that the Japanese manager rarely spoke unless someone asked him a question directly. All the others knew that this was a characteristic of Japanese culture, but they had not developed a set of norms that would constructively encourage the Japanese member's participation. Moreover, the manager from Uruguay waited until there was a brief pause in the conversation before speaking; in contrast, the American and British managers often interrupted each other. They recentered with an agreement that in the future, at the beginning of every new stage of the discussion, they would go around the table and have each person make a two-minute statement. They would assign a facilitator (a rotating role) to ensure this happened with discipline, and that facilitator also had the responsibility of ensuring balanced contributions afterwards.

By recentering around a common view of the task and situation, and around specific norms that facilitated participation, the team enhanced their Bridging and were able to provide much more valuable advice to the company.

INTEGRATING TO MANAGE AND BUILD ON THE DIFFERENCES

The final component of the MBI model is integrating the differences. It is not sufficient to have a way of understanding cultural differences and bridging the gaps by effective communication. One also needs to manage the differences effectively if they are to result in higher performance of the people who are working together. As shown in

FIGURE 3.4   MBI – Focus on Integrate

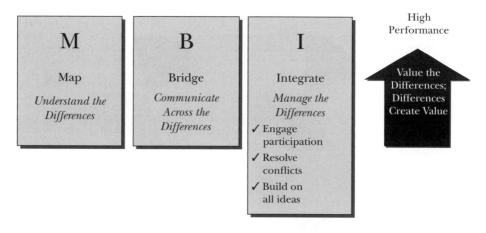

Figure 3.4, there are three main integration skills: generating participation, resolving conflicts, and building on ideas.

Generating Participation

To realize the benefits of different perspectives and ideas, it is necessary to express the ideas in the first place! Not all cultures are equally predisposed to offer their ideas openly. People from cultures with a strong hierarchical orientation, for example, are not likely to put forth their ideas in a group in which their direct superior or a higher-status person is also a member. In contrast, people from individualistic cultures are more likely to assert their ideas. The first challenge for a multicultural group, then, is to ensure that all the ideas are heard.

As foreshadowed by our multicultural team that focused on recentering, it is especially helpful if someone on the team monitors participation to notice whether there are systematic differences in participation rates. Figure 3.5 shows the pattern of participation in two meetings of multicultural teams, first in number of contributions, then in percentage of time. If there were no differences in the rates of participation, each shaded area would be equal in size. Aggregating the UK and US data shows a clear dominance of executives from these countries in both groups for both number of inputs and time. This pattern is especially clear in the second group.

There are ways of engaging all group members and facilitating their participation. In the example given earlier, the Japanese manager hardly spoke in the first half hour; his "wait" was his lone contribution during the first 45 minutes. Yet, after the break to analyze the video and recenter, one of the Americans in the group noticed his silence and

FIGURE 3.5   Levels of participation by different nationalities in two groups

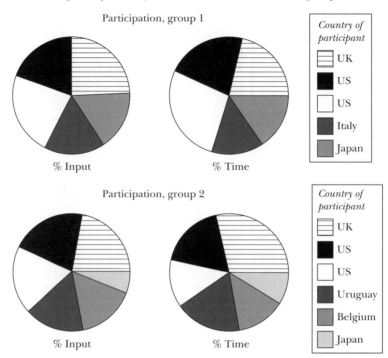

invited participation by saying, "If I recall, Sugano-san, a couple of years ago you had some experience in a merger similar to the one we are discussing. What do you think about this situation?" What followed was a highly relevant discourse, fluidly expressed, which had a big impact on the shape of the group's recommendation. When his involvement was sought, this otherwise infrequent participant made an important contribution.

To avoid relying solely on the serendipitous observation of a group member to notice the absence of participation, the group can set up routines to facilitate everyone's participation. For example, the group can use a process of going around the table to produce as many ideas as possible before discussion starts, as did the group above. Or one person can be charged with ensuring that all members have been included before an important decision is made. Another way of facilitating participation is to vary the modes of input. Some members may prefer to provide written input than to appear to be dominating or advancing their own interest by speaking in the group. Circulating written agendas well in advance of a meeting can help members prepare themselves this way and submit written responses before the meeting. Or it might be easier to provide ideas outside the context of formal meetings: in a private, face-to-face setting instead of a group meeting where the status issues may inhibit easy communication. Once they accept the possibility of having different norms for group members, most groups find creative ways to get everyone's input.

Resolving Disagreements

As more ideas from various viewpoints are expressed, there is an increasing likelihood that there will be disagreements. The way these conflicts are handled then, becomes the next cross-cultural challenge. Even the way conflict is expressed, quite apart from how it gets resolved, varies in different cultural traditions. In many cultures it is deemed inappropriate to express conflict openly. So for a manager from a culture where open expression of disagreement is valued, the first problem becomes detecting the existence of the conflict. In high-context cultures, a disagreement may be expressed very subtly or indirectly through a third party. In low-context cultures, conflict is more likely to be stated bluntly, in words of little ambiguity. When these norms are not understood, frustration or anger is likely to be the result. If I express conflict more directly, I may be frustrated by behavior that I read as sending "mixed signals" or conclude the other person is confused or cannot make up his or her mind. If I expect indirect expression of conflict, I might feel insulted by what I experience as impolite or crass comments from the other person who feels she or he is "just putting the issue on the table."

One way to deal with these issues is to use the Mapping and Bridging components of the model noted in the previous sections. Mapping provides a way to anticipate when the conflict gaps may occur; the Bridging techniques (prepare, decenter, recenter) give tools for reaching a common understanding and a common set of rules or norms for resolving the conflicts and avoiding them in the future. Effective communication is more than half of effective conflict resolution. The map of cultural differences may provide clues as to the other person's preferred ways of dealing with conflict. By decentering, you can adapt to the other's perspective without falling into the ethnocentric trap of blaming the other person or misinterpreting the meaning of actions by referencing your own cultural codes.

Building on Ideas

Even if the mapping framework is well understood, the communication skills are well developed, and participation and conflict issues are managed effectively, there is still a key component to realizing the potential in cross-cultural encounters, namely, moving forward and building on the ideas. There are cultural barriers in this phase of activity, too. As mentioned earlier, some cultural preferences would lead a person to push one's ideas (individualism), while another orientation (hierarchical) is more likely to lead to deference to authority. If you are in a group with several cultures, there might be an agreement (common rules of interaction) to surface ideas without attributing them to individuals or using an individual's ideas as a starting point for discussion. The main idea is to encourage the exploration of ideas with the conscious attempt to invent new ideas, to build on the ideas initially surfaced. A real stimulus to innovation is to try to do more than combine ideas and to avoid compromises. Finally, striving to find solutions to issues or problems that are acceptable to all (another rule for interaction or norm for behavior) is another way to increase the probability of getting synergy from the diversity in the group.

Trying to invent new ideas from those available and reaching for solutions to which every-one can agree are ideals that are difficult to accomplish. But even setting them as objec-tives will help a multicultural team achieve its potential for high performance.

The award-winning design firm IDEO has developed and refined processes that take diverse ideas and inputs, and builds on them to create highly value-creating solutions.[14] Their rules and techniques for brainstorming and prototyping are especially helpful with diverse teams. The firm's founder, Tom Kelley, says this about "brainstormers":

> Hot brainstormers may generate a hundred or more ideas, ten of which may be solid leads . . . People talk after brainstormers, sharing wild or practical ideas. A great brainstormer gives you a fantastic feeling of possibility and an hour later you walk out of the room a little richer for the experience. I think that sense of spontaneous team combustion is why we've been able to find so many unusual solutions to seemingly intractable problems.[15]

MBI CREATES RESULTS

The complete MBI model is summarized in Figure 3.6.

It is helpful to categorize six types of situations that managers face, each of which requires a different application of the fundamental MBI principles (see Table 3.2). In each of these situations, decisions must be made and implemented across cultural

FIGURE 3.6   MBI model in full

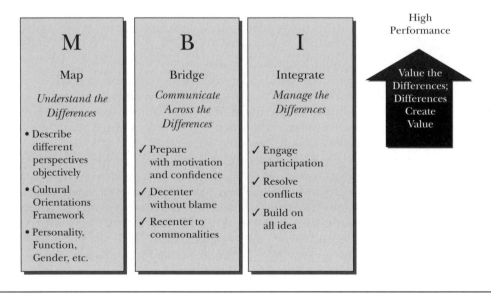

TABLE 3.2 Six arenas for synergy in cross-cultural interaction

	One-Way	*Multi-Way*
Individual Level	Arena 1: *Expatriate* Individual manager going to another country to manage a business unit or perform a specialist job.	Arena 2: *Multicultural team* Group from many countries, often cross-functional, managing across units or a multi-country project.
Organizational Level	Arena 3: *Export or import system* Take human resources, information systems, or other practice or strategy from one country into another.	Arena 4: *Global system* Develop human resources systems, organizational structures or strategies, to be implemented in many countries.
External to Organization	Arena 5: *External relationships* Customer, supplier, marketing, or other information developed in one market, adapt to another market.	Arena 6: *Multilateral systems* Conglomerates, lobbying or trade agreements, professional organizations.

boundaries. At the individual level (Arenas 1 and 2), managers must interact effectively with individuals from other cultures. People from different cultures will bring with them diverse expectations about the interaction, and effectiveness depends on understanding and building on these differences. At the organizational level (Arenas 3 and 4), managers must design systems of interaction that guide the coordinated behavior of many people. It is important for managers to know whether these systems will be consistent or contradictory with the cultural system in place. External to the organization (Arenas 5 and 6), managers work with customers, suppliers and other stakeholders in partnerships, complex negotiations, and indirectly through marketing and advertising efforts. In one-way transactions (Arenas 1, 3 and 5), managers need to take something that has been developed in one culture and put it into another one. Successful execution is based on an understanding of how things will be interpreted in the new context. In multi-way transactions (Arenas 2, 4 and 6), managers must take into account many cultural and contextual systems at the same time. Unless the differences are understood, conflict and division will characterize the situation.

MBI in Action – Adapting Systems Across Boundaries

MBI processes are critical when adopting best practices from one context to another. This is illustrated by Omar, an Egyptian proud of his humble peasant origins and founder and CEO of Smarthome Superior Plumbing Solutions. Omar developed his plumbing supplies company from nothing to become one of the main suppliers of plumbing infrastructure such as pipes and drains in the country. "It is not an exciting industry," he admits, but in a country where bringing water and taking away waste make an enormous difference to people's lives, the business creates exciting opportunities.

He was looking for tools to help take his company even further. Omar read everything he could find about management from Western sources, and realized that one tool he could use was to create a vision or mission statement. This kind of framework would help all the employees align together around a set of common ideas. With a common vision and mission, people would make better decisions and act in a way that helped the whole business. For inspiration, he read every vision and mission statement he could find, mostly on multinationals' websites from the US and Western Europe (Mapping). All of them left him cold – they would not work to align his managers. So he stepped back from the process and asked himself what vision and mission statements really need to do (Bridging). Then he thought about how to accomplish that within his own culture and with his employees (Bridging). Finally, he developed a vision based on applying the teachings of the Koran to his business, and a set of guidelines about how employees should implement Muslim values at work (Integrating). Posted on the walls of every manager's office and every meeting room is a set of statements about the importance of creating infrastructure to help do God's work on earth (Integrating). Every meeting must start with a set of reflections on how, since the previous meeting, managers and employees had helped others (Integrating).

After implementing the vision and related practices, Omar saw an increase in motivation, commitment and initiative from employees, and a concomitant increase in sales and production. He adopted some other best practices, for example, performance appraisals. His company now supplies 80 per cent of the plumbing infrastructure products in Egypt, and he exports products to Europe. The vision also helped him make and easily justify his decision to invest a significant portion of profits in infrastructure and microfinancing projects in Egypt, to help the country progress. "I can only increase my business if the country is also becoming more healthy economically."

Omar's vision and mission statements helped him align people to make and implement decisions that advance the company, and furthermore, hold people accountable for their actions and results – what any vision and mission statement is intended to do. But the four pages of his vision and mission statements are very different from those that would inspire people in most Western-origin companies. In adapting the standard management practice to his own Egyptian-Muslim context, Omar used his strong MBI skills and achieved very high results.

Who Should Adapt?

The MBI process assumes that at least some people involved in an interaction are adapting to the others. But who should adapt? This is a difficult question.

A number of factors influence the answer. As a general rule, the burden for adaptation usually rests with the party who is seen as the foreigner. The sheer force of numbers probably influences this. But this rule of the majority also misses significant opportunities for learning and inventing, as we saw in the example of the culturally-mixed team of managers discussing the acquisition.

Location is another strong factor. Everything else being equal (which is rarely the case), the guest is expected to adapt to the host. Technological dependence may alter this equation. A German joint venture in Dhaka may choose to emphasize German cultural values and management practice in spite of the location and overwhelming majority of Bangladeshi population, simply as a recognition of the need to acquire information. In fact, the power of resources in general has a strong influence on who is expected to adapt. The buyer almost always expects the seller to adapt, unless the seller has something extremely rare for which there are many willing buyers.

Individual preference may also enter the equation. An expatriate dealing with Chinese in Hong Kong may attempt to adapt to Chinese traditions, even though there is no expectation from the Hong Kong staff to do so. The motives for adaptation in this situation may range from showing courtesy to a desire to learn and to increase one's own repertoire of behavior. Furthermore, no matter where a company is operating, an attempt to adapt to others' customs will be appreciated and will have a positive influence on relations.

We usually give a different but quick and easy answer to the question "Who should adapt?": "Whoever cares about performance." There are a lot of contingencies that influence who *tends to* adapt and who is *expected to* adapt. But as our description of the MBI process should emphasize, the more everyone adapts, the more potential there is for performance to improve. If one party adapts, it is better than if no one adapts. However, if everyone adapts, performance can be even higher. Discussing "who should adapt" often becomes a negotiation of power. Discussing "how can we perform together" becomes a dialogue of empowerment.

Continuous Learning for Development and Effectiveness

Managers often feel discouraged when they realize the complexity and depth of skills needed for interacting effectively across cultures. However, there is good news. A little bit of skill goes a long way. The relationship between the MBI processes and performance is not a one-time linear equation. You don't "check the box" and get all of MBI right, then hit the button and, "ka-ching," automatically get performance. It is a much more iterative process. Doing a bit of Mapping will help you ask a couple of questions differently in Bridging. You'll get rich answers, which will lead you to avoid or manage a conflict differently, and you'll see yourself on the way to higher performance. This gives you and others more motivation and confidence, you ask more Mapping questions, engage in more Bridging, and people will volunteer some ideas you hadn't heard before. Performance looks even better. And so on.

Being able to learn continuously comes from mindfulness: paying attention to your actions, selecting your behaviors carefully, concentrating on the results, managing the impact, and learning to prepare yourself for the next set of actions. Along the way there will be some blips and dips. Experienced managers love sharing stories about these incidents with each other. Both authors and all our colleagues have experienced many of them, even recently, and we research and teach these processes!

Much more important than avoiding mistakes completely (because it is impossible), is learning. Ask questions about what you should have done. Ask them in a way that's appropriate to the culture. Provide "what if" scenarios and ask for people's reactions. Experiment when it feels safe. Then learn the new information and incorporate it into your Maps for next time.

Susan, a businesswoman, was excited about her first trip to Saudi Arabia. After a few days of different types of meetings (always accompanied by a male guide and a male host), she met with a senior woman entrepreneur and her team. During the meeting the entrepreneur invited Susan to remove her headscarf, even though there were men present. Normally Susan would have declined immediately and left the headscarf on, but there were several aspects of the situation that made it ambiguous, and she was not sure what to do. She made a decision which seemed to be appropriate, since the Saudi woman continued the meeting as before with genuine warmth, but the most important part of the learning came afterwards. Susan asked a mixed group of Saudi men and women what she should have done (without telling them what she had done). The spirited discussion lasted for half an hour, and there was no consensus. All agreed that either action would have been fine, but they disagreed about what messages would be sent by leaving the scarf on or taking it off, with arguments for both being "better" or "less offensive." The group offered many examples of factors that should be taken into account – Did she see you as an expert or as a peer? How covered was her own hair? What does she do with her relatives and outside her business context (some of them knew the woman)? What kind of statement would she have wanted you to make? Who were the men in the room? Did you get the sense she was offering this to you as a gift? And so on. They also agreed that they were fairly liberal as a group, there would be many people in the country who would disagree with them that either option was fine, and that there might be different answers if only men or only women were asked, rather than a mixed group. This led to a discussion about dynamics in different parts of the country. Susan knew when she made her decision about the headscarf that either leaving it on or taking it off could be a mistake. But the learning from the situation was invaluable and became input for the next set of interactions.

Perhaps most importantly, if you offend people or create a negative impact you didn't intend, make sure you manage that impact. That means first of all, you must be watching for these impacts with mindfulness. Become sensitive to the cues that you have inadvertently created offense, such as the other person switching the type of pronoun to a more formal one, or using more structured language and actions. If you see the signs, first apologize sincerely. A genuine and respectful apology goes a long way to creating the conditions for turning it into a learning situation. Then, being mindful, learn for next time. If you are sincere in your attempts to learn and improve, you almost always get at least one more chance and people are willing to help you learn.

In the remaining chapters of the book, we look at many different contexts for international management. Sometimes we draw on the MBI model explicitly; often we incorporate other lenses to focus on other aspects of the situation. But MBI is always assumed to be a foundation underneath the other processes, to be drawn upon in all situations.

Notes

1   Stahl, G. K., Maznevski, M. L., Voigt, A. and Jonsen, K., "Unraveling the effects of cultural diversity in teams: A meta-analysis of research on multicultural work groups," *Journal of International Business Studies*, 41 (2010) 690–709. Also see Earley, P. C. and Gibson, C. B., *Multinational Work Teams: A New Perspective* (Lawrence Erlbaum Associates, 2002).

2   Stahl et al., *op. cit.* See also Ekelund, B. Z. and Langvik, E. (eds.), *Diversity Icebreaker – How to Manage Diversity Processes* (Oslo: Human Factors, 2008).

3   DiStefano, J. and Maznevski, M., "Creating value with diverse teams in global management," *Organizational Dynamics*, 29 (2000) 45–63.

4   Stahl et al., *op. cit.*

5   Maznevski, M., *Synergy and performance in multicultural teams* (unpublished doctoral dissertation, London, Canada: The University of Western Ontario, 1994); Maznevski, M., "Understanding our differences: Performance in decision-making groups with diverse members," *Human Relations*, 47 (1994) 531–52. DiStefano, J. and Maznevski, M. *op. cit.*

6   Adler, N. J. and Gundersen, A., *International Dimensions of Organizational Behavior*, 5th Ed, (Mason, OH: Cengage Learning, 2007). Osland, J. S., Bird, A., Delano, J. and Jacob, M., "Beyond Sophisticated Stereotyping: Cultural Sensemaking in Context" *The Academy of Management Executive* 14(1) (2000) 65–79.

7   Stasser has conducted many insightful studies exploring the dynamics of sharing distributed information in teams. They are reviewed well in Stasser, G., "The uncertain role of unshared information in collective choice," in L. L. Thompson, J. M. Levine and D. M. Messick (eds.), *Shared Cognition in Organizations: The Management of Knowledge* (Mahwah, NJ: Erlbaum, 1999) 49–69.

8   Ekelund, B. Z., *Trialogue.* Also called the *Diversity Icebreaker.* This instrument and process were based on research on dynamics around diversity and how to create positive acceptance. The exercise is excellent for introducing Mapping. The instrument, background research, and other information can be found at www.diversityicebreaker.com or www.trialogue.com.

9   Briggs Myers, I., McCaulley, M.H., Quenk, N.L. and Hammer, A.L., *MBTI® Manual: A Guide to the Development and Use of the Myers-Briggs Type Indicator® Instrument*, 3rd edn. (California, USA: Consulting Psychologists Press, 1998).

10 This scheme was adapted from the work of Rolv M. Blakar. See Blakar, "Towards a theory of communication in terms of preconditions: A conceptual framework and some empirical explorations," in *Recent Advances in Language, Communication, and Social Psychology*, H. Giles and R.N. St. Clair (eds.) (London: Lawrence Erlbaum Associates, Ltd, Publishers, 1985) 10–40.

11 The first five of these are drawn from Richard E. Porter and Larry A. Samovar, "Approaching intercultural communication," in Larry A. Samovar and Richard E. Porter (eds.), *Intercultural Communications: A Reader*, 5th edn. (Belmont, CA: Wadsworth Publishing Company, 1988)

15–30. The last two are corollaries of the first five, that, according to our observations, are particularly critical to cross-cultural communication.

12   Originally discussed in an Executive Dialogue at the ION conference in Aarhus, February 2005, then followed up in several forums through Scandinavia and with Scandinavians throughout the world.

13   Smith, P. B., Peterson, M. F. and Schwartz, S. H., "Cultural Values, Sources of Guidance, and their Relevance to Managerial Behavior: A 47-Nation Study", *Journal of Cross-Cultural Psychology* 33(2) (2002) 188–208. Smith, P. B., Andersen, J. A., Ekelund, B., Greversen, G. and Ropo, A., "In Search of Nordic Management Styles" *Scandinavian Journal of Management* 19(4) (2003) 491–507.

14   Kelley, T. with Littman, J., *The Ten Faces of Innovation: IDEO's Strategies for Defeating the Devil's Advocate and Driving Creativity Throughout your Organization* (New York: Currency/Doubleday, 2005).

15   Kelley, T. with Littman, J., *The Art of Innovation* (New York: HarperCollins Business, 2002) 62.

CHAPTER 4

Managing Global Teams and Networks

Shawna moved from her native Ireland to continental Europe to lead an innovation team for a consumer goods firm. The team's mandate was to help the company spread innovations more systematically throughout the international network of subsidiaries. Shawna quickly saw that although individual projects were done well, team members missed opportunities to build innovation systems and knowledge sharing. The team worked as a group of individuals assigned in different configurations to projects; to build integration, the team needed to work together in an interdependent way.

Shawna faced significant challenges. The team of 25 was highly diverse in terms of nationality, function, and types of experience – this was important for innovation but made it difficult to integrate. Moreover, assignment to the team was considered a three-year development experience for high potentials, so about one-third of the team turned over each year. Team members worked in sub-groups on projects, and the sub-groups did not have much opportunity to interact.

Shawna started by interviewing all the team members and some important external stakeholders individually. Based on this initial input, she structured roles more clearly within the team, including the leadership role. She implemented a comprehensive set of performance expectations and an assessment system combining team priorities and stakeholder input. She began to bring the team together more often to develop common ways of working and joint priorities. She shifted the agenda of the semi-annual week-long workshops. In the past, they had focused on reporting and administrative issues as well as general team-building. Instead, Shawna had the entire team create joint knowledge books around key competency areas, which they could all then deploy. To identify the priorities and key competency areas, team members worked together in these meetings to assess all current and potential projects against the company strategy. Once the projects and basic competences were assessed, team members finished the competency books when working apart from each other, and shared them virtually. The workshops also included significant team-building activities to increase trust and communication among team members when they weren't together.

Next Shawna started to work on larger system challenges and opportunities. She put in place a clear recruitment and succession plan so the team could become more stable in terms of skills and capabilities. This also facilitated knowledge transfer in the team, and increased the company's retention of these individuals after their "tour" with the team. The team implemented a structured orientation program, which included helping newcomers to the team develop their networks and relationships in the team and among key stakeholder groups. They developed an alumni group to leverage the relationships of people who had "graduated" from the team and help make innovation more systematic throughout the firm.

Shawna addressed all the aspects important to complex teams in international organizations. She reviewed the basic dynamics of the structure, task, and social processes, and built more complex dynamics including trust and boundary-spanning in addition to the team's already well-developed innovation processes. She set up the team to manage its dispersion well, and leveraged the team's networks. The team began to achieve its higher mandate of spreading innovation more systematically.

TEAMS ARE THE BASIC UNIT OF WORK AND COLLABORATION

Most work in organizations today is done in some configuration of teams. A team is a group of people who work together to achieve a particular outcome.[1] There are different kinds of teams, each with different tasks, structures, and other characteristics. For example, a resources company identified five categories:

- **Project teams**: Teams with defined duration, clear deliverables, core membership and networking with experts and other stakeholders outside; e.g., exploration team for a new potential drilling site.

- **Management teams**: Teams with indefinite duration, clear membership representing different departments, high-level deliverables, coordination and communication are key to the mandate; e.g., global lubricants management team.

- **Production/work teams**: Teams with indefinite duration, clear membership, specific and clear deliverables, team does regular and ongoing work together; e.g. production team operating a refinery.

- **Service teams**: Teams with indefinite duration, clear membership, deliverable depends on serving other people's and teams' deliverables, team members provide regular and ongoing support to others; e.g., IT or HR support for a global business unit.

- **Action teams**: Teams with defined duration, clear deliverables, created as needed from a network of potential members, team members work together in a fast and fluid way; e.g., emergency response team for a refinery fire.

Teams have become more complex in today's international economy, and there is no simple "how to" guide that fits all teams. With the wide variety of tasks that groups of people work on jointly, managers must develop a sophisticated view of contingencies.[2]

We start by describing the inputs and processes important for international teams – those with members from multiple cultures. Then we examine the special case of virtual teams, or teams whose members are distributed across different locations. The final section of this chapter looks at network structures: connected configurations for collaboration.

EFFECTIVE TEAMS MANAGE THEIR SET UP AND THEIR PROCESSES CAREFULLY

Every team is a unique combination of people, tasks, processes, and environment, but there are two sets of characteristics that effective teams share. First, they manage some structural conditions, organizing the task and the roles in the team. Second, they manage the social processes. Single culture teams can be effective without knowing these principles, but in the international context they must be developed carefully.[3] In the team research, this is often referred to as the input-process-output approach.[4] The inputs and processes are summarized in Figure 4.1.

Structural Inputs: Set Up the Team Right, From the Start

Setting up the right conditions includes defining the task, selecting team members, identifying roles, and developing a task strategy.

FIGURE 4.1 Simplified model of team dynamics

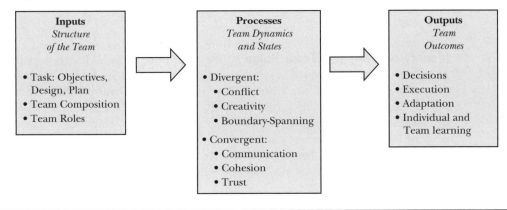

Define Task and Objectives Clearly   Team members must know clearly what their task and objectives are, in order to achieve them reliably. For example, the "savory flavors R&D team" at a fragrance and flavors company has the mandate of developing new flavors for salty (rather than sweet) foods, such as soups and sauces. The account sales team at an internet bank has the objective of selling new accounts. This sounds obvious, but many teams do not understand their objectives well or do not agree on them. Sometimes this is due to lack of clear communication from the leader, who may present a set of objectives that are clear to him- or herself but are difficult or ambiguous from the point of view of the team.

More often, team members have different interpretations of the task and objectives. For example, a specialty chemicals company launched a new industrial product, with a multi-functional team guiding the launch. Their mandate from the CEO was to launch the product successfully. The VP of marketing on the team defined this as high market share, while the financial director defined it as high profitability. These two objectives could be conflicting, and this team did not identify their different ideas until well into execution phase, when they had already created unaligned actions.

The simple lesson here is: make sure the team has a clear mandate, and don't take clarity for granted. In complex teams such as those in international settings, you will have to revisit the goals and objectives many times.

Select Team Members Carefully

Teams need the right combination of skills among members. The right combination depends on the task, and includes technical skills, functional and geographical knowledge, and skills important for managing the team processes. It is helpful to have diversity in personal characteristics among team members to boost innovation and increase the quality of decision-making. Teams are often composed based on convenience – who is available – rather than careful assignment, and sometimes the necessary skill combination is not available. As a result, teams frequently have significant skill or knowledge gaps which should be addressed by adding members or developing the necessary knowledge or skills.

Identify and Support Team Roles   Roles are sets of specific responsibilities within a group. Teams function best when different members take responsibility for different aspects. Should roles be explicitly assigned, or should they emerge? We have heard managers of teams argue strongly for both: "Our team worked well because we assigned and followed clear roles," and another team "Our team worked well because we let each person's role in the team emerge in a fluid way, shifting as necessary." Teams can perform well in either case. It is safer to assign roles, especially in a team of people who have not worked together before, or in complex situations like international teams. The best teams usually use some combination of assigning roles and adjusting them as necessary.

Plan the Task and Monitor Progress Planning and tracking are often referred to as "project management" and are the subject of many guides and software packages. Teams are more likely to achieve results if they plan clear processes with activities, milestones and deliverables, if sub-tasks are allocated clearly to members, and if the team tracks progress compared to plan.

These structural conditions provide the right inputs for effective teams. You have probably worked on many teams that did not identify all these conditions explicitly, but still performed well. This is possible if people on the team have the same basic assumptions about how teams work, and about how work is conducted. However, this is rarely the case for teams in international management. Often, managers who led teams successfully in domestic environments suddenly find themselves failing in international environments, because they have not learned to make these conditions explicit.

Social Processes: Transform Input Conditions into Performance

Social processes are those that facilitate interaction, commitment and motivation within the group. Teams need both divergent processes – those that bring in different perspectives and resources – and convergent processes – those that align the team towards a solution and coordinated action. Teams in international management settings are generally very diverse, and high diversity facilitates or increases the tendency for divergent processes while hindering convergent processes.[5]

Divergent Processes: Source of Ideas and Resources Some divergent processes, like conflict, generally decrease team performance, while others, like creativity and boundary-spanning, increase team performance.

Most conflict is negative, but not all Conflict is the expression of differences in opinion or priority due to opposing needs or demands.[6] Conflict's effect on teams is complex, with conflict usually hurting performance but sometimes helping it.[7] Teams must question each other's assumptions and ideas, and this is often best expressed in a moderate level of task-related conflict. Some teams assign a formal role of "devil's advocate" to prevent groupthink. Disagreement about people in the team and their motivations or capabilities – social conflict – tends to decrease team performance. Diverse teams in general, and multicultural teams in particular, experience more task-related conflict than less diverse teams, but they do not experience more social conflict.[8] Often, teams find it helpful to assign someone on the team, generally someone who is trusted to be neutral, a role of facilitating or mediating conflict. Chapter 3, in the section on Integrating, offers more insights about conflict resolution when working across cultures.

Creativity and innovation: Multicultural teams at their best   Innovation is developing something new that creates value. Consistent innovation requires a combination of creativity and deep understanding of the challenge the innovation is trying to address.[9] Creativity, in turn, is the consideration of a wide variety of alternatives and criteria for evaluating alternatives, as well as the building of novel and useful ideas that were not originally part of the consideration set.

Effective teams combine creativity with structured problem-solving to achieve high quality innovation. For example, the design firm Ideo uses a process called the "Deep Dive" to create innovative solutions to design challenges: anything from developing a new toothbrush to revising the way insurance claims are processed.[10] The first step is deeply examining the challenge from all points of view, paying particular attention to end-users' needs. The second step is structured brainstorming to generate as many ideas as possible. Third, the team creates prototype solutions and tests them in a variety of contexts. They combine and build on results from the prototypes, and finally create and implement a solution. In all steps, the team members encourage diversity and question assumptions, but the team maintains discipline in its focus on the problem and on a timeline and structure (convergent processes, see below).

Research has shown clearly that multicultural teams have higher creativity and innovation than single-culture teams.[11] The diversity of perspectives leads to more idea-generation, and better potential quality in idea analysis and building.

Boundary-spanning: The flow into and out of the team   Most team tasks require extensive interaction between members and various parties outside the team: to obtain resources for the team, to gather information both from within the organization and from sources outside, and to implement solutions.[12] This process is divergent because it requires connecting with people who have different needs or interests from the team members. When team members anticipate boundary-spanning and develop relationships with stakeholders outside the team, the team has better access to and cooperation with these stakeholders.[13]

One challenge teams typically face in boundary-spanning is interpreting and incorporating external perspectives.[14] Such perspectives rarely come in a form that is tailored to the team's needs. For example, a team in a global construction firm was assessing potential markets for contracts to build and upgrade hospitals; they had developed a strong reputation for this in two countries and wanted to build on this in other parts of the world as part of a growth strategy. However, different countries report health-related data differently and have very different types of health management, so the data were extremely difficult to compare across countries. The team had to develop some common indicators and assess each country on an individual basis to calculate the indicator. In the end, they were able to successfully prioritize an international strategy.

International teams, by their diversity, have strong divergent processes: higher task-conflict, higher creativity and innovation, and a broader set of external connections. These divergent processes offer a potential competitive advantage over single-culture teams. Whether they turn these social processes into final implementable performance depends on the quality of their convergent processes.

Convergent Processes: Source of Commitment and Alignment   Convergent processes are those that create unity and alignment in a team, and allow for coordinated action. Most convergent processes are helpful and important to team performance, especially communication and cohesion-building dynamics like trust. Too much convergence leads to groupthink, with the team developing high homogeneity and becoming closed to information different from their own ideas.[15] There is no research on groupthink in international teams, and in fact it is extremely rare in such teams, so we do not think you are in much danger of experiencing this problem.

Communicate to share understanding and build common knowledge   Effective communication is transmitting meaning from one person to another or others as it was intended by the sender.[16] Team performance is obviously higher when team members understand each other's perspectives and the information brought to the team. Communication is also important in ensuring that all members are kept informed of progress in the team in a continuous way. Effective communication is a very active process, requiring extensive questioning and checking from everyone involved. The Chapter 3 sections on Mapping and Bridging addressed cross-cultural communication in detail.

Contrary to expectations, a recent meta-analysis found that communication in multicultural teams tends to be just as effective as in single-culture teams.[17] It is clear that communication is more *difficult* in multicultural teams, in part due to different language fluency with the common language.[18] However, the meta-analysis results also implied that members of multicultural teams are more motivated to engage the diversity of the team, and this may help them to put more effort into careful communication. In single-culture teams, members may make assumptions about understanding that are not played out in real sharing.

Cohesion and trust: The glue that holds teams together   Cohesion and trust are positive motivations to be together and commitment to work together. They facilitate the long-term performance of a team, and are especially important for difficult, complex tasks and for implementation.

Diversity in general, and cultural diversity in particular, has a negative impact on social integration. Cohesion is easier to develop within a culture, where individuals have a relatively common sense of identity, and can more easily understand the different contributions each person brings. In multinational teams, people have less context in which to understand each other, and may even devalue each other. On the other hand, research shows that multicultural teams tend to have higher satisfaction with the team than single-culture teams do.[19] Satisfaction with the team is often a predictor of cohesion. It is possible that many people find it more interesting to work in multicultural teams, and team leaders can use this interest to build cohesion.

Trust is a belief among team members that others in the team would make decisions that optimize the team's interests, even in each other's absence. Trust increases motivation and commitment to the team, and thus the quality of contributions and communication processes. In addition, trust makes teamwork more efficient.[20] In a global account team, representatives of the supplier in each country must work with local subsidiaries of the customer in such a way that the global brand is maintained and enhanced. From time to time, that may mean particular country representatives making exceptions to team agreements. If country representatives feel committed to the team so they make the best decisions possible, and if team members trust each other to be committed, then the account team will get the best combination of customer service and profitable value creation.

Trust cannot just be switched on (although it can be lost quickly), and many teams are disappointed when they come away from their team launch without complete trust. Trust must be generated through a series of experiences, building from predictability and reliability (I know I can rely on you to do what you committed to do) to deep-level personal trust (I can rely on you to make big decisions for me). Ironically, to build trust, members must take risks. Team members can only demonstrate to each other that they will act in the team's interests if other team members let them take unsupervised actions. If you are leading a team, it is a good idea to set up a series of minor tasks in the beginning of a team's life together, that will help create trust that the team can rely on later.

Managing Faultlines: A Special Case of Divergence and Convergence   Global teams face yet another challenge that is less relevant for single-culture teams: managing faultlines. Faultlines are rifts in teams created by alignment of different types of diversity.[21] For example, a global team may consist of two production engineers, two marketers, and two R&D scientists, from the US, Japan, and Germany. If the engineers are from the US, the marketers from Japan, and the scientists from Germany, then the functional and cultural divisions are aligned and the forces towards divergence may be too difficult to overcome. On the other hand, if each of the functions is represented by people from different countries, the sub-groups will be less evident and the group will find it easier to balance divergent and convergent processes.

On a team that was developing a new global pricing strategy for the company's service offerings, all the finance expertise on the team came from the headquarters country. The other members of the team assumed that whatever the finance people suggested represented the headquarters' point of view, so the others on the team were unwilling to question the finance members. The company eventually took one of the headquarters people out and brought in a finance director from a moderate-sized subsidiary on a different continent, and this changed the dynamics significantly in a positive way.

Effective Teams Adapt and Learn

There is no easy formula for team performance, and most teams' mandates or situations change as they go along. Teams that are set up well and manage divergent and convergent processes well are generally able to adapt to the situation as they work together. The most effective teams incorporate mindful practices such as after-action reviews and process reviews on a regular basis.

For example, a global airline cargo management team, created from a merger of two airlines, started off with clear roles and a set of task processes for first merging the two sets of operations, then developing and implementing a plan to win a larger share of the cargo market. As the nine team members from six countries and four different functions began to work together, they managed the structural inputs and social processes well. They defined the different parts of their mandate and revisited the definition as they worked on the task. They assigned roles and developed and followed a task plan. The early part of the task, integrating the operations, had some relatively simple aspects, which they tackled first. As they worked on the integration, they learned more about each other's knowledge and cultural backgrounds. They implemented parts of the integration in their own divisions and saw the good results. At this point, they started experimenting with shifting roles, diving more deeply into innovation and unexpected solutions. In the next stages, which were more difficult, they experienced market resistance to the merger and challenges with customer alliances. But the trust and knowledge they had built up earlier helped them support each other and find good solutions to these challenges. Every few weeks they took time to reflect on their processes, and took action to correct the course if necessary. The team exceeded their market share goals and began setting their sights on the next targets.

VIRTUAL TEAMS: THE JOYS AND CHALLENGES OF DISTANCE AND TECHNOLOGY

A virtual team is one whose members work together more over technology than face-to-face. Most professionals work in one or more virtual team. Although virtual teams are ubiquitous today, they are still quite new to the management landscape. Some teams perform well, others fail miserably. As a result, most managers are unsure about how to lead such teams reliably. In this section, we describe what makes virtual teams so difficult to manage, the dynamics these teams should focus on, and how to turn those dynamics into high performance.[22]

Virtual Teams: Just What are We Dealing With?

Many virtual team leaders focus on the technology of virtual teams. But the characteristics that really challenge virtual teams are more difficult to see: dispersed configuration and diverse composition.

Dispersed Configuration: From Time Zones to Infrastructure

Virtual team members are distributed widely, often around the globe. Some of the consequences are obvious. You may be familiar with the Tokyo-Berlin-Rio conference call scheduling dilemma! A more subtle challenge is with different infrastructures: communicating seamlessly over different network types is often impossible. Moreover, team members are embedded in different contexts. They deal with different legal and political infrastructures, social relations, and climates.

Team dispersion demands strong coordination and conscious processes. If the team is not well-organized, members cannot work interdependently. Unless team members explain their infrastructures and contexts to each other, communication cannot be effective. On the other hand, high-performing virtual teams use dispersion to their advantage. For example, team members can use the 24-hour clock to develop tasks asynchronously and use the discipline of coordination to move the task forward steadily.

Diverse Composition: Intended and Unintended Differences Members of virtual teams are usually assigned because of their geographic, functional, or some other type of expertise. This assignment inevitably creates high levels of diversity on characteristics like culture and language, personality, and values. As we discussed in Chapters 2 and 3, team members therefore bring different expectations to the team regarding how to interact with each other and how to engage in the task. For example, team members from Japan or Brazil may prefer a clear hierarchy in the team, with a specific leader who manages the team's actions, takes final decisions, and represents the team outside. Team members from Sweden or Canada will likely be more comfortable with a fluid leadership structure and different people taking the lead for different parts of the task. Unless these diverse perspectives are managed continuously, the team will experience conflict that can destroy it. But the high level of diversity also presents opportunities for applying expertise and creating innovation, and teams that work effectively capture this synergy and turn it into performance.

The Triple Challenge Dispersed configuration and diverse composition combine to create three challenges for virtual teams: complexity, invisibility, and restricted channels (see Figure 4.2). With more dynamics to manage, virtual teams are much more complex than face-to-face teams. They face physical invisibility – team members cannot see each other, and non-verbal communication is therefore missing. But they also face mental and emotional invisibility. Being apart from each other creates blocks to perception, and it is much harder to practice empathy or decentering. Communication channels are highly restricted. They are physically restricted: members must choose among a limited number of technologies and coordinate their choices. They are also mentally and emotionally restricted: members often work in second (or third)

FIGURE 4.2   Challenging conditions in global teams

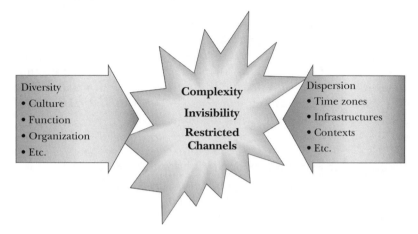

languages and translate ideas across cultures, sometimes stripping those ideas of their richness.

Most teams focus on how to use technology to overcome the challenges of the conditions. However, successful teams first focus on a particular set of dynamics based on the team effectiveness principles identified above, applied specifically to virtual teams.

Virtuous Cycles: Pursuing Three Processes Simultaneously

Virtual teams must focus on three dynamics: shared knowledge, trust, and ongoing communication. These are difficult to accomplish, but teams that do so create cycles of effectiveness. Virtual teams usually begin with a basic level of each of these dynamics. Then they either build on the dynamics or destroy them, as shown in Figure 4.3.

Shared Knowledge: Foundation for Good Decisions   Most teams start with a basic level of shared knowledge. This includes agreement on the goals, often from a mandate given to the team, and general knowledge about each other's potential contributions, perhaps from their job titles or reputations. High-performing teams take this shared knowledge and build on it. They use diversity and dispersion to learn about how the goal is interpreted in different contexts. With trust and ongoing communication, they create a deep understanding of multiple causes of the issue, and a rich portfolio of possible solutions. Low-performing teams don't test their shared understanding past the first basics. Inevitably, when members are working in their own places, they encounter different interpretations of the task and develop different ideas of what to prioritize. Because they do not share these evolving interpretations, misunderstandings arise and lead to serious conflicts.

Trust: Foundation for Good Execution   We discussed the importance of trust above; in virtual teams it is even more critical. Most virtual teams start with a basic type of reliability. People are willing to give each other the benefit of the doubt.[23] This shallow trust can either grow into something stronger or can degenerate into lack of trust. High-performing virtual teams use shared knowledge and ongoing communication to build personal trust. They believe that each member's priorities and values coincide with those of the team, and that individual members can make good decisions on behalf of the team. Low-performing teams make decisions and take actions that create a culture of blaming and mistrust within the team.

Ongoing Communication: Foundation for Good Flow   Again, most teams start out fine on this dynamic. After the team launch there is a flurry of emails, postings, and phone calls. High-performing teams use trust and shared knowledge to create communication that is decentered – focused on the receiver's perspective (see Chapter 3 on Bridging). Such teams might tell stories about customers to illustrate their ideas, and share visual information like photographs or videos. Low-performing teams do not develop such rich communication. In combination with their lower trust and lack of shared knowledge, their messages become less and less frequent. When they do communicate, it is usually minimal information, such as spreadsheets or PowerPoint reports, and not supplemented with contextual explanations.

As shown in Figure 4.3, the three dynamics of shared knowledge, trust, and ongoing communication work together. Teams cannot develop or ignore one or the other without affecting the rest.

FIGURE 4.3a   Dynamics of shared knowledge, trust, and ongoing communication: The starting point

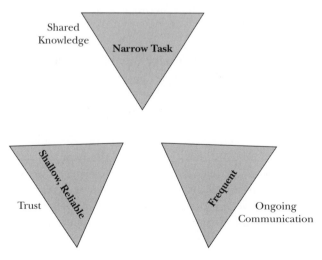

FIGURE 4.3b Potential positive dynamics   **FIGURE 4.3c** Potential negative dynamics

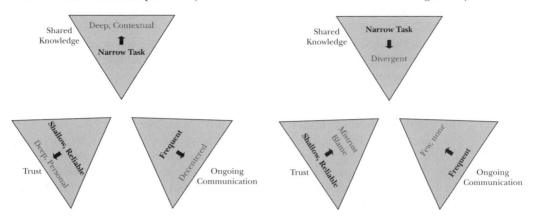

FIGURE 4.3d Virtuous circles of positive dynamics drive high global virtual team performance

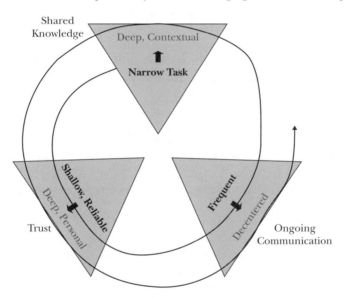

Managing Virtual Teams: Leading Virtuous Cycles

Advice to virtual teams is often confusing, and even outdated when a new technology emerges. We've identified three principles that apply to all virtual teams: organize and discipline, match technology to process, and create a heartbeat.

Organize and Discipline: A Lifeline for Virtual Teams
Face-to-face teams can get away with being unorganized and undisciplined. When members see each other, they catch up on the task, and they muddle through an agenda even without preparation

or clear process. For virtual teams, lack of organization and discipline is deadly. High-performing virtual teams set up their norms for organizing and disciplining early in the team's life, and follow them with commitment. They also understand that the definitions, milestones, norms, and roles will change as the team and the task evolve. Such teams use the organization and discipline to build shared knowledge, trust and ongoing communication so they can revise the team's structure as necessary.

The Right Technology: Match Richness with Message   Virtual teams are faced with a wide array of technologies and applications. However, there is no correlation between specific technologies and performance. Some good teams use only email and telephone calls, others use high-tech voice and video over internet and shared live websites. High-performing teams use a menu of technologies and select the right one for the team process at a given time.

The more you are building trust and shared knowledge, the more you need rich media that allow multiple modes at the same time, such as voice, text and visual. This includes face-to-face or web-based video. High quality videoconferencing is not always necessary; what's important is capturing context and some personal contact. On the other hand, the more you are engaging in routine work, the more you can rely on less rich media. Tracking progress and sharing routine reports can be done with email or shared websites that are checked regularly.

Create a Heartbeat   When should we get together in person? Leaders often assume that high-performing teams get together whenever things become complex, for example, a situation of intense conflict or when it's important to make a big step on a task. Our research[24] and experience, however, suggest otherwise. Quite simply, high-performing virtual teams get together on a regular schedule, creating a heartbeat for the team.

Teams should set a schedule of regular meetings, perhaps once a quarter or twice a year. These meetings can be planned in advance to coincide with events such as professional conferences or large management meetings. Heartbeat meetings should focus on the major dynamics: building shared knowledge, trust, and ongoing communication. A two-day agenda of presentations sharing PowerPoint results from the last quarter will do nothing to help the team. But a two-day agenda of customer visits, site visits, and discussion of difficult cases to share knowledge and advice will pump the equivalent of high quality oxygen into the team's circulatory system.

The heartbeat rhythm does not need to coincide with major decision points or milestones. A high-performing team can handle intense conflict and heavy deliverables in virtual mode if it has developed shared knowledge, trust, and ongoing communication. Rhythm is critical. Like a human heartbeat, a team's heartbeat should be adjusted depending on the situation. If the team is less fit – for example, if there are new members or if trust has been damaged through a difficult situation – then the heart should beat faster than if the team is highly fit. If the team's task is more difficult – includes more ambiguity, more strategic importance, or the environment changes unexpectedly – then the heart should beat faster than if the team's task is simpler or more predictable.

Ideally, heartbeat meetings are in person. A well-developed team may have a slow face-to-face heartbeat supplemented with interim virtual heartbeats. We have also seen successful teams that cannot meet face-to-face, who develop strong heartbeats using virtual technologies. These teams consciously use ongoing communication to develop shared knowledge and trust. For example, members use simple multimedia technologies – digital cameras and webcams – to share what is going on in their separate worlds, and they explicitly develop social relationships by sharing family and personal information as they increase their trust.

Virtual Teams are Complex, but can Create Great Value

We are often asked "What's the secret?" as if there is some simple key that will unlock virtual team performance. Unfortunately, there is no such key. Collaborating across dispersion and diversity brings challenges. But it also brings opportunities that are worth the investment. Beyond their task mandate, virtual teams expand our possibilities. In today's flat organizations, well-managed virtual teams create development experiences with exposure to other cultures and situations. When virtual teams try to replicate their face-to-face teams, they are usually disappointed. But when they develop new skills to address the challenges discussed here, they achieve high performance and create competences that the organization as a whole can benefit from.

BEYOND TEAMS: CONNECTING NETWORKS FOR SOCIAL CAPITAL[25]

How big can a global team be? A global brand manager for a large consumer electronics group said, "My team has 100 people; that is probably too much, but that's the real group of people who need to work together on this." A global supply chain manager for an industrial parts manufacturing group said, "I have purchasing teams, production teams, logistics teams, and integration teams, and they all need to work together at different times. Which sets of teams should I apply these principles to, and how, when they are always shifting?"

The idea of "team" tends to limit us to thinking about a group of people that is relatively stable over time, doing a single task. However, most collaborations in international organizations are not really that stable or one-dimensional.[26] It is helpful to think in terms of social networks and the social capital they carry.

FIGURE 4.4   An account team's networks: team, firm, and client

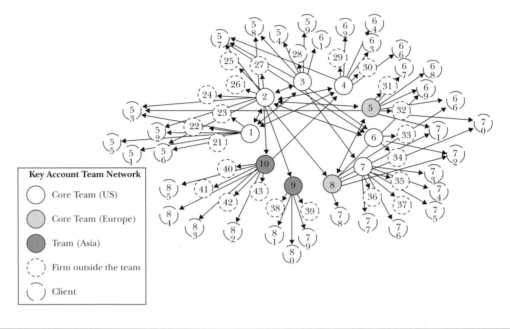

Networks are Maps of Social Connections

A network is a set of relationships among people. We visualize networks by drawing them as a set of points representing people (or organizations, or teams, or other social entities), with lines linking them to represent relationships. Figure 4.4 shows the network of a 10-person account team for a marketing and advertising firm.[27] In the center are the 10 core members, from the US, Europe and Asia. Team member 1 is the Managing Director, 2 is the Assistant Director, and the others are relatively equal in the team hierarchy. The arrows among them show information relationships among the core members of the team: who goes to whom for advice about the client and the task? The second layer adds relationships between team members and others in the firm: who do the core team members go to, outside the team but within the firm, for advice about the client and the task? The third layer adds relationships between the team members and people in the client firm – who do the core team members go to at the client firm for advice about the client and the task?

This network view shows many things that a simple team perspective cannot. For example, the managing director of the account does not interact with many of the account team members, and it may seem he is a negligent team leader. However, as we see by the network, he does interact frequently with the most senior people at the client, and this helps the success of the team. Another important insight is related to team members 9 and 10 in Asia, the newest location for this account. The assistant director goes to them whenever she needs information from them. But members 9 and 10 are otherwise not integrated into the core team. The two Asian representatives go only to people in their own office and in the client's local offices to work on the account. Their contacts at the client don't overlap with anyone else's, so if they were to leave the team, the team would lose these client contacts. Learning and synergy opportunities are also being missed. After seeing this map, the assistant director started incorporating the two Asian members into more team meetings.

Social Capital: The Assets in Relationships

Relationships are important for many aspects of business performance. To assess these relationships, it is useful to draw on the notion of social capital: the assets in networks of relationships that can be valuable to achieve objectives.[28] Like other assets, building social capital requires investing, and the payoff may be immediate or long-term. Using social capital can increase it, and not using it can decrease it. Unlike other assets though, social capital exists entirely in a relationship between parties. One person cannot own social capital by him- or herself.

Social networks, like the structure shown in Figure 4.4, are holders and carriers of social capital. Social capital flows along the connections to and through people to other parts of the network, to get things done. Social capital moves four types of resources through networks:[29]

- Information flows.
- Influence for decision-making.
- Reputation and credibility.
- Identity.

Relationships that increase information flow, provide influence, clarify credentials and reinforce identity enable the actor to access and use social capital to enhance their performance.

In the marketing account team described above, all four aspects of social capital – information, influence, credibility, and identity – were facilitated by social networks. Team members used their relationships to influence people whose cooperation they needed, and to facilitate information flow. Relationships with the client were important for obtaining the information and detecting its validity. Relationships among team members were important for sharing information and creating a comprehensive picture of the client firm's needs. Team members with strong influence encouraged other team members to increase their commitment to the client and the team, providing better solutions for the client. Relationships with the client were also used to influence the client's propensity to accept the firm's advice. Team members' relationships with their professional associations influenced their credibility, and the senior leader in this team derived enormous credibility from the quality of his relationships with other senior leaders in the firm and senior managers at client firms. Finally, the marketing and advertising experts' identity as professionals was enhanced when the team produced a market plan and brand idea that won awards in the industry.

Network Structure: Not All Networks are Created Equal

To understand which organization structures are best, we look at the characteristics of strength and density.

Connections between people, or ties, can be weaker or stronger.[30] Weak ties are those among people who have met briefly, perhaps exchanged business cards, and connect with each other infrequently; or, they may have connected more frequently but without a close relationship. Weak ties are good for accessing information, such as learning about new products or customers, or for looking for job candidates or jobs. They are relatively easy to maintain. Strong ties are those among people who have known each other longer, have a personal relationship, maybe even deep trust in each other. Strong ties are good for getting in-depth information, scarce resources, and commitment to new ventures. Strong ties are relatively difficult to maintain.

Internet social networking sites such as Facebook, LinkedIn, Twitter and Tumblr[31] show connections among people. They have developed innovative ways to indicate and leverage strength of ties. Facebook is aimed at linking together social networks of friends. On Facebook, when you accept someone as a friend, he or she can add personal things to your site that others can see. Most Facebook users accept as friends only people with moderately strong relationships. LinkedIn was developed to build networks of professionals, especially in business. LinkedIn emphasizes that you should only accept as connections people you know and trust, since others who can see your network will be able to see and possibly leverage those connections. LinkedIn provides mechanisms for recommendations and endorsements, which is another way to indicate strong ties. If I recommend or endorse you, our relationship is likely stronger than if I do not. Twitter and Tumblr are social networks used more for knowledge-sharing and commenting about current events and other trends, from the deeply serious to the very lighthearted. As social media sites come and go, different ways of building and using social capital over technology emerge and shift.

Density is a measure of how interconnected people are with each other. The more everyone is connected to everyone else, the higher the density. In high-density networks, information is passed quickly. There tends to be redundancy in information, as everyone is talking to the same sources. In low-density networks, information is passed less efficiently and may miss network members. However, low-density networks tend to access a broader set of resources and information, with less overlap.

Strength and density combine to create many different types of networks. Two important patterns are fishing nets and safety nets. Fishing nets are lower-density structures with many relatively weak ties.[32] Like "real" fishing nets, they can be cast in the right

FIGURE 4.5 An international engineering company's cross-business unit, cross-geography fishing net

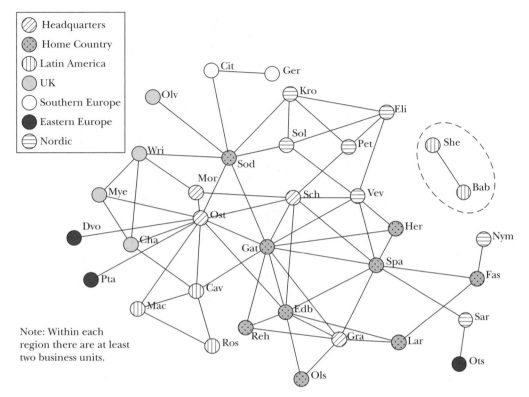

Note: Within each region there are at least two business units.

place to cover an area and catch things in the area. Fishing "social" nets catch ideas, job candidates, customers, suppliers, and other opportunities. They can work when the network owner is not actively involved, but they must be checked from time to time in order to bring in the catch. These nets must be maintained at regular intervals, checking that the connections are still in place and replacing those that have ripped. A real fishing net that is too dense brings in too many fish that are too small; not dense enough and it doesn't catch anything. Likewise, a fishing social network that is too dense brings in too much of the same kind of information. One that is not dense enough brings in too little information or resources.

Figure 4.5 shows a global engineering company's fishing net. This company has quite good fishing nets, with connections broadly distributed across all geographies and specialties. But this diagram highlighted two members from Latin America, "She" and "Bab," who were not connected to the rest of the company. Their operations had developed expertise in mining that would have been very valuable to the rest of the company, but it was not being "caught" by anyone else. After they saw this diagram, managers in the company worked to repair these holes and transfer more information. Global teams should assess their fishing net to ensure it is catching and holding the right resources, and build fishing nets where necessary.

FIGURE 4.6 An investment banker's safety net for business execution

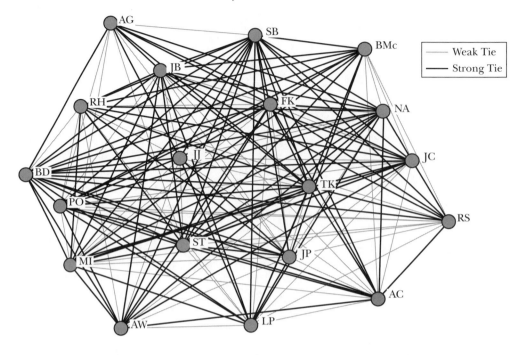

Safety nets are higher-density structures with relatively strong and flexible ties. Like "real" safety nets, they catch people when they fall, and bounce them back up again. They are rarely used, but must be carefully maintained in case they are needed. Human safety nets usually include family members and a few close colleagues. Some people think it's best never to use a safety net, but we disagree. In fact, when one is training in trapeze and tightrope, the first instructions are always about how to use the safety net. Experts say "If you're not using your safety net during training, you are not learning enough."[33]

Figure 4.6 shows one manager's business network, clearly structured as a safety net. This manager is an investment banker in a highly volatile country, and knows that structuring his business network in this way is critical to achieving success in the business.[34] One of the peripheral members of the network is his golf instructor, whom he is introducing to everyone else in his network to facilitate interaction during a leisure activity.

All teams should have safety nets, as well as fishing nets. The core team itself may be a safety net. One top management team of a global company we worked with realized that members' divisional roles left them feeling isolated and frustrated, with nowhere to turn for advice. They began to create relationships among themselves to become the safety net for each other, and explicitly used the safety net to help the company take some bold but important steps in a coordinated way. Although the company is in an industry that has been hit hard by the current global turmoil, they are much better positioned than their competitors in terms of coordination and strategy.

There are many other ways of looking at social networks and social capital that are very useful, and we encourage such teams to consult the many good references on this topic.[35]

COMPLEX, LARGE, DISTRIBUTED GLOBAL TEAMS: AMBITIOUS CONFIGURATIONS TO ACHIEVE AMBITIOUS GOALS

The most determined global organizations combine global team, virtual team, and social network configurations and processes to achieve ambitious goals. Here is an example to illustrate.

The organization coordinates research and implementation projects to improve sustainable agriculture around the world. More than 200 local projects are distributed on all continents, with the majority in Asia, Africa and South America. A team of people at headquarters oversees the projects and funding. In each region, a representative coordinates and monitors local projects. The headquarters team thought there was more potential for learning across projects, and for coordinating projects to achieve joint outcomes across regions that shared waterways and climate. However, they were worried that creating multiple teams and adding the burden of coordination to those teams might take away effort from the immediate challenge of better farming in local projects. They designed and implemented a configuration that combines all the principles in this chapter.

- Members of the core team spend more time in the field, learning from local and regional projects. They meet in person as a whole group only twice a year, for a week each time. They meet monthly for a half-day scheduled conference call as a whole team (sometimes they are able to do these meetings in person), and ad hoc in subgroups to share ideas and follow up on particular aspects of projects.

- Each of the members of the core team meets with their regional team twice a year, for two full days. These meetings are scheduled for the opposite quarters of the core team. They are held at a different site within the region each time, and regional team members learn about each other's countries and projects.

- Once a year, related to one of the core team meetings, 20 representatives from various local projects meet for three days. The 20 representatives are selected to highlight a diverse spectrum of projects in different stages who can learn from each other. Attendees are selected who have high social capital within their local areas, so they will pass on what they have learned and motivate others to collaborate.

- Once every three years, the organization has a large conference with representatives from as many projects as possible, as well as external experts, suppliers, and other parties who can learn from and help the projects.

The implementation of this interaction strategy is complex. But so is the goal, and ambitions are high. By managing the various levels and types of teams and the entire network in a strategic way, the goal is more likely to be achieved. Once routines are in place, it is actually easier to manage – with discipline and focus – than it is to describe. Most people in the network do not need to see the whole network of teams.

The role of the core team shifted from assessing, funding, and monitoring projects, to managing the relationships among projects. This was a difficult shift for some members of the core team. In the future, selection to the core team will reflect the new criteria. The organization is already seeing the results of the efforts in new innovations of sustainable agriculture, combining ideas from unlikely places.

Managers facing complex international coordination appreciate the combination of the team and network perspective since it helps them find and manage patterns in the complexity of their task. They know the task is difficult and that simple solutions and principles will only go part of the way. Even if the perspectives here are not simple to apply, they are systematic, and they provide ways of working towards performance and assessing progress.

TEAMS IN INTERNATIONAL MANAGEMENT COMBINE THE OLD AND THE NEW

As work in international firms becomes more interdependent, the need for coordination increases. The most common way to coordinate is with teams. Most managers are part of multiple teams of different configurations, with at least some of those teams having members distributed across space. It's important to set the team up well from the start, with the right task, composition, roles, and planning. To turn those inputs into performance, managers must lead and facilitate divergent and convergent social processes, adapting as the team works together. The inputs and social processes are part of leaders' "old" classic knowledge; however, managers of global teams must be able to lead them very well. The newer skills that are important in global organizations are managing virtual teams, and managing with networks in mind. Today's internet-raised generations will likely lead with yet an additional set of team skills. Teams will never disappear, and good global leaders will keep evolving with them.

Notes

1 Earley, P. C. and Gibson, C. B., *Multinational Work Teams: A New Perspective* (Mahwah, NJ: Lawrence Erlbaum Associates, 2002).

2 Maznevski, M. L. and Athanassiou, N. A., "A New Direction for Global Teams Research: Introduction to Special Issue," *Management International Review* (2007). Maznevski, M. L. and Chui, C., "Leading global teams," in Mendenhall, M. E., Osland, J. S., Bird, A., Oddou, G. R., Maznevski, M. L., Stevens, M. J. and Stahl, G. K., *Global Leadership,* 2nd edn. (New York, NY: Routledge, 2012).

3   Maznevski, M. L. and Jonsen, K., "The value of different perspectives," *Financial Times, Mastering Uncertainty*, March 24, 2006, 11.

4   Earley and Gibson, *op. cit.*

5   Stahl, G. K., Maznevski, M. L., Voigt, A. and Jonsen, K., "Unraveling the effects of cultural diversity in teams: A meta-analysis of research on multicultural work groups," *Journal of International Business Studies* 41 (2010) 690–709.

6   Tjosvold, D., *Working together to get things done: Managing for organizational productivity* (Lexington MA: Lexington Books, 1986).

7   Jehn, K. A., "A multimethod examination of the benefits and detriments of intragroup conflict," *Administrative Science Quarterly*, 40 (1995) 256–282. Jehn, K. A., "Enhancing effectiveness: An investigation of advantages and disadvantages of value-based intragroup conflict," *International Journal of Conflict Management*, 5 (1994) 223–238. De Dreu, C. K. W. and Weingart, L. R., "Task versus relationship conflict, team performance, and team member satisfaction: A meta-analysis," *Journal of Applied Psychology*, 88 (2003) 741–749.

8   Stahl et al., *op. cit.*

9   O'Reilly, C. A., Williams, K. Y. and Barsade, S., "Group demography and innovation: Does diversity help?" *Research on Managing Groups and Teams*, 1 (1998) 183–207.

10 Kelley, T., Littman, J. and Peters, T., *The Art of Innovation: Lessons in Creativity from IDEO, America's Leading Design Firm*, 2nd edn. (New York, NY: Doubleday, 2007).

11 Stahl et al., 2010, *op. cit.*

12 Ancona, D. G. and Caldwell, D. F., "Bridging the boundary: External activity and performance in organizational teams," *Administrative Science Quarterly*, 37 (1992) 634–661.

13 Freeman, R. E., "The stakeholder approach revisited," *Zeitschrift für wirtschafts- und unternehmensethik*, 5 (2004) 228–241. Driskat, V. U. and Wheeler, J. V., "Managing from the boundary: The effective leadership of self-managing work teams," *Academy of Management Journal*, 46 (2003) 435–457.

14 Maznevski, M. L. and Athanassiou, N. A., "Bringing the outside in: Learning and knowledge management through external networks," in Nonaka, I. and Ichijo, K., (eds.), *Knowledge Creation and Management: New Challenges for Managers* (Oxford: Oxford University Press, 2006).

15 Janis, I. L., *Victims of Groupthink: A Psychological Study of Foreign-policy Decisions and Fiascos* (Boston: Houghton Mifflin, 1972).

16 Maznevski, M., "Understanding our differences: Performance in decision-making groups with diverse members," *Human Relations*, 47 (1994) 531–52.

17 Stahl et al., *op. cit.*

18 Maznevski, M. L., Canney-Davison, S. and Jonsen, K., 2006. *Op. cit.* Klitmøller, A., Schneider, S. C., and Jonsen, K. 2013. "Common language differences in global virtual teams: The role of media and social categorization," Academy of Management Annual Conference Proceedings.

19 Stahl et al., *op. cit.*

20 Govindarajan, V. and Gupta, A. K., "Building an effective global business team," *MIT Sloan Management Review*, (Summer 2001) 63–71.

21 Lau, D. C. and Murnighan, J. K., "Demographic diversity and faultlines: The compositional dynamics of organizational groups," *Academy of Management Review*, 23 (1998) 325–340. Maloney, M. M. and Zellmer-Bruhn, M., "Building bridges, windows and cultures: Mediating mechanisms between heterogeneity and performance in global teams," *Management International Review*, 46(6) (2006) 697–720.

22 The structure of this section is based on research conducted by M. Maznevski with A. Baan, Arie Baan Consulting.

23 Jarvenpaa, S. L. and Leidner, D. E., "Communication and trust in global virtual teams," *Organization Science,* 10(6) (1999).

24 Maznevski, M. L. and Chudoba, K. M., "Bridging space over time: Global virtual team dynamics and effectiveness," *Organization Science,* 11(5) (2000) 473–492.

25 This section draws on research conducted by the authors with N. Athanassiou, Northeastern University.

26 Maznevski and Athanassiou, 2007, *op. cit.*

27 Athanassiou, N. A., Maznevski, M. L., and Walker, P. Unpublished study.

28 Adler, P. S. and Kwon, S-W., "Social capital: Prospects for a new concept," *Academy of Management Review,* 27(1) (2002) 17–40. Lin, N., "Building a network theory of social capital," *Connections* 22(1) (1999) 28–51. Cross, R. and Parker, A., *The Hidden Power of Social Networks* (Cambridge, MA.: Harvard Business School Publishing, 2004).

29 Lin 1999, *op. cit.*

30 Granovetter M. S., "Economic action and social structure: The problem of embeddedness," *American Journal of Sociology* 91(3) (1985) 481–510.

31 www.facebook.com, www.linkedin.com, www.tumblr.com, www.twitter.com. Accessed May 4, 2013.

32 Also referred to as networks with structural holes, Burt, R. S., *Structural Holes: The Social Structure of Competition* (Cambridge, MA: Harvard University Press, 1992).

33 Various circus school participants, personal communications.

34 Research by Shaner shows that foreign direct investments in stable and predictable environments perform better if the business unit has a fishing net type of network with customers, suppliers, and others in the business environment. However, in unstable and unpredictable environments, the business unit performs better with a safety net type of network. Shaner, J., "The relation between external business networks and performance in foreign investments," (unpublished doctoral dissertation, University of Lausanne, 2005).

35 We particularly recommend Cross, R. and Parker, A., *The Hidden Power of Social Networks: Understanding How Work Really Gets Done in Organizations* (Cambridge, MA: Harvard Business School Press, 2004). Cross, R., Borgatti, S. and Parker, A., "Making invisible work visible: Using social network analysis to support strategic collaboration," *California Management Review,* 44(2) (2002) 25–46. Cross, R., Nohria, N., and Parker, A., "Six myths about informal networks and how to overcome them," *MIT Sloan Management Review,* 43(3) (2002) 67–75. Cross, R., Ehrlich, K., Dawson, R., and Helferich, J., "Managing collaboration: Improving team effectiveness through a network perspective," *California Management Review,* 50(4) (2008) 74–98. Narasimhan, A., and Conger, J. "Capabilities of the consummate networker," *Organizational Dynamics,* 36(1) (2007) 13–27.

PART 3

CHAPTER 5

Executing Global Strategy[a]

Today's global organizations need skilled managers. Cultural understanding and good intercultural skills are important managerial competencies. However, as a manager in the global economy you will need more than intercultural skills. You also have to understand how the intercultural context may influence your company's strategy, structure, administrative systems, and operations.

STRATEGY EXECUTION IS EMBEDDED IN CONTEXT: KNOW YOUR ASSUMPTIONS

The formulation and implementation of a strategy requires understanding market demands, competitors, and external constraints such as government policies. Managers interpret information from their external environment, combine this interpretation with an understanding of the organization's internal strengths and weaknesses, and translate the implications into appropriate organizational action that will lead to desired goals. However, in addition to choosing, for example, markets and manufacturing sites, important organizational actions include choosing structures, work systems, and administrative mechanisms to motivate employees toward the desired goals.

Since a company's knowledge and practices are not always completely documented, or made explicit, there is a great deal of implicit or tacit knowledge required to manage a company effectively.[1] Executives need to be aware of the implicit knowledge or

[a]The authors would like to acknowledge Professor Nick Athanassiou for his contribution to this chapter, which is based on his in an earlier version of the text; and also to thank Professor Bert Spector for his contribution.

assumptions underlying their firm's strategy, structure, systems, and practices. These practices are influenced by both organizational culture and national culture. Culture, the "shoulds" and the "oughts" of life or business that people usually cannot articulate, is acquired through the socialization process, which creates common experiences, shared mental models, and accepted ways of operating – the way things should be done. Using domestic strategy, systems or practices, unmodified, in another country may lead to unforeseen negative consequences. Therefore, global executives need to understand how their assumptions about organizing and managing may differ from those in their company's home country.

As a company spreads beyond its home country and creates a global network, top managers need to recalibrate their cultural "filters" through education and the acquisition of personal experience. Specifically, this should include knowledge about their different market environments, company activities in these countries, and the linkages among this network of activities. The experiences and the understood but unwritten information, as well as the explicit policies and practices shared by a top management group, create the operational and cultural filters used to decode, interpret, and understand context-dependent information flowing from the company's various markets and operations. With properly interpreted information, global executives can make informed strategic decisions and influence the design and implementation of culturally-sensitive organization structures and systems to achieve strategic goals.[2] Executives can put into use the global mindset they have developed.

Most companies have a particular organizational heritage that has evolved within the culture of their home countries. This means that a potential cultural bias may exist in their strategy, systems, and practices – "the way things are done in the headquarters' home country." For example, Lincoln Electric, renowned in the United States for its highly skilled and extremely productive employees, used a unique piecework incentive system to pay workers primarily on the number of quality pieces that they produced.[3] Working faster and harder meant a higher salary. This system was instituted around 1907 by James F. Lincoln, who strongly believed in the individual human being and in the equality of management and workers. Driven by his philosophy and beliefs about human motivation, he created the system that he believed would generate the best productivity and utilization of the company's human resources. This system was a significant contributor to the company's productivity and profitability. But the question to be answered is "Could it be transferred to another culture without modification?"

Global Strategy Execution: Science + Art = Craft

This chapter addresses Lincoln Electric's question, which is shared by every manager implementing business in another country. We start by introducing a tool to identify and analyze what needs to be aligned – and how – in order to implement effectively. We look at the nature of work tasks and coordination structures, and the systems that align them. Then we look at how organizations are embedded in their context, and the influence of culture on organizing and implementing. Next we provide an overview of strategy, to examine how alignment needs to adapt to different strategies. This is not a book about strategy, but it is impossible to discuss implementing strategy without taking a brief look at strategic choices. We review the traditional structures and processes for developing a global presence, and we identify some recent trends with these structures. We close with a note about the importance of organizational adaptation and management judgement.

If management were a science, we simply would have to learn the laws regarding management. Unfortunately, laws regarding management have not yet been discovered and may never be. If management were an art, we could rely on the intuition and insight of individuals, and we could probably do little to create managers in the numbers our organizations require. We would rely on a few naturally gifted people.

We prefer to think of management as a craft, an undertaking that requires knowledge of facts and principles and an ability to interpret these in their cultural context. It also requires the development of experience and judgment to aid in the correct interpretation of situations. One can learn about and practice management to improve upon our craft domestically and globally.

ALIGNING THE ORGANIZATION TO EXECUTE

In this section we present a model for identifying and analyzing the most important aspects of an organization to align internally for effective execution.[4] We will develop the organizational alignment model first in a culture-free mode without considering how culture may affect management practices and systems, and then we will consider the impact of culture. The basic components of the model for internal alignment are shown in Figure 5.1.

In this section we look at tasks and coordination – the foundation for building structure. Most of the rest of this book is about people, and the next chapter in particular focuses on selecting and developing people for international business.

Tasks are the Building Blocks of Organizing

Global organizations are complex and have many jobs or tasks that need to be done. These tasks have different characteristics requiring different skills which mean employing people with different educational backgrounds, knowledge bases, and skills. Think of the differences between accounting, marketing, R&D and manufacturing, for example. There are usually patterns of differences, or systematic variances, between people in these various functional departments. The idea that segments of a company are

FIGURE 5.1   Organizational alignment model: internal alignment

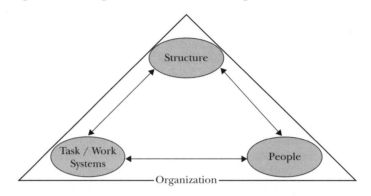

organized for specific tasks and that some people by education, experience, and attitude seem more appropriate for some jobs rather than others, is the concept of differentiation or the "difference in cognitive and emotional orientation among managers in different functional departments."[5] This concept encompasses the specialized knowledge required for the tasks as well as the differences in attitude and behavior of the people in the jobs. As the complexity of an organization increases, it is likely that the differentiation increases as well. As this happens, the potential for departments to pursue their own particular goals increases, as does the likelihood for potential conflict. Therefore, it is important to coordinate these functional areas. This is not always easy in large corporations, since people may be separated physically and psychologically by their personal predispositions and orientations.

Once there is a differentiated organization capable of executing the required tasks, then integration is needed. The concept of integration includes the coordination of activities and interrelationships and conflict resolution, as well. Integrating mechanisms include task forces, teams, liaison people, product or project managers, product management departments, and matrix organization designs. These are structural responses to the increasing coordination needs of an organization.

What Level of Interdependence is Required?   To ensure the proper coordination, managers also must be aware of how each area is dependent on the others to achieve its tasks and responsibilities. There are three basic types of internal interdependence in organizations, and most complex organizations exhibit all three types.[6] The simplest is *pooled* or simple interdependence. This means that each part of an organization can pursue the achievement of its goals relatively independently from other parts and still contribute to the overall objectives of the organization, as shown in Figure 5.2. This is a situation "in which each part renders a discrete contribution to the whole and each is supported by the whole."[7] For example, in a department store, personnel from the furniture department do not necessarily have to interact with people from sporting goods for each to fulfill its objectives. Each can contribute, independently, to the goals of the

FIGURE 5.2 Pooled (simple) interdependence

FIGURE 5.3 Sequential interdependence

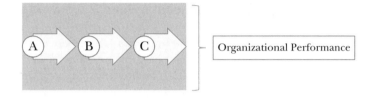

store. Each however, is supported by the human resource department and the accounting department, for example.

Higher up on the complexity scale is *sequential* interdependence. As the name implies, one group must accomplish its task before the next one can begin. There is a predetermined and ordered progression by which some tasks must proceed. In manufacturing a relatively standard product one can see a progression from the design department to engineering to purchasing to production scheduling and then to manufacturing. On the assembly line of an automobile, for example, the car's frame and axles are assembled before the engine or the body is attached. A specific task, "A" must be accomplished before the next task, "B," is begun and so forth. This is depicted in Figure 5.3.

An even more complex form of interdependence is *reciprocal*, which means "the output of each becomes the input for the others."[8] Rather than having discrete linear relationships between groups, the relationships are continuous and almost circular in nature. For example, in creating sophisticated technology systems, production must understand what the researchers have developed, but the development engineers must also understand the constraints on manufacturing. Similarly, both the researchers and the engineers must understand the customers' needs in order to accurately forecast delivery dates. As can be inferred from this simple example, reciprocal interdependence creates an iterative process in which the required level of inter-group communication is high and the potential for conflict increases dramatically. Think of an advertising agency working on a new account. Copywriting, photography, art, production, finance and the account executive constantly meet to decide on the latest iteration of the ad. Each has to understand the constraints on the others. And if, when the customer sees the ad, changes are required, the interactive process starts all over again. Reciprocal interdependence is depicted in Figure 5.4.

FIGURE 5.4   Reciprocal interdependence

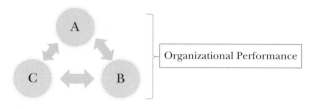

Coordinate According to the Interdependence Need: The Foundation for Structure

As the complexity of organizations increases, the need to coordinate and control the activities of diverse groups of individuals also increases, and formal control mechanisms such as accounting, auditing, and management information systems are important. Most organizations systematically collect, analyze, and disseminate information on production, finances, and personnel. Budgets are developed, refined, and monitored. Like other mechanisms, these provide messages about what is required or valued.

For example, requiring Manufacturing to concentrate on costs and Sales on customer satisfaction could in some circumstances produce high levels of dysfunctional conflict. Manufacturing would want long productions runs to minimize down time and re-tooling costs, while Sales might want runs stopped to meet a valued customer's urgent need for another product. Both need to understand the other and act in a coordinated fashion if either is to satisfy their objectives.

The managerial issue is how to coordinate the various types of interdependence. At the simplest level, for example, with pooled interdependence, standardization by rules and budgets can be used. A department is given a budget, a set of operating procedures, hours of operation, and a set of well-defined tasks to do, and measured on its results against set objectives. With sequential interdependence, coordination is usually also accomplished with plans and schedules.

However, at the level of reciprocal interdependence, special structural integrating roles such as project teams or product managers are employed, and coordinating mechanisms such as task forces are often used. Direct, face-to-face communication or coordination through mutual adjustment, is usually required as well.[9] These methods are summarized in Table 5.1.

A problem-solving approach to resolving conflict is generally regarded as the most appropriate way to contribute to organizational effectiveness. This means that managers confront problems rather than avoid them or smooth them over. As they confront them, they recognize that the conflicts may be rooted in legitimate task differences and different viewpoints held by different specialists. Managers should avoid letting situations develop where functions attempt to prevail and win out over others. Win-lose situations

TABLE 5.1 Matching interdependence, coordination, and the task environment

Interdependence	Coordination	Task Environment Characteristics
Pooled (simple)	Standardization: rules, regulations	Relatively simple, static, certain, predictable, unchanging (stability)
Sequential	Plans: schedules, budgets, milestones	Multiple inter-related components, frequent but manageable changes (complexity)
Reciprocal (complex)	Mutual adjustment: constant communication; often face to face	Multiple inter-related components, rapidly changing, unpredictable, multiple interpretations, cause and effect uncertainty (dynamic complexity)

can be very destructive for organizations. Managers should attempt to resolve conflicts so that the organization as a whole wins.

ALIGNING THE ORGANIZATION EVERYDAY: THE CRITICAL ROLE OF SYSTEMS

It is one thing to set up the right tasks and systems, with the right people. But every day people make decisions and take actions, and each decision and act can support the alignment or hinder it. Systems, such as structure, reward, and control systems, help to maintain the alignment. Each of these systems sends an employee some type of message about what is expected of him or her. These systems' signals are important. Quite often different systems give people different messages or signals. Ineffectiveness often results when individuals cannot reconcile those different messages. Often they pay attention to the messages of one system to the exclusion of messages coming from another.

We do not intend to deal with particular tools in depth here. Our aim is to help you select and implement the right systems for you, given the criteria of aligning for implementing strategy. Our goal is to explore how, if used effectively or ineffectively, such systems can create fits or misfits between people and their jobs, or between people and the organizations in which they work.

Organizations are Socio-technical Systems

Organizations are systems and need to be understood as such. In practical terms this means that what happens in one part of the organization has implications for, and probably affects, other parts. Organizations are socio-technical systems, meaning that they have both social and technical components. The "technical" component is the numerous technical and/or functional tasks of the business. These include acquiring inputs such as capital and raw materials, as well as using specific technology and work processes to create finished products or services. Each of the major functional areas of an organization – such as production, marketing, or finance – also is a system within the larger "technical" organizational system. Each has a set of tasks and operations necessary to the functioning of the entire organization.

The "social" component is the human element, the people – the individuals and groups, with their skills, needs, feelings, expectations, experience, and beliefs – who carry out the tasks and operations. Managers have to align the connected and interdependent parts of social and technical elements of a company and solve problems that arise within and between the two in order to achieve the organization's strategic goals.

As an example, let's look at a firm we will call ABC Financial Printing in the financial printing industry. When a company had an Initial Public Offering (IPO) or there was a merger or acquisition, ABC had long provided transaction services, such as completing and filing required documents with regulators like the Security and Exchange Commission. This was a highly customized service based on relationship selling by a sales force, and this service had very high margins. The sales representatives who were hired to sell transaction services were aggressive self-starters who liked the substantial salary, bonuses, and glory that came from being successful in the high margin, relationship-oriented transaction business.

Then, in 2002, the Sarbanes-Oxley Act required firms to file numerous routine, standardized periodic reports that were time-consuming to prepare. As a result, financial printing companies like ABC, pushed by competitors that were offering a low cost "do it yourself" product, introduced a compliance service for their customers to meet the requirements of Sarbanes-Oxley. The compliance service was a lower margin offering than the transaction service. However, in terms of company revenue, it was growing to become a very important part of a firm's business.

ABC Financial Printing developed a range of products such as computer programs to address this market. However, it had difficulty in motivating its sales representatives to sell these products. They did not have the technical skills to sell the new products. Neither the characteristics of the sales people, nor the reward and evaluation systems, fit the demands of the new market or its customers for compliance business.

Organizations should be designed so that the behavior elicited by the management systems matches the needs of the organization. All too often, procedures are imposed without due consideration of the job at hand, simply because, *de facto,* they just "have become company policy." In such situations, the administrative heritage of the company may become the controlling factor, with the jobs and the people forced into fitting the existing systems, when it should be the other way around.

These management systems are tools, not ends in themselves. For best performance, there should be a fit, or *alignment,* between the people and the jobs that they do.

Managers can use administrative "tools" to strengthen this alignment between people and tasks. These tools channel the activities of employees; they are social-relational tools as much as they are technical tools. Judgment is required in assessing the likely impact of administrative systems on people and in adjusting these systems accordingly to support task achievement and organizational results.

Aligning Tasks with People

The first, extremely important fit is between the tasks to be performed and the skills of the people who perform them. The people and tasks they are working at are organized using various divisions of labor and structures to achieve coordination, efficiency, and effectiveness. Structure is the set of relationships between people in an organization and is one mechanism that communicates to organization members what behavior is expected of them, what tasks to work on, what not to do, what goals to work towards, with whom to work, whom to obey, and whom to direct. This includes such things as hierarchy, teams, and rules and procedures.

Structure, for example, determines relationships between people at various levels of responsibility, while budgets and performance appraisals direct behavior toward specific tasks and goals. The other alignment "tools" include selection criteria and processes, development programs, allocation of rewards and sanctions, information and control systems, and performance evaluation methods.

Getting the Right People in: Recruiting and Selecting   The people brought into an organization through its recruitment and selection systems can have a very dramatic effect on organizational alignment. The most obvious effect is on the pool of knowledge, skills, and attitudes. Selection is the mechanism by which a pool of candidates is narrowed to the number of job vacancies. Several sources of assessment error can enter these decisions. The one most frequently described is the "just like me" error in which the successful candidate is the one who is closest in skills and personality to those making the decision. Although it might augur well for the fit between the person and his or her boss, this type of decision might not provide the required congruence between person and task. Selection, like recruitment, involves a careful analysis of both the job(s) and the organization to determine the right type of person.

Rarely does a selection decision alone provide a perfect person–task (P–T) or person–organization (P–O) fit. P–T fit is the traditional focus of employee selection, the skills and abilities to do the job; while P–O fit is concerned with a person's compatibility with broader characteristics of the organization, such as culture, values, and colleagues.[10] If it is only to find out how things are done in the company, most employees need some form of training or development to make them effective performers. So even if the fit is perfect, it is not likely that condition will last for long. Continual development is needed as conditions change.

Encouraging Performance: Performance Appraisal and Rewards Two of the most talked about and studied management systems are performance appraisal and rewards. Appraisal processes are seen in many forms and administered in many ways. However, at the core there are several common purposes:

- Communicate expectations or standards of performance.

- Provide feedback on how well one is doing against expectations or standards.

- Identify areas of developmental need and develop a plan of remedy.

- Provide information and documentation for decisions about salary, promotion, or discipline.

Rewards come in different forms and in different ways for different people. One person's reasons for working are different from another's. Basically, rewards fall into one of two categories: intrinsic, those that come from doing the job itself or being directly part of the work environment, and extrinsic, those more tangible aspects provided by others. More job autonomy is an example of the former, while getting a raise is an example of the latter.

Rewards have different meanings for different people. Some rewards (particularly the financial reward) have instrumental value, helping us get other things of importance such as food and shelter. Rewards often serve as a signal that one's contribution or presence is valued: a form of recognition. They can serve as a signal to others of one's value, thereby enhancing self-esteem. Individual needs determine which of these meanings are most important at any one time and which reward will have the desired effect.

In designing and administering reward systems from the employee's perspective, several issues are important. From the organization's perspective, it is important to ask the following questions about rewards:

1 Are they competitive? Can the organization attract the people it wants vis-à-vis its competitors? Are the rewards commensurate with what the employee brings to the job in terms of skill, knowledge and aptitude?

2 Are they sufficient? Do employees get enough of the right things to satisfy their needs? Is the sum of both the intrinsic and extrinsic rewards enough to motivate, and retain employees?

3 Are they equitable? Is the internal distribution of rewards fair? Are they commensurate with the required attitude and effort?

4 Do they motivate the right task behavior, or do they create a disincentive? Do they motivate for a sustained period of time?

With a range of options, how do you decide which type of system is most appropriate? The answer to these questions should come from the analysis of the organization and the environment in which it operates. Once a strategy is developed, goals have been established, and the key tasks have been laid out, the people required can be identified and the correct systems instituted.

Organizations Have Cultures Too   Organizations also have cultures that may facilitate or hinder the work of the company, and management is responsible for shaping the culture of the organization. A set of values and philosophy will develop in every organization, whether it is created explicitly with careful forethought, or whether it happens implicitly without specific guidance and is perhaps less effective. Management's values can encourage a culture of trust, problem solving, and adaptation to another country or one of mistrust, obedience, and domination.

Lincoln Electric, for example, based on founder James Lincoln's values and philosophy, created a corporate culture of rugged individualism, productivity, and innovation. Workers were responsible for their own success.

If values provide the content of the culture, managers' styles shape the climate and feeling for how other managers and subordinates relate – the day-to-day process of taking action and solving problems. Management style can create an atmosphere of openness and sharing, or one of insecurity and fear. The challenges facing today's organizations would seem to call for flexible, innovative organizations and for managers whose personal styles can create or contribute to those characteristics.

The management at Lincoln Electric did not believe in hierarchical distinctions, and sought to erase them.[11] There were no reserved parking spaces for managers, and they ate in the same cafeteria as the workers. There also was an Advisory Board of elected employee representatives which met twice a month with Lincoln executives. Management was approachable and had an open door policy. The result was trust between the workers and management.

Aligning the Organization with Systems: Each Part Affects the Others

In summary, people are selected for certain skills and attitudes, trained and educated (developed) to improve these skills, evaluated on how they do their jobs, and rewarded. Evaluation and reward systems, development, budgets, and control systems are also used to motivate people. To make sure that the tasks of the organization are coordinated and carried out in the best possible way, companies use various structures. Too often decisions about the administrative systems are made as a result of unexamined assumptions about motivation, rather than of an understanding of the organization in its context.

Managers must understand that if they make a change in either the task or the people, their action may have ramifications for the other and implications for overall results – and not always the ones intended. This is one of the properties of a system; a change

FIGURE 5.5 Organizational alignment: Internal with systems

in one part affects the other parts. This is why a systemic and integrated perspective of organizations is essential in diagnosing problems and considering courses of action. The internal organizational alignment model with systems is shown in Figure 5.5.

ALIGNING TO THE ENVIRONMENT

Christopher Alexander, in writing about the process of design of physical things such as buildings or transportation systems, commented on the need for fit or alignment:

> Every design problem begins with an effort to achieve fitness between two entities: the form in question and its context. The form is the solution to the problem; the context defines the problem. In other words, when we speak of design, the real object of discussion is not the form alone, but the ensemble comprising the form and its context.[12]

Relating this to global organizations, the form is the result of decisions managers make about how to structure tasks and coordinate them, who to hire, how to reward them, and so forth. The context is the global environment in which it operates. The context (environment) makes demands on the form (organization), and meeting the demands of the environment is "fitness" or alignment. To achieve alignment, managers need to understand their organization and its context.

External complexity affects managers also, as our discussion of globalization earlier in this book pointed out. These organizations are part of an environment or context that is comprised of social, political, and economic institutions and technology that affect them. Internationally, the social, political, and economic institutions in the host country may be very different from those in the home country. Also the (national) cultural assumptions about "how things should be done" or the "right way to manage" may differ as well. Firms also have competitors, and they compete in the same environment by developing a sustainable, competitive strategy.

Managers are responsible for the functioning of these complex human systems. Obviously, the complexity faced by a manager and his or her responsibility varies by job and by level within the organization. People at the highest levels generally are more concerned with forces outside of the organization and linking the organization to its external environment, while people at lower levels are more concerned with internal operations. However, with globalization and having operations in many countries, people at all levels are now being exposed to the complexities of how other cultures affect both external and internal organizational environments.

Managers also have to judge the potential effectiveness of home country management systems and practices in relation to host country cultural assumptions. For example, in the conduct of domestic business North American companies tend to decide about strategy, structure, and systems with the use of rational, economic cost-benefit analyses. Decisions may be based on discussions that reference and build on implicit sets of shared cultural assumptions; all managers of the domestic companies are assumed to share these (although they don't necessarily). Yet these assumptions of common viewpoints must be challenged and questioned when a manager operates in multiple national markets.

Geert Hofstede has commented that "theories reflect the cultural environment in which they were written" and asked the question, "To what extent do theories developed in one country and reflecting the cultural boundaries of that country apply to other countries?"[13] Hofstede's own answer was that his research "seriously questioned the universal validity of management theories developed in one country – in most instances here, the United States."[14] Management concepts and practices are explained by theories regarding organization, motivation, and leadership. Therefore, theories of management and the derived management systems and practices may work well in the culture that developed them because they are based on local cultural assumptions and paradigms about the right way to manage.

Consider Lincoln Electric again. With its origins in the Midwest of the United States, it created a set of administrative systems based on a culture of strong individualism. When Lincoln transferred, unchanged, its US manufacturing, labor selection, compensation and incentive systems abroad, it experienced relative success in markets that were culturally "close," or similar, to the USA – Canada, UK, Australia – and problems in others that culturally were more "distant," or less similar – Brazil and Germany. A new generation of internationally experienced top managers emerged, who understood the extent to which Lincoln Electric's operations were dependent on its American context and roots. Only at this point were the company's strategy, organization structure, and systems modified to allow for cultural differences. Then, Lincoln's international business began to recover.[15]

Cultural Influences Assumptions about Strategy and Systems

An organization's management systems and processes have cultural assumptions incorporated into them. Although there is some debate as to whether cultures around the world are converging or diverging and in what areas, there is no doubt that, in the realm of systems and practices preferred in a given country, culture influences preferred behavioral style and the management systems that are acceptable or even desirable. The practices of one country (such as hiring friends and relatives in many Latin countries) are often unacceptable or even ridiculed in another (such as hiring friends and relatives in the United States and Canada). Earlier chapters provided numerous examples of how culture influenced management systems and processes.

Our earlier discussion about alignment and the alignment model could be used by any executive formulating and implementing strategy in his or her home market. Unless they are operating in a very multicultural domestic context, they don't necessarily give much thought to cultural influences in their domestic operations. But they must learn to do so when crossing cultural borders both within and between nation states. When firms start operating in different cultural environments, the ability to create alignment can change – often dramatically.

An additional element of judgment is required of global managers who must work across national boundaries. As described earlier, global business is distinguished from domestic business by home vs. host country cultural differences; differences in policies and operations among national governments; and the degree of integration that must take place among operating units. Administrative systems should be adaptable to changing conditions and work forces and not be ends in themselves. Furthermore, the fit that they create needs to be dynamic. This means that as strategies, competitive environments, or geographic locations change, then structures, systems, and policies also need to be reevaluated and modified as necessary.

Consider again, for example, Lincoln Electric's experience with its individual-oriented, piece-rate incentive and bonus systems in factories in Europe and Brazil. Lincoln Electric's executives found that in Europe, managers were opposed to piecework and preferred more vacation time to extra income from bonuses. In Germany piecework at the time was illegal, and in Brazil bonuses paid in two consecutive years became a legal entitlement.[16] These culturally based conflicts went against the very systems that had helped Lincoln Electric become so successful in the United States.

The values underlying administrative systems, in this case reward systems, may not be obvious. It might be easier to conclude that workers were the problem instead of examining the assumptions underlying an incentive scheme. Another question to ask is, What would be the effect of a highly individualized compensation system such as Lincoln Electric's in countries such as those in Eastern and Central Europe, whose political/cultural systems have reinforced collectivist values under several decades of Communist rule?

Similarly, what are the cultural assumptions underlying practices such as empowerment, self-directed work teams, and 360-degree feedback? How would they work in hierarchical versus individualistic cultures?

However, there are counter-examples of managerial systems that are successful despite their lack of alignment with the local culture. It is important to remember what we said earlier: cultures are not monolithic and there is a distribution of values, beliefs, and ways of doing things in each one. Brannen and Salk described three broad categories of people that exist simultaneously in each culture and who display mainstream cultural attributes to varying degrees – probably depending on the issue domain: cultural-normals (the typical or "average" person of that culture); hyper-normals (people who believe and follow very strongly the espoused values of a culture); and marginals (those who believe less strongly or differently).[17] Because there is likely a distribution of beliefs and assumptions in any population, practices from the corporate headquarters' home culture may be able to be transferred globally. Moreover, sometimes there are unexpected alignments between culture and systems. For example, McDonald's successfully adapted its business model and systems to Russia, in part, because there was a fit between the restaurant tasks and the Russian culture.[18]

Cultural Influences Assumptions about Structure

Organizational structures are also not free from the influence of culture. Each structure carries with it identifiable assumptions about the legitimacy of certain practices and relationships and defines the locus of authority, responsibility and bases of power differently. Each legitimizes a different pattern of communication and interaction. In addition to "fitting" better with certain competitive situations or product characteristics, some structures may be more acceptable than others in a given culture. For example, matrix organization, a structure in which a person has two bosses, has cultural assumptions built into it. It violates the principle of unity of command that some hierarchical cultures may believe is correct, and because of the existence of potentially competing interests, it can force conflict into the open, which some cultures may avoid.

André Laurent believed that the national origin of managers affected their views of proper management and also that educational attempts to communicate alternative management processes and structures would fail unless the "implicit management gospels" that they carried in their heads were addressed.[19] Although there are many managers of all nationalities who do not like the matrix form of organization (including in the United States), the French seemed to have a particular aversion to it. Laurent became convinced of this when he was trying to explain matrix organizations to French managers, to whom the idea of reporting to two bosses was "so alien that mere consideration of such organizing principles was an impossible, useless exercise."[20]

A common American attitude is that constructive conflict can be positive. It forces issues into the open and differences of opinion help in understanding problems, in providing different solutions, and in increasing creativity. In the US, organizational structures are not designed to decrease all conflict. However, not all cultures view conflict the same way. Stella Ting-Toomey's research shows that cultural variability (individualism vs. collectivism, power distance and high vs. low-context communication patterns) provides "lenses" through which conflict is viewed; individualists use an outcome-oriented model while collectivists follow a process-oriented model.[21] Where Americans or other individualistic, low-context cultures may embrace conflict as potentially beneficial and engage the associated structures like cross-functional teams and matrix organizations, collectivistic, high-context cultures may seek to avoid open conflict and may prefer hierarchical cultures with more clear responsibilities. Ting-Toomey states:

> For individualists, effective conflict negotiation means settling the conflict problem openly and working out a set of functional conflict solutions conjointly. Effective conflict resolution behavior (e.g., emphasizing the importance of addressing incompatible goals/outcomes) is relatively more important for individualists than is appropriate facework behavior. For collectivists, on the other hand, appropriate conflict management means the subtle negotiation of in-group/out-group face-related issues – pride, honor, dignity, insult, shame, disgrace, humility, trust, mistrust, respect, and prestige – in a given conflict episode. Appropriate facework moves and countermoves are critical for collectivists before tangible conflict outcomes or goals can be addressed.[22]

In another study comparing French and American managers, Inzerelli and Laurent discovered that American managers held an instrumental conception of structure, while the French held a social conception.[23] The instrumental viewpoint sees positions in a company ordered in terms of task requirements and relationships between positions as being instrumental to achieving organizational objectives. In an instrumental view, authority is impersonal and comes from a person's role or function, implying equality of persons involved. Subordination is the acceptance of the impersonal, rational, and legal order of the organization. In contrast, the social viewpoint sees positions defined in terms of social status and authority, and relationships are hierarchical. Authority comes from status, and it could extend beyond the function. Superior–subordinate relationships are personal, implying superiority of one person over the other, and subordination is loyalty and deference to the superior.

Numerous other examples of the impact of values on systems and management styles were provided earlier in Chapters 2 and 3, on culture and inter-cultural effectiveness. You may want to go back and review those discussions.

What's the Verdict? Can Existing Practices, Systems and Management Styles be Transferred or Adapted?

Executives must decide whether existing practices, systems, and management styles can be transferred from one culture to another, or whether they must be changed and adapted when they appear to be in conflict with the norms of another culture. The alignment model showing alignment to the environment is shown in Figure 5.6.

FIGURE 5.6   Aligning the organization with the environment

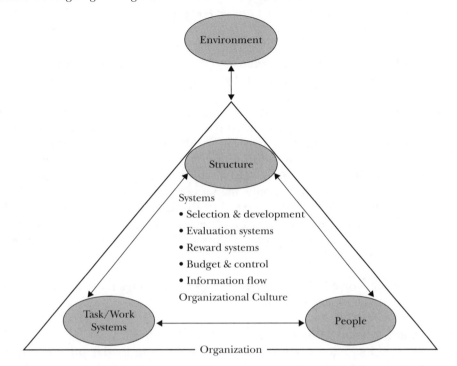

The answer is not always to change the system, even if it is different than that in the host country. In Rome, you do not always need to do as the Romans have always done! Sometimes people in another culture simply need to be trained to use a system (remembering, of course, that the best training format may be influenced by the culture). However, neither is the answer to always assume that training is all that is required. Each response has a proper time and place.

The decision regarding transferring, adapting, or possibly even creating a new hybrid practice should be the result of careful, informed judgment based on understanding the cultural biases of management systems and the cultural norms of the country in which the operations are located. Are there rules? Not really, but careful analysis can help sort out the issues and help managers solve the problem. First, one must remember that cultures are not monolithic and in every culture there is a distribution of values. There are variations within cultures, and culture is not deterministic. Some people will adhere strongly to the norms of their culture, while others will not. You could find champions within the culture, who are eager to do something a bit different from their cultural norm. It also means that if certain cultural values are a critical part of an organization's model for success, then managers can use the selection system to find employees who display these characteristics.

Questions such as "How important is it that we do it identically to the way it's done at home?" can guide your decisions. It may not be important that the procedures are exactly the same; rather, results may be more important. Just because it is the way headquarters does it, or wants it done, does not mean that it is right for a different cultural environment.

What Does the Business Need?   The most important questions are around the business imperatives: tasks that must be done well for the firm to make money.[24]

An example is Carlos Ghosn, who turned around Nissan by doing everything he was not supposed to do in Japan. Ghosn said, "[A] lot of advice I received from outside was, 'You cannot do this, you cannot do that, you cannot do this – because you are in Japan.'"[25] In a culture of lifetime employment, seniority, and interlocking business relationships, he eliminated 21,000 jobs, closed plants, introduced bonuses and stock options, had younger people managing older ones, and reduced the interdependency with suppliers in the *keiretsu*. In this case it is important to recognize that Nissan was in a crisis and in times of crisis traditional norms may not apply. The important point is that managers must understand the situation they face and not rely on stereotypes.

So should you adapt? It all depends on the business imperatives of the company and its industry. Three examples are:

Adapt to your partner.   Take for example a local American auto parts company that entered into a joint venture in North America with a Japanese company to learn about just-in-time manufacturing, a technique in which the Japanese company was a leader. The American company had a short-term orientation to cost control, and as the joint venture progressed, it became uncomfortable with the Japanese partner's longer term orientation and wanted to institute a tighter control system, which, however, interfered with its original objective for the joint venture – learning. In this situation, whose way should be followed? The Americans wanted to learn from the Japanese, who were clear experts. The Japanese way should take precedence.[26]

Keep your own practices.   The experience of a Canadian bank, the Bank of Nova Scotia, in Mexico is a different example. When the Mexican banking system was about to collapse after the economic crisis in 1994, the Mexican government put up for sale most of the Mexican banks. The Bank of Nova Scotia bought Inverlat.[27] In 1982, Mexico's banks had been nationalized and they remained essentially government institutions for many years. It was a period of stagnation despite substantial innovations in technology and practices in the global banking industry. Many Inverlat managers claimed that their bank had generally deteriorated more than the rest of the banking sector in Mexico, and overall had failed to create a new generation of bankers who understood and reflected the changed conditions and times. The bank had been lending primarily to the government, and managers were unfamiliar with the challenges of lending to the private sector, and therefore failed to collateralize their loans properly or to ensure that covenants were being maintained. The existing managers did not have the knowledge or the capacity to manage the critical credit assessment function.

In this situation, whose practices were going to be followed? Banks make money by lending money, and the credit function is critical, or what we think of as a business imperative. Whatever the Mexican culture, the Canadians were the experts in this situation, and their practices should dominate.

Create a new way.   The head of production for Nestlé Malaysia wanted to take the adequately-performing factories to a new global standard of production.[28] He had had good experiences with semi-autonomous work teams (SAWTs) in a previous assignment, and thought they would work well in this situation. He considered it to be a business imperative: he thought it necessary to empower production teams to make decisions about their own production improvements, and coach them to align their decisions with the business and customer needs. However, the Malaysian employees were not exactly used to low-hierarchy team-based initiatives, and common wisdom was that implementation would be a failure. Malaysian culture is very high on hierarchy, and the multi-ethnic culture is not prone to trust among the different ethnicities. The manager went ahead with implementing the initiatives, but modified the implementation *process* significantly and in ways that were unique to Malaysia. The initiative caught the eye of the global head of production for Nestlé, who combined it with other initiatives to create a new global system of production (and other systems) for Nestlé, which allowed for global standardization around business needs with local adaptation around the process of achieving them.[29]

Aligning Dynamically Requires Judgement

We encourage you to use the Organizational Alignment Model as an analytic tool, remembering that both organizations and the environment are dynamic. The model simply provides an initial analytic tool of possible solutions and direction for action. Structures and management systems should be tools to help organizations and their employees succeed. There is no simple formula for choosing effective structures and systems. Use judgment in assessing the likely impact of systems on people in jobs and in adjusting the systems to support job achievement and organizational results. Successful implementation means finding the right combination of strategy, structure, and systems that motivates people to strive for high performance. It involves listening to, understanding, and working with people from different cultures in the organization.

STRATEGY IN GLOBAL ORGANIZATIONS

The final component of the alignment model is strategy. A strategy defines the way an organization chooses to relate itself to its external environment. It encompasses such things as the firm's chosen niche in its industry and the control of critical factors for competing successfully in that niche. The final organizational alignment model, showing the role of strategy in executing and aligning, is shown in Figure 5.7.

FIGURE 5.7   Complete Alignment Model: Aligning the organization with strategy and the environment

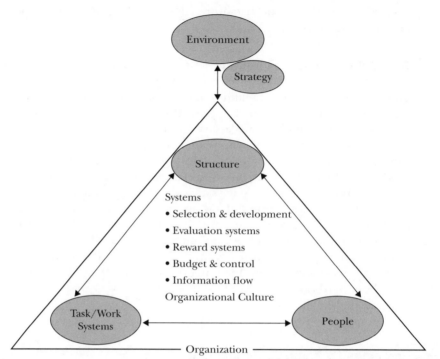

To be successful in a business or industry there are certain activities that an organization must do well. These key success factors vary from industry to industry and from one industry segment to another. For example, if you are producing a commodity product, it might be critical to have a secure source of supply and efficient production or processing operations so you can be the low-cost producer. If you are producing highly differentiated products, advertising, marketing, and product development are likely to be the critical activities. If you are in the aerospace industry, your R&D capability and the ability to manage contracts to produce on time and within budgets may be key success factors.

You have to know what you must do well in a business to succeed, and you must recognize that these factors vary from industry to industry. Although one could say "you have to do everything well," that truism would not reflect the specific competitive situation within an industry. Any firm may need finance, production, marketing, sales, and human resource capabilities, but the relative emphasis or importance of each of these may vary according to the nature of the business. Once you understand how you have to compete in your business, you can translate this into the tasks that must be performed within the organization. Once you know what tasks need to be done and how they should be done, a structure and set of administrative mechanisms can be implemented to get the jobs done properly.

This is not a chapter about formulating strategy but, rather, executing strategy. However, it is necessary to have a basic understanding of a firm's strategy (or any planned changes to a strategy) to evaluate it in relation to the potential fit with the internal structure, administrative mechanisms, and the skills and abilities of the company's human resources. It is critical that the administrative systems are consistent with an organization's strategy.

Business Strategy: The Most Fundamental Business Decisions

There are multiple levels and types of strategy: corporate, business, international, and functional strategies. Corporate strategy, in a diversified company, is about deciding what businesses the company engages in; where in the world it should operate; and how these businesses should be managed to create value.[30] Both business and corporate strategy tell you what the company does and, just as importantly, what it doesn't do. It also tells executives where to put resources. Peter Drucker said strategic management is "analytical thinking [formulation] and a commitment of resources to action [execution]."[31]

We will focus here mostly on business strategy: that is the level of strategy that must be aligned for executing effectively. In a single business company or in a business unit of a diversified company, business strategy, also called competitive strategy, refers to how a company creates competitive advantage by offering better customer value than its competitors.[32] There are multiple strategic frameworks, and our intent is not to explain all of them but to present a few that we have found particularly useful as we work with managers.

Porter's Generic Competitive Strategies for Product Focus Probably the best known and most widely used competitive strategy framework is Porter's.[33] He identified three generic strategies: cost leadership (low cost), differentiation, and a focus strategy. Cost leadership requires keeping costs (and, therefore, prices) low through an emphasis on tight cost control, efficient operations, low overhead, and leveraging the benefits of a well-managed supply chain. Industries that produce products such as sugar, chips for calculators, or other commodity-like offerings usually fit in this category. In retailing, for example, companies like Walmart and IKEA come to mind.

Differentiation means creating differences in your products or services that customers are willing to pay a premium for. Differentiation can be created in multiple ways, such as through prestige or brand image, proprietary technology or state-of-the-art product features, or outstanding service networks, for example. Examining the first category, prestige or brand image, one can think about automobiles: Mercedes stands for engineering; BMW is the driving experience; and Volvo is safety.

Focus, or market segmentation, means choosing a narrow niche in an industry and tailoring a strategy to serve clients in this niche.[34] However, even this strategy has to be a cost leadership or differentiated one. Southwest Airlines, Ryanair, and IKEA are examples of a focus strategy with cost leadership, and Ferrari a differentiated one.

Hax and Wilde's Delta Model   Hax and Wilde argue that Porter's framework does not capture all the ways in which companies compete in a dynamic networked economy and that customers, suppliers, and complementers are important contributors and should be included.[35] Their framework includes Porter's focus on product characteristics, but they go beyond the product focus to look at customer value.

They propose three strategic options: best product, total customer solutions, and system lock-in. The first two are relatively straightforward. Best product (BP) competition is essentially low cost or differentiation based on product economics. Total customer solutions (TCS) competition is based on customer economics, and the challenge is to reduce customer costs or increase their profits.

System lock-in (SLI) competition is based on system economics. Companies may bundle products and services and customize them to the needs of their customers or do joint product development, for example. SLI locks in complementers, locks out competitors, and develops proprietary standards. This means considering all the meaningful players in a system that contribute to the creation of economic value.[36]

What is a "complementer"? An easy way to think about complementers and SLI competition is to think about the software industry. Microsoft, for example, provides an operating system such as Windows 8 for computers. Then there are a number of companies that develop applications for use with that operating system. These companies are complementers and, because of their involvement and products, they contribute to the value of the total system. Or think of Apple's iPhone and the apps (applications) available for it developed by complementers.

Complementers also exist outside of high tech industries. An example is the ubiquitous K-Cup used in the Keurig brewing systems for coffee, tea and hot cocoa. Well-known brands such as Starbucks, Celestial Seasonings, Wolfgang Puck, Caribou Coffee, Gloria Jean's, Swiss Miss, Twinings of London and Dunkin' Donuts all use K-Cups to package their products.[37] The more name brands that package their products in this format, the greater the value the system creates for Keurig and the more difficult it becomes for competitors to gain market share. The dynamics of SLI are captured in the Delta model which is summarized in Figure 5.8.

There are many other models for making strategic choices, and we encourage you to use the ones that make most sense for your industry and competitive context, while taking the time to question your assumptions from time to time as the environment changes.

FIGURE 5.8   Delta model of customer strategies

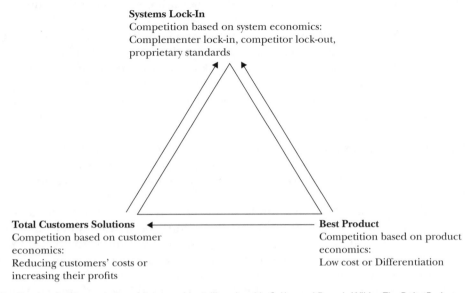

Systems Lock-In
Competition based on system economics:
Complementer lock-in, competitor lock-out,
proprietary standards

Total Customers Solutions
Competition based on customer
economics:
Reducing customers' costs or
increasing their profits

Best Product
Competition based on product
economics:
Low cost or Differentiation

Source: Reprinted with permission of Palgrave Macmillan, Arnoldo C. Hax and Dean L. Wilde, *The Delta Project*,
p. 31, 2001.

Business Models: Making the "How" Choices

We said in an earlier section that corporate strategy was the decision about what business a company should engage in and that a business (competitive) strategy referred to
a company's competitive advantage by offering better customer value than its competitors. Three questions to ask about strategy are *who, what* and *how*: who are our customers, what is our product or service, and how is it delivered?

A business model is how a firm creates and captures value and earns a profit in a competitive environment.[38] Simply stated, it is how a firm delivers its value proposition to
customers and how it makes money. An example should help in understanding the concept of the business model.

Think about retail booksellers in the late 1990s.[39] Barnes & Noble Booksellers was
founded in New York in 1917 and by 1987 had become a national chain in the United
States. In the late 1980s and early 1990s, it evolved the concept of the suburban super-
store, which generated 96% of its retail sales. The company offered a comprehensive
selection of books and music (the *what*) using experienced staff in spacious stores, complete with cafes that sold Starbucks coffee (the *how*). It became a destination for people,
a sort of town meeting place, and its business model was to deliver its products and services to customers in brick and mortar stores that were open certain hours. Although

it opened its first online book superstore on America Online in 1997, Amazon.com received the prize for developing the new business model in this industry.

Founded in 1994, Amazon.com went public in 1997 and by 1999 it generated over $1.6 billion in sales. Amazon.com turned the retail bookselling industry upside down. Its business model was to deliver books to customers anytime and anyplace, using the Internet. It created an online community of customers by allowing people to write their own book reviews and share them. Amazon.com continued to modify its strategy by morphing from being a book retailer to being an online shopping portal.

This example shows how companies in the same industry, selling the same products, can have vastly different business models to deliver their products and services. And the people, skills, and systems for each model to function are vastly different.

Another example to help understand the concept of business models is found in the movie rental business.[40] Blockbuster was founded in 1985 when the market was dominated by local "Mom & Pop" shops. These outlets required a deposit for the bulky VHS or Betamax tapes. Blockbuster introduced the membership model, opened stores across the US and members could rent videos from any of its stores. Like its competitors of the time, it charged late fees. By 1999 it was the largest video rental company in the world. Its business model and scale replaced that of the local shops. Blockbuster filed for bankruptcy in 2010, and in 2011 it was bought by DISH Network.

The introduction of DVDs in the mid-1990s made the videotape technology obsolete and contributed to Blockbuster's demise. Even though Blockbuster rented DVDs, Netflix had arrived with a different strategy and business model. It delivered movies by mail from a central location, eliminating the need for brick and mortar stores. However, Netflix itself eventually faced competition: video streaming services like Amazon Video on Demand, Hulu and Apple iTunes; and Redbox, which offered extremely cheap video rentals from kiosks in convenient, high-volume traffic locations such as supermarkets. Using this business model, Redbox captured 25% of the rental market by 2010.[41] This example also shows that a company does not need to have a technologically-sophisticated business model like Amazon.com to displace existing companies and be successful.

Aligning the Business Model: The Example of Global Multi-Products Chile   Now we link the concept of a business model to the Organizational Alignment Framework and show how changes in an existing business model may necessitate organizational realignment. A more complex, international example in which culture played a role was the experience of Global Multi-Products in Chile.[42]

Global Multi-Products had a strategy of continuous introduction of new, innovative products based on proprietary technology that had high margins. Approximately 30% of its sales came from products introduced in the previous few years. Historically, it used a "best product strategy" in which the value proposition for the customer was: buy our products because they are the best quality based on the latest technology, and they are reliable.

To deliver on this strategy, it excelled in R&D, where the new products originated, and it had a formal program of research and development with 40 technology platforms that were the seedbeds of the company's new products. Historically it distributed its products through separate product-related business units. We could characterize the company's business model as investing in R&D; developing proprietary technology and high-margin products; manufacturing them efficiently; and continually introducing these new "best products."

Then the competitive environment in Chile changed. Small sole proprietorships were largely replaced by big American retailers and local retailers developing similar super-store models. Previously, local superstores represented approximately 60% of retail sales. The superstore segment, local and foreign, grew quickly to represent over 90% of the company's business, and power shifted from the manufacturer to the customers: large retailers. The level of sophistication increased among purchasing managers, and they expected more from their suppliers, such as more advertising and lower prices. Products that traditionally had margins averaging around 80% now had margins not very different from those of competitors. Finally, customers wanted to reduce the number of Global Multi-Products' sales representatives with whom they were dealing. They wanted to see one face representing the manufacturer.

At the time that one of the authors was involved with Global Multi-Products' local organization in Chile, it was in the process of transitioning from a Best Product strategy to a Total Customer Solutions (TCS) strategy, which had been forced on it by the shift in power to the new, large retail customers who were interested in increasing their return on investment.

The new strategy became one of providing solutions to its customers and making money by selling more products at lower margins (still based on proprietary technology and efficient manufacturing). Internally in Global Multi-Products this change meant that more integration was required among business units and that employees had to work horizontally across the organization and in teams to analyze customer operations in order to provide solutions for them. This program sought to reorient the sales and marketing effort around the needs of customers, instead of the company's product groups. Global Multi-Products also developed a program of strategic relationships with customers to conduct joint R&D to develop new products that could benefit both partners. The company was now competing on the basis of its organization as well as its technology to provide solutions for its customers.

To compete on the basis of creating value to the customer by providing "solutions," companies have to learn to work more effectively, or in some cases even learn to work horizontally across the organization to leverage all their capabilities. Corporate culture, entrenched interests, existing evaluation and reward systems are among the barriers to change. In Global Multi-Products Chile, it was not a simple change to implement.

Organizational Realignment in Chile: There were a number of barriers getting in the way of the necessary changes. These barriers can be organized using the Organizational Alignment Framework in the following categories:

- *Organizational structure:* Strategic Business Units, product groups and distribution-based selling (some products were sold through product groups to distributors), hierarchy, and functional "silos" worked against cooperation. Teams had to work laterally across these groups.

- *Organizational culture:* heads of functions had a great deal of autonomy and it was almost a "feudal" system.

- *Top management team:* executives had no skills with group/team processes and there was no trust among them. They were concerned with their authority, and there was resistance to change.

- *Society/national culture:* There was status consciousness on the part of executives, reflecting Chile's high power distance culture.

- *Political history:* A legacy of distrust and not speaking out was left over from the Pinochet era.

- *People:* The sales representatives' status, lack of required new skills, title, education, age/seniority all worked against their being successful in the new environment. Sales Reps were low status jobs in this culture, and the people in them did not have the necessary skills and training to interact with the new, more sophisticated purchasing executives of the "big box" stores. The company had to find new Sales Reps, provide them with new titles, and improve training.

- *Rewards:* The reward system did not encourage selling someone else's products or working together in teams. The behavior required of Sales Reps was to continually introduce new products and let go of the old ones, which the reward system did not encourage.

It took the Managing Director a number of years to implement the organizational changes necessary to re-align the Chilean organization with its new business model.

Companies are Becoming More Customer-focused

It is easy to talk about globalization, global strategies, and being customer-centric, but it is not easy to put these ideas into practice. It has been the authors' experience over the past years working with a number of companies in various industries such as defense, financial printing, telecommunications, financial services, fast-moving consumer goods, construction and development, and even law enforcement that they all were experiencing the need to provide "solutions" and to develop organizations that were customer-centric. This need to behave differently was driven in all cases by changes in the organizations' external environment. For some it was the appearance of new competitors with new products and business models that sparked the need to coordinate across functional or business areas. For others, such as financial services firms, both the consolidation of the global players into the Big

Four and increased regulation (Sarbanes-Oxley and other changes) affected their customer orientation. For the law enforcement agency it was the appearance of new criminal or terrorist network organizations posing new threats that drove the change.

However, the characteristic they all had in common was that they all had difficulty working horizontally across the organization and coordinating information and activities effectively to improve performance in these new environments that they faced.

Culture's Influence on Strategy

It takes a deep understanding of a company's strategy and management systems and an understanding of the history and culture of the host country to execute a strategy globally. And it takes time.

What happens when a company takes its strategy "on the road" so to speak – when it begins implementing it in another country? What appears to be obvious and straightforward in a firm's home market or in another international location may not work in a new country. What an executive takes for granted at home may not apply in another country. Consider the TJX Companies Inc., the world's leading off-price retailer of apparel and home fashions, operating multiple businesses through four divisions: The Marmaxx Group (T.J. Maxx and Marshalls) and HomeGoods in the U.S.; TJX Canada (Winners, HomeSense, and Marshalls); and TJX Europe (T.K. Maxx and HomeSense); and in December 2012, it acquired Sierra Trading Post, an off-price internet retailer.[43] TJX's value-oriented retailing business model delivers a rapidly changing assortment of fashionable, quality, brand name merchandise at 20 to 60% below regular department and specialty store prices. It can do this because it relies on opportunistic buying, disciplined inventory management, and a low expense structure, with its stores located in community shopping centers. Its stores are flexible spaces with no permanent, fixed store features. Its core target customer is a middle- to upper-middle-income shopper, who is fashion and value conscious and fits the same profile as a department store shopper.[44]

Customers entering the T.J. Maxx Store in Newport, Rhode Island, for example, would encounter this business model by driving to a shopping mall, parking their car in a spacious parking lot and taking a shopping cart as they entered the store, which they would push to hold all the merchandise they selected in their "exciting treasure-hunt shopping experience."[45] This is a straightforward, common experience in the United States in this type of retail store. However, this mode of operating has a number of built-in, culturally influenced assumptions which include:

- Customers can and will drive to the mall where there is plenty of parking.

- Customers will need and use a shopping cart in order to purchase many items.

- Customers can identify the value inherent in their purchases because they can recognize the brand name and its reduced selling price in the store.

When TJX opened its first European stores in the United Kingdom and the Netherlands, it discovered that many of its customers only bought one or two items because the idea of using a shopping cart or "buggie," as they referred to it, was foreign to them, and they initially refused to use them. In the Netherlands, there were more obstacles to overcome than in the UK, including language and culture. TJX was not able to replicate the brand/value proposition in the Netherlands as customers did not easily recognize the value offering – the brand versus price trade-off. The business model did not work there as it did in the United States.[46]

Monsanto is another example of the potential non-transferability of strategy. It introduced genetically modified soybeans into Europe based on its experience and the lessons it learned in the United States. It encountered significant resistance and had to realize that the lessons learned in the United States could not necessarily be generalized to other locations.[47] Monsanto's mastery orientation did not fit with a more prevalent harmony orientation in Europe.

One's cultural filters and possible lack of experience with, or knowledge about, a particular country may influence the assumptions used in developing international expansion projects. Very often, costs are underestimated at the start of the project and this mistake does not become apparent until later, when they outweigh the expected benefits. An experienced entrepreneur observed that "No one ever lost money on a spreadsheet. You can torture the numbers until they confess."[48] This comment attests to an apparent common tendency to make new projects or ventures look attractive by underestimating the time necessary for revenues and profits to materialize or by optimistically forecasting the initial and ongoing costs of operating internationally.

A spreadsheet analysis is only as good as the assumptions that go into it. It's important to remember that it is not reality, only a representation of reality. As the philosopher Alfred Korzybski stated, "The map is not the territory." Someone in the company has to understand the territory. Someone has to travel to another country to negotiate a contract, arrange a distributorship, or work with people from another culture to make a project or joint venture a reality. Once this person leaves the office to negotiate the contract in Europe or to start up the plant in Southeast Asia, what really takes place? There are a lot of questions to ask and answers to find before the business becomes a reality.

The previous sections have developed the organizational alignment framework and linked it to strategy and business models. We also discussed executing competitive strategy and business models in global organizations. Now we turn our attention to global strategy: the strategic decisions about developing a global presence and positioning a company and its value chain in global markets to take advantage of location economies while adapting to local differences.

DEVELOPING A GLOBAL PRESENCE

Globalization, in business and economic terms, is often characterized as the erosion of national boundaries that have accelerated due to deregulation and technology. Trade liberalization has opened borders across which capital moves easily since foreign direct investment (FDI) restrictions have been relaxed. Airline travel as well as reliable, inexpensive communications and sophisticated information services and technologies have shrunk the globe so effectively – diminishing physical boundaries – that corporations are able to manage, control, and coordinate activities of far-ranging operations. It is possible to do business almost anywhere through a web site, as the representative of one small, family-owned Japanese company learned. While in Boston she was able to successfully conclude sales to Saudi Arabia and Pakistan without ever going there.

Both responding to and feeding the trend of globalization, companies are "globalizing" in search of growth. Some companies continue to search for growth by expanding into new international markets and some by integrating and expanding their current global operations, creating what the UN has called "an international production system."[49]

We do not intend to pursue in detail an exposition of the advantages and disadvantages of each strategy or structure that corporations could use in globalizing. There are many books and readings on the topic of international organization that comprehensively cover these issues.[50] However, beyond considering the advantages or disadvantages of the various strategies or structural forms a company can use, one must recognize the cultural values and assumptions upon which these structures may be based that has been our focus and has been discussed earlier.

In this section we briefly highlight some decisions about strategies, structures and systems that companies face as they become more global: balancing global integration and local responsiveness, organizing for global effectiveness, new market-entry modes, international joint ventures and alliances, global account management, global virtual teams and reverse innovation.

The Classic Dilemma: Global Integration Versus Local Responsiveness

Two fundamental forces influence global companies: those pushing towards global integration and those pulling towards local responsiveness.[51] Forces for global integration, such as the need to secure commodities or the cost of investment in R&D or new facilities, push companies to minimize duplication of functions and to increase efficiencies by placing specific value-chain activities in the most suitable locations around the world.

The ability to concentrate each value-chain activity in the best location has been enhanced by the erosion of national borders. This allows companies to capitalize on their competitive advantage in the particular activity and the host country's comparative advantage vis-à-vis other countries.[52] For example, the USA's Silicon Valley is considered by global technology companies to be a prime location for R&D operations because of the high concentration of professionals, educational institutions, and companies with leading-edge knowledge and expertise that nurture each other's learning. Similarly, countries in Southeast Asia have become locations of choice for manufacturing technologically intensive components because of the quality-cost-availability profile of their local labor forces. At the extreme, companies could locate each activity in a region from which the firm could best serve the rest of its global activities. This creates complex interdependencies among the firm's multiple and often culturally diverse geographic locations and poses unique cross-cultural challenges for managers.

The requirement for local responsiveness appears when a company has to tailor its business model, re-align its administrative systems, and adapt products to meet the needs of a specific national market. Because of different preferences for certain products and services or different government regulations and systems, it is rarely possible, in the long term, to operate in another country exactly the same way as at home. Four elements tend to promote localization of strategy: non-tariff barriers, such as requirements to have a local partner or local standards for products; foreign-exchange shortages; cultural differences that influence consumer tastes and preferences even as some products become global; and flexible production technology that reduces the cost advantage of large-scale production while permitting greater local customization.[53] Moreover, cultural preferences that influence how people work and how they relate to each other, as well as government policies regarding human resource practices, may favor localization of structures and systems.

To achieve local responsiveness, the value-chain activities of the company are tailored to a particular country's needs, and a successful company will adapt at least some elements of its operations to the local culture. Value-chain activities could be tailored to each locality.

In addition to balancing globalization and localization, a successful global organization engages in global learning, that is, the transfer and sharing of new ideas and knowledge among units.[54] A new production technology, marketing strategy, or product feature designed for one market can often be transferred to other markets. The challenge is to be able to identify synergistic links among units and to transfer knowledge and skills effectively. The proper organizational structures and systems, as well as the right individuals, play an important role in facilitating global learning.

Generic International Strategy Choices   All companies that operate globally are subject to the pressures of global integration and local responsiveness. The degree to which a company must respond to these forces depends heavily on the characteristics of the industry in which it competes and influences its multinational strategy. One common classification scheme that is based on the integration-responsiveness framework identifies four strategies: the global, the multi-domestic, the international, and the transnational.[55] This is shown in Figure 5.9.

A company that follows a strategy highly dependent on global integration for many of its value-chain activities and that is locally responsive for few of them is following a *global strategy*. Such a company is usually characterized by a high degree of complex interdependencies among its subsidiaries and has a governance structure that is tightly

FIGURE 5.9   International strategy choices

High		
Cost pressure or global integration pressure	Global standardization strategy	Transnational strategy
	International strategy	Multi-domestic or localization strategy
Low		

Low	Pressure for local responsiveness	High

Source: Adapted from Charles Hill, *International Business: Competing in the Global Marketplace*; Irwin McGraw-Hill, 2000 and Charles Hill, *Global Business Today*, McGraw-Hill Irwin, 2014

and centrally controlled. Its managers have to be culturally aware and its senior management is likely to be dominated by a cadre of seasoned-career foreign-assignment veterans who share similar corporate values. Companies like Ericsson (telecommunications) and Sony (consumer electronics) have been identified as companies with global strategies.

A firm that follows a *multi-domestic strategy* is one that is minimally dependent on global integration but highly dependent on local responsiveness for many of its value-chain activities. A multi-domestic strategy enables a firm to tailor its strategy, product, and operations to specific markets but does not optimize global efficiency. These organizations may operate differently in each country; in an extreme case, each country or region would have its own manufacturing, marketing, and research and development. These firms can be thought of as a confederation of loosely-coupled organizations with strong local control and weak central control. The managers of multi-domestic subsidiaries often function as independent "feudal lords" who may or may not be expatriate managers depending on the company's administrative heritage. Unilever, Procter & Gamble, and KFC, while not representing the extreme end of the spectrum, tend to use multi-domestic strategies.

Third, a multinational that depends minimally on global integration and minimally on local responsiveness follows an *international strategy*. Essentially, it replicates its home market systems in each of its foreign subsidiaries. These companies are very centralized and their subsidiaries are simply outlets for headquarters' decisions. The product categories most suitable to such a strategy would include commodities. For example, grain businesses (AMD, Cargill) are large organizations that deal with commodity products that are traded around the world on the basis of price. Also, the ball bearing industry to a certain extent can be seen as an industry suitable to an international strategy. For this industry there are many consumers (any manufacturer of machinery that has moving parts) and an undifferentiated product that depends on technical specifications that are applicable anywhere in the world.

Finally, a firm that is simultaneously globally integrated and locally responsive is following a *transnational strategy*. This strategy distributes the global responsibility for specific activities to the managers who manage the subsidiary to which the activity has been assigned. Each country manager may report to different persons with different worldwide activity responsibilities. The local responsiveness is achieved by managing each distributed value chain activity with enough flexibility so that the local manager can make the essential compromises necessary to achieve as high a local market fit as possible. The transnational strategy is extremely costly to implement and requires managers who are cross-culturally and interpersonally skilled and flexible. Few – if any – truly transnational corporations exist, but many are aspiring and progressing in that direction, including Nestlé, Shell, and Matsushita.

When formulating a strategy, the ideal balance of global integration and local responsiveness and how best to implement global learning depend on many factors. Rather than present a single ideal solution (since none exists), our orientation is to help you develop insights into issues involved in implementing strategies, structures, and systems to increase the chances of making informed decisions when entering new markets and managing in other countries.

Structures for Globalizing

Typical structures for international involvement include international division, geographic (regional) division, product or project division, matrix, and transnational. Each of these structures has its strengths and weaknesses and would be appropriate for different situations. The two main factors that influence strategic choice of structure are the pressures for local responsiveness and the forces pushing toward global integration, as discussed in the previous section. Two additional criteria to be considered in the choice of an appropriate structure are the extent to which a company's sales and profits are derived from foreign operations and the complexity of the company's product line.[56]

Basic categories: International division, matrix, or transnational?

International division. In this structure, all business conducted outside the firm's home country is organized through one division. This form is often a starting point for firms that are beginning to internationalize and that probably have relatively little international business as a percentage of total revenues. As the overseas involvement of a firm increases, the international division structure may evolve into a geographical division structure in which all products for a particular region are grouped together. This structure is typically more suitable with a multi-domestic or an international strategy. In the product or project division structure, responsibility for all markets around the world is given to a specific product line or project division. This form tends to be adopted by multinationals that are involved in multiple product lines or businesses overseas.

Matrix structure. This structure is used when companies have two dimensions of its business that are important such as geography and product and one cannot be subordinated to the other. In theory, matrix permits combining a simultaneous focus on country preferences and product features for example, but in practice, matrices are difficult to implement and manage. A structure in which a manager reports to two bosses can create ambiguity, tension and conflict, and often these structures fail. Companies that can manage them effectively find that it allows them to deal with the complexities of the real world that they face and provides them with a performance advantage. Managing them well requires trust, flexibility, teamwork and a culture of conflict resolution focused on problem solving. And in some cultures with a strong hierarchical value-orientation, matrix may violate the "one boss" chain of command orientation.

Transnational organization.   This organization tries to simultaneously capture the responsiveness of local organizations and the efficiency and global competitiveness of the more centralized structures by maintaining what could be called a "federal" structure.[57] These organizations are often referred to as network organizations characterized by high degrees of autonomy between headquarters and business units, and between business units. Strong multilateral communication which does not necessarily have to pass through a central headquarters unit permits coordination and knowledge sharing.[58] These distributed business units are usually components of a larger corporation.

However, it is useful to keep in mind that the distributed units could also be independent companies functioning as an economic network that permits smaller corporations to compete globally. Regardless of whether the organization is a large global company or an economic colony of smaller ones, the network organization merits special focus because it has become increasingly common and important.

A New Form? Network Organizations   Some observers believe that the network has become the most important emergent organizational structure.[59] Borgatti has defined a network organization as:

> . . . a collection of autonomous firms or units that behaves as a single larger entity, using social mechanisms for coordination and control. The entities that make up a network organization are usually legally independent entities (separate firms) but not always. Some of the entities may be wholly owned subsidiaries. They can even be divisions within the company, but treated as separate companies that sell to outside customers.[60]

In addition to their unique structure they are considered to be very adaptable. They are "fast and flexible in responding to changes in the underlying environment."[61] Their appearance (or reappearance in the management literature if one thinks about Japanese *keiretsu* or Korean *chaebol*) has been brought about by advanced communication and information technology as well as by organizational restructuring.[62] Although Borgatti sees network organizations as a blend between vertical integration and market disaggregation, others suggest that they are qualitatively different from classic market or hierarchy models of traditional economics. A networked organization combines many or all types of organizational units in relationships of varying degrees of ownership and relationship intensity with the home country's headquarters. Matrix and networked forms are mostly adopted by large diversified companies and tend to be costly to implement and maintain.

Although flexibility and adaptability are admirable characteristics, Vega-Redondo modeled network organizations and found that there was a limit to the environmental volatility that they could handle before they were overwhelmed and a more rigid structure was required again.[63]

However, prior to reaching a tipping point, networks have some comparative advantages. Business conditions that favor networks include:[64]

- Frequent transactions. Infrequent transactions can better be handled by market mechanisms.
- Uncertainty in the demand for new products or services.
- Buyer requirement for customization.
- Task complexity.

Networks can provide the advantages of balancing strategies in a matrix organization and the flexibility inherent in alliances with other organizations. For example, a network organization might include global research and development in some product areas and local R&D in others, global marketing for some product lines and local marketing for others, and so on. It could also have several different types of alliances for projects having different roles in the firm's overall strategy or for product lines at varying stages of development. Examples might include companies such as Levi Strauss, Toyota or Astra Zeneca, all of which have outsourced many of their primary activities and have become the "lead firms" in a production chain.[65] Other companies, for example, could include Nike, which outsources the making of its products in order to focus on design and marketing, and Apple, which outsources its hardware manufacturing.[66] However, as might be expected, managing a complex, networked structure spanning multiple countries, cultures, and time zones is a complicated undertaking and difficult to do well. Chapter 4 provides some additional insights about network structures, in the context of global teams.

Choosing a New Market-Entry Mode

Independently of the international strategies or organizational forms selected, companies entering new markets must decide on the appropriate business form, or entry mode, for each overseas market.[67] Entry modes establish the legal form in a foreign market; the extent to which the multinational owns the organization; the degree to which it maintains operating control; and the extent to which this new organization is part of a set of business relationships that extend beyond a one-country market.

There is a large range of entry and ownership forms. Options vary in terms of the amount of capital, other resources invested, and managerial involvement required in the host country. At one extreme, limiting a company's investment and set of activities, is the exporting of products or licensing of technology to other companies in the foreign market. There also are market-entry modes that require capital and human resources investment but permit full control of the wholly-owned businesses or subsidiaries that can be acquired or developed as new, "greenfield" sites. A third set of market-entry alternatives includes hybrid modes, such as a variety of equity joint venture and strategic alliance forms. An international equity joint venture involves creating a new entity owned jointly by two or more "parent" organizations to enter a market where at least one of the parent organizations is nonresident. Management responsibilities are contractually delineated. The percentage of equity held by each parent generally defines who has formal strategic control. A strategic alliance is an agreement between two or more companies to engage in cooperative activities without equity involvement. For example, a strategic alliance may involve a contractual agreement to cross-sell complementary products or to engage in other activities on a cooperative basis. Passenger airlines have formed global strategic alliances to share reservation systems, complementary routes, aircraft purchasing and technical specifications, maintenance facilities and crews, ground services staff, and even pilots and cabin crews.

Costs and benefits are associated with each of these operating modes and ownership structures. The costs to be considered usually include capital, management time and commitment, impact on strategy, and the cost of enforcing agreements. Some benefits include repatriation of profits, political security, contribution to parent-company knowledge, and local distribution capability.

The chapters about culture earlier in the book are applicable when you are working with people from other cultures in exporting or licensing agreements as well as in subsidiaries, acquisitions, international joint ventures or alliances.

International Joint Ventures (IJVs) and Other Formal Alliances   Formal alliances, including equity-sharing joint ventures, are one of the most important modes for entering new markets, so it is worth taking a few minutes to look at these special situations.

Joint ventures are used for many reasons. Companies may need to share financial risk, respond to government requirements, secure access to natural resources, acquire particular technical skills, gain local management knowledge and experience, or obtain access to markets and distribution systems. From a multinational's perspective, two important reasons for using joint ventures are to understand and have access to local markets and to have local general management knowledge, skills, and experience in the joint venture company.

In establishing joint ventures, managers often make some common mistakes. There can be a tendency to concentrate on the end result and desired outcome and not to think carefully and critically about the process through which these results will be obtained. Executives need to invest in the personal relationships that must be built to create a joint venture and commit the time and effort necessary to make the venture successful. They need to think more clearly about joint venturing, which is a process orientation.

Another common mistake is to emphasize the "visible" inputs to the decision and the "tangible" aspects of the business. These visible inputs include the legal structure of the venture, the financial considerations of ownership and pro forma operating statements, and the market analyses – all the things managers (and specialists like lawyers and accountants) learned in school and deal with daily. These are important considerations that require attention, and they are necessary for success, but they are not sufficient to ensure it.

There are many operational issues beyond the legal and economic ones that may not be given enough careful forethought and may be left to be resolved as problems arise, which often is too late. The "invisible," "intangible," or "non-quantifiable" components of a venture, like trust, commitment, and partners' expectations, often are overlooked or ignored, possibly because they may not be part of a manager's prior training or mind-set. The situation of international joint ventures is like an iceberg in that approximately one-seventh of it is visible above the water's surface and six-sevenths is below the surface. The result of not knowing what is hidden can be disastrous for companies as well as for ships.

Alliances are not an automatic solution to a lack of experience with, or understanding of, another culture, as executives sometimes think. An additional cultural interface, besides the one with the external marketplace, is created with the partner in the venture. Perhaps the most critical decision to be made in establishing an international joint venture or alliance is the choice of a partner, as Geringer explains:

> Selecting partners with compatible skills is not necessarily synonymous with selecting compatible partners . . . . Although selecting a compatible partner may not always result in a successful JV, the selection of an incompatible partner virtually guarantees that venture performance will be unsatisfactory.[68]

How does one choose a partner? Where does one look? What characteristics should a partner have? What are one's expectations? What are the potential partner's expectations? There are a number of criteria that should be considered: "complementarity of technical skills and resources, mutual need, financial capability, relative size, complementarity of strategies and operating policies, communication barriers, compatible management teams, and trust and commitment between partners."[69]

The role of relationships in strategy and international joint ventures is worthy of special comment. Often in North America, relationships are viewed as instrumental, as a means to ends, if they are thought of at all in a business context. In contrast, much of the world outside the United States and Canada values relationships in and of themselves. They form a basis of trust and linkage upon which a business activity may be built. Relationships are a major determinant of strategy, if not part of the strategy themselves. Given such striking differences in outlook on relationships, it is not surprising that partnership problems are one of the most frequently cited reasons for joint-venture failure.[70]

Some Special Forms for Globalizing

Global Customers and Global Account Management[71]

The foregoing discussion would make it appear that all the decisions to be made about operating globally were at the discretion of a company's management – which markets to enter, the countries in which to set up operations, and the type of strategy to follow. However, there is another factor driving firms to establish subsidiaries or enter joint ventures in international locations: the emergence of global customers and their requirements.

The customer dimension has become more important to companies and many are organizing operations around their customers.[72] In the automotive industry, for example, large auto manufacturers are requiring their parts suppliers to be close to production and assembly plants to support just-in-time production systems. As a result, traditional parts suppliers are establishing joint ventures and manufacturing operations in foreign locations for their customers. One company we have worked with was told by their customer, a "Big-Three" auto manufacturer in Detroit, that to continue supplying parts, it had to be no more than two hours away from the assembly plant in Mexico.

In addition to the globalization of customers, the factors fueling this trend include a preference for partnerships and fewer suppliers, a desire for solutions to problems not just products, the ease of e-commerce, and the increase in the power of buyers. The emergence of global customers who have integrated their purchasing on a worldwide basis is driving multinational companies to consider another structural variation, global account management.

Although not a new concept, global account management is appearing more frequently in industrial, high-technology and some consumer goods companies. If a global customer is of sufficient importance, a supplier may decide to implement a global account management structure and to create the necessary reporting relationships on top of already existing structures and reporting lines. Although it sounds good in theory, in practice it is difficult and time consuming to implement since it means new ways of working and a shift in responsibilities and power balances.

The key tension to manage is between the global account managers (GAMs) doing what is best for the customer and the country sales managers doing what is best for the local country organization. Three broad approaches can be identified:

1 The balance of power lies with country sales managers. Global account managers act as coordinators across countries, but the account ownership remains at the local level. Global account managers act as information providers, influencers, and coordinators, but they do not have decision-making power over sales to their account.

2 There is a "matrix organization" in which global account managers report both to their local sales manager and to a corporate executive responsible for global accounts. This is probably the most common arrangement, seen in such companies as ABB, 3M, HP, and Intel. In cases of conflict, such as the GAM spending time building sales to the global customer in another country, it is up to the local sales manager and the corporate executive responsible for global accounts to agree on a solution. The matrix is typically not completely balanced, in that the local considerations usually take precedence over the global or vice versa.

3 The balance of power lies with the global account managers. This structure is currently fairly rare, but it is starting to emerge in a few companies. The logic of this structure is that global customers are more important than local sales, so the company is organized first and foremost around those customers. Examples include top-tier automotive suppliers such as Magna and Bosch and contract electronic manufacturers such as Solectron and Flextronics, because their activities are structured around a few large customers.

Emerging structural forms such as global account management put high demands on managerial sensitivity and skills. One example of developing capability with this form of organization is Schneider Electric, a recognized world leader in electrical distribution, automation, and control. In June 2007, Schneider Electric received the Strategic Account Management Association's (SAMA) award for outstanding corporate performance in strategic customer management. Strategic Account Management is a dedicated program for global enterprises interested in developing special relationships with key suppliers that shortens communication and decision-making cycles across Schneider globally to quickly provide solutions and services. In 2007, Schneider worked with 70 multinational companies as strategic accounts. In 2012 that number had grown to 91 including Air Liquide, GlaxoSmithKline, IBM, Lafarge, Marriott, Nestlé, Procter & Gamble, Total, Toyota and Walmart.[73,74] Schneider offers its strategic accounts the following:[75]

- Coordination across multiple business units regardless of languages and cultural issues.

- The ability to manage global sales agreements involving several countries.

- Long-term partnership in global purchasing, logistics, processes.

- A single interface or point of entry to Schneider to coordinate account activities worldwide.

- An opportunity for appropriate customized offers.

- Privileged meetings with top management to discuss technological trends and develop business opportunities.

Global account managers have to have traditional account management skills and solution selling competence but, since they also are operating across national and organizational boundaries, they need to be able to build relationships and establish trust; and to be culturally adaptable. The implementation of a global account management structure and the systems to support it require daily use of all components of the MBI model of interpersonal and team effectiveness. Finally, it stretches the capacity of organizational designers and of more conventional managers who have to share power and be much more flexible than in the past.

Strategic Use of Global Virtual Teams   Teams have become a common organizing structure for global companies. The use of global teams has increased dramatically as companies have invested resources in technological infrastructure to connect technical expertise and local knowledge for the purpose of achieving shared global business objectives.[76] We discussed the management of diverse and dispersed teams in detail in Chapter 4. In this section we will discuss briefly the strategic potential of global virtual teams.

The idea of using global virtual teams is an attractive and promising one, and companies often see them as a way to save time and money in designing and developing new products, for example. However, similar to matrix or global account management, global virtual teams are not easy to manage successfully. Many companies don't appreciate the complexity introduced by the interaction of the task, contexts, members, culture, time, and technology;[77] and many managers, team leaders, and global team members may not have the requisite "cultural acumen"[78] necessary to function in this mode.

Research has shown that teams, on average, outperform individuals on complex, nonroutine tasks. The strategic ideal then is to use global teams to take advantage of this potential for superior performance to create a competitive edge. The objective is to make use of the expertise, experience, perspectives and local knowledge that exist in the diverse employees and contexts of a global company, as well as their networks, as resources to facilitate cross-project learning and knowledge transfer.

A classic example was the design of the Boeing 777 airplane. Boeing used global virtual design teams. It had members from more than 12 countries linked together by work stations. It was the first jetliner to be 100% digitally designed. The airplane was "pre-assembled" on the computer, eliminating the need for a costly, full-scale mock-up. Boeing designed and launched an airplane with greater fuel efficiency, at less cost, and faster than teams using a paper-based design approach could have.[79]

The potential for strategic benefit and competitive advantage exists from using global virtual teams as the Boeing 777 example makes clear – but only if the process is understood and managed appropriately as was discussed in Chapter 4.

Reverse innovation.   As companies continue trying to grow they are increasingly looking to emerging markets for that growth. Important questions are: What products and price points will work in these new markets? Govindarajan and Trimble argue that companies fall victim to their *dominant logic* and engage in *glocalization* and, as a result, are not successful. The dominant logic is "the assorted orthodoxies that govern the thinking of key enterprise decision makers"[80] and glocalization is the belief that the firm has already innovated products for its rich markets and that "firms can tap emerging markets simply by exporting lightly modified versions of global products developed for rich-world customers – mainly lower end models with fewer features."[81]

To continue their growth, companies have to learn how to be successful in emerging markets – another example of a statement easier said than done. There are companies that have engaged in reverse innovation successfully such as Logitech, Procter & Gamble, EMC, GE Healthcare, and Pepsico.[82] The structural solution is to put local growth teams in place in the market that report directly to the CEO. However, actually achieving success means having the right managers in place, as we will discuss in the next chapter, who have the ability to understand these cultures and who will take the time to listen to the requirements of their potential customers. These managers have to be able to function as anthropologists in order to understand the world the way their customers do; how they use products; and what features are desirable. Rather than initially imposing an externally developed analysis and derived understanding, they should develop an indigenous perspective on their products and the market by engaging in participant observation and some time in immersion. As the colloquialism, "it's not rocket science" implies, asking questions about how customers use products and their features should not be complicated, but it apparently is when the dominant logic overwhelms common sense.

EXECUTING GLOBAL STRATEGY: THE IMPORTANCE OF JUDGEMENT AND LEADERSHIP

In this chapter we have identified the key things that managers need to keep in mind as they implement global strategy. We shared a model of the elements to align within the organization, including the task, the people, and the structure. We provided ways of thinking about tasks and structure (people are the focus of other parts of the book), and explored the systems and tools managers can use for creating alignment on a daily basis. We examined the relationship between organizational alignment and the environment, including the role of strategic choices and business models.

While this chapter provides useful tools and ways of thinking, let us not forget our metaphor of management as a craft. This chapter provides the science, based on research and experience. You, the leader, provide the art; and your experience provides the judgement that helps combine the art and science into a craft. As we have said many times in this chapter, alignment is not a static state. In fact, misalignment can stimulate creative discussions that eventually result in a more powerful realignment. The principles of alignment are always important; the configuration should be adaptable.

Notes

1 Nonaka, I. and Takeuchi, H., *The Knowledge Creating Company* (New York: Oxford University Press, 1995).

2 Athanassiou, N., *The impact of internationalization on top management team characteristics: A tacit knowledge perspective* (unpublished doctoral dissertation, The University of South Carolina, 1995); and Athanassiou, N. and Nigh, D., "The impact of company internationalization on top management team advice networks: A tacit knowledge perspective," *Strategic Management Journal,* 19(1) (1999) 83–92.

3 O'Connell, J. and Bartlett, C., "Lincoln Electric: Venturing Abroad," Harvard Business School Case 9 - 398 - 095.

4 This organizational design framework and analytic model has been adapted from a number of writers on the contingency theory of organizations: Thompson, J. D., *Organizations in Action* (New York: McGraw-Hill, 1967); Lawrence, P. R. and Lorsch, J. W., *Organization and Environment* (Homewood, IL: Richard D. Irwin, 1969); Galbraith, J. R., *Designing Complex Organizations* (Reading, MA: Addison-Wesley, 1973); Lorsch, J. W. and Morse, J. J., *Organizations and Their Members: A Contingency Approach* (New York: Harper & Row, 1974); Galbraith, J. R., *Organization Design* (Reading, MA: Addison-Wesley, 1977); Lorsch, J. W., American Management Association, "Organization Design: A Situational Perspective," *Organizational Dynamics* 5 (1977); Galbraith, J. R. and Nathanson, D. A., *Strategy Implementation: The Role of Structure and Process* (St. Paul, MN: West, 1978); Kotter, J. P., Schlesinger, L. A. and Sathe, V., "Organization Design Tools," in *Organization: Text, Cases and Readings on the Management of Organizational Design and Change* (Homewood, IL: Richard D. Irwin, 1979). See also Lane, H. W., "Systems, Values and Action: An Analytic Framework for Intercultural Management Research," *Management International Review* 20(3) (1980) 61–70.

5 Lawrence, P. R. and Lorsch, J. W., *Organization and Environment* (Homewood, IL: Richard D. Irwin, 1969).

6 Thompson, J. D., *Organizations in Action* (New York: McGraw Hill, 1967).

7 Ibid., p. 54.

8 Ibid.

9 Ibid.

10 For a review of this literature see Sekiguchi, T., "Person–Organization Fit and Person–Job Fit in Employee Selection: A Review of the Literature," *Osaka Keidai Ronshu*, 55(1) (March 2004). http://www.osaka-ue.ac.jp/gakkai/pdf/ronshu/2004/5501_ronko_sekiguti.pdf. Accessed March 21, 2013.

11 "Lincoln Electric: Venturing Abroad, " n. 3 above.

12 Alexander, C., *Notes on the Synthesis of Form* (Cambridge, MA: Harvard University Press, 1964) 15–16.

13 Hofstede, G. H., " Motivation, Leadership, and Organization: Do American Theories Apply Abroad? " *Organizational Dynamics*, 8(2) (Summer 1980) 50.

14 Ibid., p. 62.

15 Hastings, D. F., "Lincoln Electric's harsh lessons from international expansion," *Harvard Business Review* 77(3) (February – March 1999) 162–178.

16 "Lincoln Electric: Venturing Abroad," n. 3 above.

17 Brannen, M. Y. and Salk, S., "Partnering across borders: Negotiating organizational culture in a German – Japanese joint venture," *Human Relations* 53(4) (2000) 451.

18   Shea, C. and Lane, H. W., "Moscow Aerostar," Ivey case 9A92C010, Ivey Publishing. See also Puffer, S. M., McCarthy, D. and Zupelev, A., "Meeting of the Mindsets in a Changing Russia," *Business Horizons* (November–December 1996) 52–60; and Vikanski, O. and Puffer, S. M., "Management Education and Employee Training at Moscow McDonald's," *European Management Journal* 1(1) 102–107.

19   Laurent, A., "The Cultural Diversity of Western Conceptualizations of Management," *International Studies of Management and Organization* 13(1–2) (1983) 75–96.

20   Ibid. at 75.

21   Ting-Toomey, S., excerpted from the chapter (194–233) "Constructive Intercultural Conflict Management" in Ting-Toomey, S., *Communicating Across Cultures* (New York: The Guilford Press, 1999).

22   Ibid. p. 211; http://books.google.com/books?id=ndZy_EWD0LUC&pg=PA211&lpg= PA211&dq. Accessed March 22, 2013.

23   Inzerilli, G. and Laurent, A., "Managerial Views of Organization Structure in France and the USA," *International Studies of Management and Organization* 13(1–2) (1983) 97–188.

24   This statement is a good example of the North American instrumental orientation.

25   Brooke, J., "Speaking the Language of Success," *New York Times*, October 23, 2001.

26   Geringer, J. M. and Miller, J., "Japanese-American Seating Inc. (A)," Ivey case no. 9A92G004 (London, Canada: Ivey Publishing,).

27   Slaughter, K., Lane, H W. and Campbell, D., "Grupo Financiero Inverlat," Ivey case no. 9A97L001 (London, Canada: Ivey Publishing).

28   Maznevski, M. L. and Gleave, T. 2011. Magdi Batato at Nestlé Malaysia (A): Introducing team-based production. IMD-3-2199. And Magdi Batato at Nestlé Malaysia (B): First the systems, now the people. IMD-3-2200. Lausanne: IMD.

29   Buechel, B. and Coughlan, S., 2011. Nestlé Continuous Excellence(A): Beyond cost savings. IMD-3-2212. Lausanne: IMD

30   Afuah, A., *Business Models: A Strategic Management Approach* (New York, NY: McGraw-Hill Irwin, 2004) 12–13. Thompson, A. A. and Strickland, A. J., *Crafting and Executing Strategy* (New York, NY: McGraw-Hill Irwin, 2001) 53.

31   Drucker, P. F., *Management: Tasks, Responsibilities, Practices* (New York: Harper, 1974) 123.

32   Ibid.

33   Porter, M. E., *Competitive Strategy* (New York: McGraw-Hill, 1980).

34   Dess, G. G., Lumpkin, G. T. and Taylor, M. L., *Strategic Management* (New York, NY: McGraw-Hill Irwin, 2005) 169.

35   Hax, A. and Wilde, D., *The Delta Project* (New York and United Kingdom: Palgrave, 2001). See also a summary article, "The Delta Model: Adaptive Management for a Changing World," *Sloan Management Review* (Winter 1999) 11–28. An updated and extended version of the original book is Hax, A., *The Delta Model: Reinventing Your Business Strategy* (New York, NY: Springer, 2010).

36   Hax, A. and Wilde, D., *Sloan Management Review* (Winter 1999) 13.

37   For a complete list of the brands that package their products in K Cups see the Keurig website, http://www.keurig.com/. Accessed March 29, 2013.

38   Dess, G. G., Lumpkin, G. T. and Taylor M. L., n. 31 above at 277.

39   This example relies on information from the following sources (accessed March 29, 2013): Barnes & Noble company website, http://www.barnesandnobleinc.com/our_company

/history/bn_history.html, and Frey, C. and Cook, J., "How Amazon.com survived, thrived and turned a profit: E-tailer defied predictions it would do none of those," *Seattle Post – Intelligencer*, Wednesday, January 28, 2004, http://seattlepi.nwsource.com/business/158315_amazon28.html. Accessed November 26, 2008; and also "Amazon posts its first annual profits e-tailer defies predictions it would never do it" http://www.highbeam.com/doc/1G1-112667107.html. Accessed March 29, 2013. Also "Using Economies of Scale to Make the Sale," Economics of Selling Online, September 12, 2008. http://shielddigital.com/economicsofsellingonline/2008/09/. Accessed March 29, 2013.

40 This example is adapted from "Netflix Inc.: Streaming Away from DVDs" by Luis Dau and David Wesley; Ivey case 9B12M040.

41 Ibid. p. 2.

42 Lane, H. W. and Campbell, D., "Global Multi-Products Chile," Ivey case no. 9A98C007, (London, Canada: Ivey Publishing). Although this is a disguised case, the company is real and is a Fortune 100 company.

43 http://www.tjx.com/about-tjx.asp. Accessed March 24, 2013.

44 Ibid.

45 Ibid.

46 Personal communication from Ted English, previously CEO of TJX Companies at the time the company entered Europe.

47 Wesley, D., Spital, F. and Lane, H. W., "Monsanto Europe (A) and (B)," Ivey Publishing, Case nos. 9B02A007 and 9B02A008, 2002.

48 Jesus Sotomayor, Mexico City, 2003, personal communication.

49 *World Investment Report 2000: Cross-border Mergers and Acquisitions and Development*, United Nations, New York and Geneva, 2000.

50 See, for example, Bartlett, C. A. and Ghoshal, S., *Managing Across Borders: The Transnational Solution*, 2nd edn. (Boston: Harvard Business School Press, 1998); and Prahalad, C. K. and Doz, Y. L., *The Multinational Mission: Balancing Local Demands and Global Vision* (New York: The Free Press, 1987).

51 Bartlett and Ghoshal; Prahalad and Doz, n. 50 above.

52 Kogut, B., "Designing Global Strategies: Comparative and Competitive Value-Added Chains," *Sloan Management Review* 26(4) (Summer 1985) 15–28.

53 Ibid.

54 Bartlett and Ghoshal, n. 47 above. For an interesting case example of mutually beneficial learning between newly acquired local companies and the headquarters of the global new owner, see "Merging Two Acquisitions: How Minetti Built a High Performance, Cohesive Organization (A) and (B)" cases, IMD-3-1484 and 3-1485.

55 Hill, C., *International Business: Competing in the Global Marketplace* (New York, NY: Irwin McGraw-Hill, 2000).

56 Bartlett and Ghoshal, n. 50 above; and Stopford, J. M. and Wells Jr., L. T., *Managing the Multinational Enterprise: Organization of the firm and ownership of the subsidiaries* (New York: Basic Books, 1972).

57 Beaman, K. V. and Guy, G. R., "Sourcing Strategies for the Transnational Organization," *IHRIM Journal* (July/August 2004) 30.

58 Ibid., at 31.

59 Faulk, J., "Global network organizations," *Human Relations*, Vol. 54(1) (2001) 91.

60 Borgatti, S., "Virtual/Network Organizations," http://www.analytictech.com/mb021/virtual. htm, February 5, 2001. Accessed March 26, 2013.

61 Vega-Redondo, F., "Network organizations," EUI Working Paper, ECO 2008/09. January 21, 2008.

62 Faulk, n. 59 above.

63 Vega-Redondo, n. 61 above, at 1.

64 Borgatti, n. 60 above.

65 Strange, Roger, "The Outsourcing of Primary Activities: Theoretical Analysis and Propositions," *Journal of Management & Governance.* 15(2) (2011) 249-269; http://www.springerlink.com/link.asp?id=102940. Accessed March 27, 2013.

66 Steven Pearlstein, "Outsourcing: What's the true impact? Counting jobs is only part of the answer," *The Washington Post,* July 01, 2012. http://articles.washingtonpost.com/2012-07-01/business/35486822_1_inventory-control-mitt-romney-lenovo. Accessed March 27, 2013.

67 Beamish, P. W., Killing, J. P., Lecraw, D. J. and Morrison, A. J., *International Management: Text and Cases,* 2nd edn. (Burr Ridge, IL: Richard D. Irwin, 1994).

68 Geringer, J. M., "Partner Selection Criteria for Developed Country Joint Ventures," *Business Quarterly,* 53(1) (1988) 55.

69 Ibid.

70 Beamish, P. W., *Multinational Joint Ventures in Developing Countries* (London: Routledge, 1988).

71 This section is adapted from Birkinshaw, J. and DiStefano, J. J., "Global Account Management: New Structures, New Tasks," Chapter 14 in Lane, H. W., Maznevski, M. L., Mendenhall, M. and McNett, J., *The Blackwell Handbook of Global Management: A Guide to Managing Complexity* (Blackwell Publishers, 2004). Used with permission.

72 Galbraith, J., "Building Organizations Around the Global Customer," *Ivey Business Journal,* 66(1) (September/October 2001).

73 Schneider Electric Receives SAMA Award for Outstanding Corporate Performance in Strategic Customer Management, http://www.schneider-electric.com/sites/corporate/en/press/press-releases/viewer-press-releases.page?c_filepath=/templatedata/Content/Press_Release/data/en/shared/2007/06/20070619_schneider_electric_receives_sama_award.xml. Accessed March 28, 2013.

74 Schneider Electric, *Financial and Sustainable Development Annual Report,* 2012; p. 21; http://www2.schneider-electric.com/documents/presentation/en/local/2013/03/schneider_electric_annual-report-2012.pdf. Accessed March 28, 2013.

75 http://www.schneider-electric.com/sites/corporate/en/customers/original-equipment-manufacturers/global-accounts/global-accounts.page?xtmc=global%2520oem%2520accounts&xtcr=7. Accessed March 28, 2013.

76 Lane, H. W., Maznevski, M. L., Mendenhall, M. and McNett, J., "Introduction to Leading and Teaming," in *The Blackwell Handbook of Global Management: A Guide to Managing Complexity* (Blackwell Publishers, 2004) 171–173.

77 Cohen, S. G. and Bailey, D. E., "What makes teams work: Group effectiveness research from the shop floor to the executive suite," *Journal of Management* 23 (1997) 239–290. These authors among many others have identified that team effectiveness is a function of factors related to task, group, and organizational design factors, environmental factors, internal processes, external processes, and group psychosocial traits.

78 Javidan, M. and House, R. J., "Cultural acumen for the global manager: Lessons from Project Globe," *Organizational Dynamics* 29(4) (2001) 289–305.

79 Benson-Armer, R. and Hsieh, T.-Y., "Teamwork Across Time and Space," *The McKinsey Quarterly*, 4 (1997) 19–27.

80 Govindarajan, V. and Trimble, C., *Reverse Innovation*, Harvard Business Review Press, (2012) 31.

81 Ibid., p. 5.

82 These companies are examples in *Reverse Innovation*, n. 80 above.

CHAPTER 6

Talent Management: Selecting and Developing Global Managers

Given the scarcity and the importance of global managers (or leaders), sophisticated talent management – the selection and development of global managers – is becoming increasingly vital to international organizations. As we discussed in Chapter 1, global leaders need a set of competences beyond those required for "normal" domestic leadership; and as we discussed in Chapter 5, it is critical to align the right people with the tasks and structures of global management. So before examining global talent management itself, we revisit our discussion on the characteristics of the complex global environment.

GLOBAL MANAGERS MANAGE COMPLEXITY[1]

The current environment facing companies is a mélange of global competitors, multiple countries, and governments with differing social, legal, regulatory, and political constraints and physical infrastructures in addition to numerous cultures and languages; all facilitated by technology and more tightly linked than ever in the past. Lane, Mendenhall, and Maznevski identified several characteristics which together function as a foundation for the increasing complexity of globalization: multiplicity, interdependence, and ambiguity. Each of these characteristics is difficult to manage by itself but they also are interrelated which presents an even greater challenge. And as if that were not enough, they are continually in flux.

Interdependence. With fast and easy movement of capital, information, and people, geographically distributed units are no longer isolated. Globalization has created a world of complex political and economic interdependence. The global financial system crisis in 2008 that started in the United States with the sub-prime mortgage defaults is a perfect illustration of this increased interdependence. However, companies are finding that they must enter into interdependent arrangements through offshoring, outsourcing, alliances, and network arrangements related to their value chains in order to stay price competitive or continue to create value. Interdependence is not only a feature of the external environment; it also is something companies create themselves through alliances, for example, to cope with the challenges of the competitive environment.

Multiplicity. With globalization, executives deal with more organizations, governments, and people. Importantly though, many of these entities are also different from the executive's own organization, government, and people, and from each other as well. Globalization is not just about "more"; it's about "more and different."[2] There are more competitors, partners, different types of organizations such as networks, and customers with different needs in different markets. Companies have more operations in more locations to manage and, of course, have more governments in these locations to contend with as well.

Ambiguity. Although there may be plenty of information, the meaning or implications of the information may not be clear. It is a condition of multiple meanings, incorrect attributions, erroneous interpretations, and conflicting interests. Situations, intentions, corporate actions, and individual behaviors can be interpreted in many different ways, and implications for action can be confusing. The problem is not the need to obtain more information and apply probabilities to the outcomes; that is uncertainty. Ambiguity involves not being able to understand and interpret the data in a way that guides action effectively. Ambiguity goes beyond uncertainty. Three aspects of ambiguity contribute to the complexity of globalization:

- Lack of information clarity. Information itself can be unclear – sometimes sources may use different indicators to analyze the same subject, coming to different conclusions. Or data may simply not be available.

- Cause-effect relationships. This is confusion about the relationship between means and ends, inputs and outputs, actions and outcomes.

- Equivocality. This is a condition in which multiple interpretations of the same facts are possible. Given a set of facts, there can be two or more possible meanings, but to identify the "right" interpretation is difficult.

There is also the multiplier effect: *Multiplicity x Interdependence x Ambiguity = Dynamic Complexity.*[3] Tightly-linked, complex global organizations operating in a tightly-coupled global environment potentially become more vulnerable as interdependence increases.[4] For example, a single email sent simultaneously to several locations in the world can not only be interpreted differently, but also forwarded to several other destinations, each generating varied interpretations and, possibly, actions. The increase in complexity leads to a decrease in buffers, slack resources, and autonomy of units. There is also less time to contemplate corrective action. Ambiguity makes problem diagnosis and action planning difficult. Problems appear and must be resolved. "Now" has become the primary unit of time in the world of global managers.

If customers, governments, interest groups, and competitors were passive then a corporation could manage the complexity by simply adding more managers and computers. That would be an increase in detail complexity.[5] The increase in interdependence and multiplicity leads to more ambiguity. Ambiguity makes understanding multiplicity difficult. And so on. Such a scenario can create messy situations for executives but this is the reality of global managers.

Flux. As if multiplicity, interdependence, and ambiguity were not enough on their own, the whole system is always in motion, always changing. And it seems to be changing at a faster rate all the time.

Eliminate or Amplify?

There are two alternative ways for dealing with increased complexity: eliminating input variety, or amplification. Elimination of variety is the reduction of environmental input achieved by not being able, or willing, to see and understand the nuances in the environment, or by creating situations of certainty that delude executives into thinking they can be controlled.[6] Such ostrich-like behavior does not usually bring success.

Amplification[7] means increasing the number of decision-makers. Generally speaking, more decision-makers or team members provide greater "variety decoding" potential. Yet simple amplification will not necessarily work. If, for example, executives operating out of a corporate headquarters in Norwich, Connecticut cannot generate the requisite variety in their decisions to match the variety existing in a global marketplace, simply increasing the size of the team may not work. If multiple decision-makers are highly homogeneous, with similar outlooks, a similar vested interest in the outcome, and reliance on the same selected sources for their information, they may be fooled. That is, they may think they are facing less variety than they actually are.[8]

Organizational structures have become more and more complex, with more managers and more multi-dimensional matrices. The more complex structures become, the more unwieldy they are. Moreover, they cannot always adapt quickly to new circumstances, since they are designed to fit a particular set of contingencies. More complex sets of policies may not work either. In a continually changing, dynamically complex environment, the policies have to be changed continually and thus lose their effectiveness.

The appropriate response to complexity is through the deliberate development of human requisite variety.[9] Ashby said: "Only variety can destroy variety."[10] In human information processing terms, development of requisite variety means that when there are complex, ambiguous inputs coming from the environment, organizational decision-makers (managers) must have the cognitive complexity, and firms need the organizational capacity, to notice these inputs, decode them, and process them. Simply, this means that global organizations need to employ managers capable of recognizing, understanding, and interpreting correctly events and information from the global marketplace, to respond adequately to the external variety or complexity. To respond to today's global complexity, organizations must find the right people to decipher the informational content in the environment and create the appropriate organizational processes for managing the complexity and executing action plans. Weick and Van Orden stated: "Globalization requires people to make sense of turbulence in order to create processes that keep resources moving to locations of competitive advantage."[11]

Effective Global Managers are the Key to Responding to Complexity

A global mindset enables executives to manage the complexity of globalization. In an earlier chapter we defined the global mindset as:

> The capacity to analyze situations and develop criteria for performance that are not dependent on the assumptions of a single country, culture or context; and to make decisions and plan action appropriately in different countries, cultures and contexts.

When managers have the capacity to think across cultures and contexts and make decisions based on that analysis, they can use the variety and resources within the firm to respond to threats and opportunities in the environment. Jack Welch called this the globalization of intellect: "The real challenge is to globalize the mind of the organization . . . I think until you globalize intellect, you haven't really globalized the company."[12]

As companies globalize, managers face increasing complexity. The challenges require a more complex view of the world, put into action through the mechanism of a global mindset. Without this approach, managers may be prone to deciding on the wrong, simple solutions to their problems. As the American journalist H. L. Menken observed "for every complex problem there is a simple solution. And it is always wrong."

The global mindset is not an additional managerial capability; it is a different capability. What does it really mean for executives to think globally? Begley and Boyd suggested thinking "glocally," which means to be able to think globally, be able to think locally, and be able to do both simultaneously. At the heart of the global mindset is the ability to see and understand the world differently than one has been conditioned to see and understand it. We particularly like a quote from Marcel Proust who expressed the essence of the global mindset when he observed that "The real voyage of discovery consists not in seeking new landscapes, but in having new eyes." A global mindset is a meta-capability that permits an individual to function successfully in new and unfamiliar situations and to integrate new skills and knowledge with existing bases.

This definition does not include, for example, specific business knowledge or skills. It is helpful to see a global mindset as separate from business knowledge, which tends to be developed in a more traditional way through formal education and business experiences. Business knowledge helps a manager understand the business; a global mindset helps the manager understand the context in which the business operates. It is also helpful to differentiate a global mindset from skills. Skills put into action the knowledge and perspectives gained from the business understanding and the global mindset. Business knowledge, a global skill set and a global mindset all are critical for effective performance in global companies; but they are not the same thing.

There is little doubt that dealing with the complexity of global operations requires having managers with the orientations, competencies and skill sets beyond those required in domestic organizations. The challenge is to find or develop managers with business knowledge and experience, a global skill set and a global mindset. Acquiring and retaining people who can function effectively in this new context becomes a critical human resource management undertaking.

The process of finding and developing globally-minded managers with the requisite skills is more difficult than it might appear. High-potential individuals must be carefully selected and prepared for their international assignments so that they can achieve the necessary professional development. Their repatriation process must be managed responsibly so that they remain with the organization to use their new skills to help it attain its strategic objectives.

GLOBAL TALENT MANAGEMENT[13]

A McKinsey & Company study, *The War for Talent*, published in 1998, identified "the war for senior executive talent [as] a defining characteristic of the competitive landscape for decades to come";[14] and probably ushered the term "talent management" into the management lexicon. Fifteen years later, what has changed? In its 2012 report, McKinsey states that "Worldwide, and in organizations of every type, 'people processes' are failing to keep pace with a changing business landscape . . . The talent shortage has not diminished."[15] Stahl et al. state that building and sustaining a talent pipeline is one of the biggest challenges facing companies everywhere.[16] However, it is no longer sufficient just to build a talent pipeline. Companies must combine it with a mobility strategy to move managers where they are most needed. As they continue to look for growth, companies are looking to emerging markets. According to the IMF, by 2014 emerging markets will have overtaken developed economies in terms of share of global GDP.[17] Given the demographic profile of aging populations in many developed countries, market expansion into emerging markets is a growth requirement for firms – and not just to the

BRIC countries. Companies are now exploring the CIVETS and the Next 11 countries.[a] A recent report by PwC states:

> The rapid pace of globalization continues to make expanding a company's global footprint into new and emerging markets a necessary business response. And expansion hinges on how effectively key individuals are deployed to international locations to support overall business goals and objectives. To retain these key individuals, companies must recognize the importance of both global mobility and talent management programs and take steps to link the two.[18]

International Assignments Come in Many Shapes and Sizes

International assignments are generally considered essential for career development and they have increased in importance over the past few years. According to an article in the Wall Street Journal, managers aiming for the C-suite will need multiple international assignments and not just in developed countries.[19]

Historically used in a management control role, for decades expatriates went abroad for usually two to three years, very often accompanied by a trailing spouse who did not have a career or expect to work. It was viewed as an interesting or exciting opportunity and a possible chance to make additional money or save money because of tax treatment. Surviving the assignment often was a measure of success. That scenario has changed. Today managers are transferred (to and from the parent company) to learn about affiliated operations in other countries, to fill a skills gap, to transfer knowledge and technology, to launch projects, to facilitate integration of the global value chain, to transfer corporate culture, and for management development.

Expatriates now are more likely to have a dual-career partner. Brookfield Global Relocation Services in its 2012 Survey Report found that 49% of the spouses/partners were employed before the assignment but only 12% continued to be employed during the assignment.[20] Career impact on their partners and loss of income has become a consideration as executives think about accepting an international assignment.

Another change has been an increase in measuring the performance of international assignees in order to gauge the effectiveness of the managers and the return on investment (ROI) of international assignments. Although still not widely practiced, companies are attempting to understand and measure the cost-benefit tradeoff of international assignments. Some companies use specific assignments or projects which can be assessed as completed or not, while others attempt to measure more formally the successful completion at the expected cost.[21] Companies are increasingly tracking the costs of international assignments and requiring clear statements of the assignment's objectives,

[a]BRIC's: Brazil, Russia, India, China; CIVETS: Colombia, Indonesia, Vietnam, Egypt, Turkey, South Africa
Next 11: Indonesia, Vietnam, Egypt, Turkey, Mexico, South Korea, Bangladesh, Iran, Pakistan, Nigeria, Philippines

pre-approval by business units and possibly HR. Some companies are doing cost-benefit analyses; but companies that measure ROI are in the minority.[22]

International assignments are important tools for the coordination and integration of organizational resources which are essential activities for successful strategy implementation in geographically dispersed companies embedded in differing cultural environments. Although it is true that numerous electronic communication and data processing system options allow the creation of sophisticated enterprise information systems to coordinate dispersed operations and the activities of suppliers and customers, cultural nuances of information that provide the deepest comprehension of market-specific knowledge may not be transferable electronically.

Tacit knowledge, which is deep-rooted and usually not codified, explains the most important nuances of operations in a particular cultural context. This knowledge is acquired experientially and must be shared through face-to-face interactions. Firms gain sustainable competitive advantage from executives acquiring experiences and lessons that are held as tacit knowledge and then shared across the organization.

Given the dispersed nature of multinational organizations, knowledge-sharing is particularly difficult. Some solutions to this challenge include the use of short-term assignments as well as cadres of expatriates and inpatriates (an employee transferred from a foreign country to a corporation's home country operation or headquarters) to acquire and share this tacit knowledge that exists within the organization. Used strategically, short-term assignments, inpatriation, and expatriation can be used to implement projects, fill positions and, as a management development experience, to provide high-potential employees with a global orientation – or all three. These employees create global relationships, inside and outside the company, in addition to explicit and implicit or tacit operating knowledge. The relationships and knowledge then become essential to the value creation process in global operations.[23]

We have dealt with some companies that were increasing the number of inpatriates to headquarters. These inpatriate assignments were usually short-term, two to three months at headquarters for a special project. This had a double advantage of exposing the inpatriate to headquarters' processes, concerns, and perspective, while allowing headquarters' personnel to become acquainted with cultural orientations and views of divisions from around the world. At the same time, some of these firms were establishing formal policies that required international experience as a prerequisite for consideration for promotion to senior ranks, thereby "localizing" management and eliminating many of the perks that were formerly needed as incentives for executives to accept international assignments.

One of the criticisms of the North American international human resource management literature has been its heavy, some would say almost exclusive, focus on expatriates. Although expatriates on long-term assignments (one year or longer) are very common and probably still the majority of international assignees, numerous surveys of multinationals also have shown an increasing trend of using "non-standard international assignments," which include frequents flyers, commuting, rotations, virtual, and short-term (up to 12 months) assignments. The use of local managers to reduce costs has increased. In Brookfield's 2012 survey, most respondents answered that localization was the option being considered for the future.[24] The people in these new arrangements are often called "flexpatriates," and research is just beginning to understand the implications for managing the assignments effectively.[25]

A major reason for the rise in nonstandard assignments is the expense associated with relocating expatriates and their families. Expatriates' salaries are usually higher than those of local managers, and they usually receive benefits to make an overseas move attractive. Benefits often include items like housing or a housing allowance, moving expenses, tax equalization, and schooling for children. Many of these benefits are not usually provided to local employees. In addition to lowering costs, having fewer expatriates has reduced conflict between expatriate employees and local employees.

Localization has also become a viable option with the increase of host country managerial and technical capabilities. In many developing countries, larger pools of better educated management talent are appearing. In developed countries, where sufficient management talent exists, there are employment and immigration laws with which a firm must comply. Companies are also now using third country nationals (TCNs) more frequently to reduce labor costs and are converting the status of expatriates to local employees, thereby reducing costs.

Selecting the Right Managers

Finding appropriate candidates for international assignments is a challenge, as is preparing them and their families for successful assignments.

In 1973, published research showed that managers were selected for international assignments based on their proven performance in a similar job, usually domestically.[26] The ability to work with foreign employees was at or near the bottom of the list of important qualifications. Unfortunately, 40 years later the situation has not changed dramatically. Very often technical expertise and knowledge and previous domestic performance are used as the most important selection criteria. However, they should not be given undue weighting relative to a person's ability to adapt to and function in another culture. It does no good to send the most technically qualified engineers or finance managers, for example, to a foreign subsidiary, if they cannot function there and have to be brought home prematurely. Caligiuri stated that:

> . . . selection for international work starts where other systems stop in that only those individuals who have a demonstrated competence for the tasks and duties of the job are considered. In essence, international assignment selection attempts to take a group of "qualified individuals" and determine who can effectively deal with the challenges inherent in working with individuals, groups, and organizations that may approach work in a very different way. Not everyone with a proven record of professional success in a domestic context for a given

job title will have what it takes to be successful in an international context — even doing the same job with the same job title.[27]

Given the importance of selecting and assigning the right candidates to these international jobs, one would think that companies would have very thorough processes. Although some undoubtedly do, this does not appear to be the case overall. Brookfield Relocation Services, in its 2012 report, found that only 28% of its surveyed companies had a formal career management process in place. And only 19% of its respondent companies used candidate assessment tools to evaluate suitability for international assignments.[28] In fact, Worldwide ERC has stated that "over 80% of companies do not conduct assessments on either candidates or their accompanying family prior to sending them on an overseas assignment. The few companies that assess assignees focus primarily on areas impacting job performance."[29]

Kealey developed a useful model for thinking about overseas effectiveness that focuses on adaptation, expertise, and interaction.[30] He states that for a person to be effective, he or she "must adapt – both personally and with his/her family – to the overseas environment; have the expertise to carry out the assignment and be able to interact with the new culture and its people."[31]

Success in an international assignment, what we think of as managerial effectiveness, is the ability to live and work effectively in the cross-cultural setting of an assignment. Effectiveness is a function of professional expertise; plus the ability to adapt to one's host country; plus intercultural communication skill to interact with the locals; and situational readiness, such as having a family that is willing, able, and probably excited to take the assignment or not having aged or sick parents to care for.[32] Our shorthand notation for this is $E = f\ (PAIS)$ which stands for *Effectiveness = f (Professional expertise, Adaptation, Intercultural interaction and Situational readiness)*.

Effectiveness on the job is *the* important outcome for an international assignment. Many studies have used outcome variables such as expatriate satisfaction with an assignment as a surrogate for performance. An international assignee who is satisfied with his or her assignment is not necessarily an effective manager nor is a manager with previous international experience necessarily effective, although such managers are likely to be more satisfied in their assignment. Previous experience is related to increased satisfaction, ease of adjustment, and less stress, all of which are good. However, global companies need effective managers and an ineffective one can damage relationships in the host country. Poor performance in an international assignment also can result in high professional and personal costs to the individual and his or her family. Therefore, all the variables in $E = f\ (PAIS)$ are important.

Women as Global Managers

The international assignment of female executives has become an issue as more women have graduated from business schools and are in line for senior management and international careers. It is also a relevant concern both under employment equity guidelines and legislation in some countries like the United States and Canada. The overall percentage of female international assignees has been rising. In its survey of 123 companies (55% headquartered in the Americas; 42% in Europe, the Middle East, and Africa; and 3% in Asia Pacific), Brookfield Global Relocation Services found that the percentage of female expatriates was 20%. This was 4% above the historical average.[33]

Nancy Adler conducted some of the early, pioneering research on female expatriates.[34] Her research showed that, contrary to conventional wisdom at the time, women did want careers as international managers. In a recent class of MBAs one of the authors asked the women in the class how many wanted to be international managers. In a class of 90 students that was approximately 30% female, the response showed 100% interest in international careers.

One lesson learned about women expatriates is that a common problem is more a perceptual one with men in the home country rather than the behavior of men in the foreign country. Men in the company's home country tend not to select women for international assignments in order to protect them from imaginary difficulties in foreign countries. However, Adler learned that a foreign woman is not expected to act like a local woman and being foreign was more noticeable than being female.

Our advice is to send the best person for the job. If a woman is the best person to be sent on an international assignment, then she should be sent. However, she should be at a senior level and have significant decision-making responsibility so that executives in the foreign company will understand that she is a senior executive and the person that they must deal with. Finally, being a woman expatriate in some countries is undoubtedly more difficult than in others and companies have a responsibility to prepare women well for the challenging assignments in difficult countries, and support them once there.

Training and Preparing for an International Assignment

The training that a person undergoes before expatriation should be a function of the degree of cultural interaction which they will experience. Two dimensions of cultural exposure are the degree of integration into a culture and the duration of stay. The integration dimension represents the intensity of the exposure. A person could be sent to a foreign country on a short-term, technical, troubleshooting matter and experience little significant contact with the local culture. The same person could be in another country only for a brief visit to negotiate a contract, but the cultural interaction could be very intense and might require a great deal of cultural fluency to be successful. An expatriate assigned abroad for a period of years is likely to experience a high degree of interaction with the local culture simply from living there.

The framework shown in Figure 6.1 suggests that, for short stays and a low level of integration an "information-giving approach" will suffice.[35] This includes, for example, area

FIGURE 6.1 Relationship between degree of integration into the host culture and rigor of cross-cultural training, and between length of overseas stay and length of training and training approach.

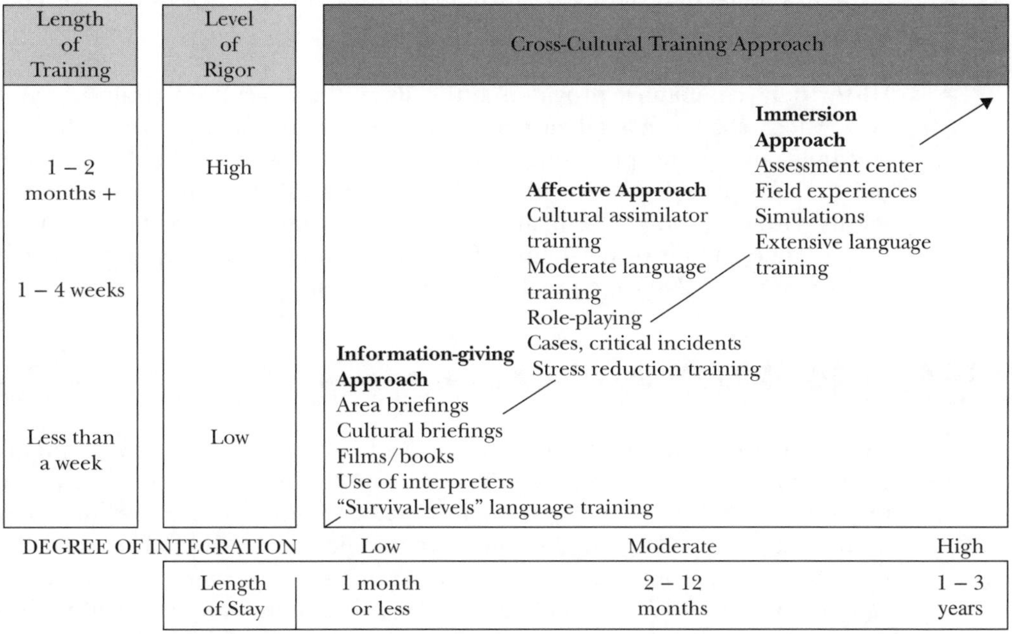

Length of Training	Level of Rigor	Cross-Cultural Training Approach		
1 – 2 months +	High			**Immersion Approach** Assessment center Field experiences Simulations Extensive language training
			Affective Approach Cultural assimilator training Moderate language training Role-playing Cases, critical incidents Stress reduction training	
1 – 4 weeks		**Information-giving Approach** Area briefings Cultural briefings Films/books Use of interpreters "Survival-levels" language training		
Less than a week	Low			

DEGREE OF INTEGRATION		Low	Moderate	High
	Length of Stay	1 month or less	2 – 12 months	1 – 3 years

Source: Reproduced with permission of John Wiley & Sons.

and cultural briefings and survival level language training. For longer stays and a moderate level of integration, language training, role plays, critical incidents, case studies, and stress reduction training are suggested. For people who will be living abroad for one to three years and/or will have to experience a high level of integration into the culture, extensive language training, sensitivity training, field experiences, and simulations are the recommended training techniques. Effective preparation would also stress the realities and difficulties of working in another culture and the importance of establishing good working relationships with the local people.

The Canadian International Development Agency (CIDA) developed a useful approach to training for situations in the top right-hand corner of the figure. After extensive predeparture training, expatriates are sent abroad. Shortly after they begin in their new posting, more training is provided to them along with their new co-workers, thus facilitating a productive integration. During the expatriates' stay abroad, periodic "refreshers" or debriefing sessions are held. Finally, the expatriates are actively involved in repatriation training both prior to and after their return home. The expatriate's spouse and family are also provided with similar training and resources.[36]

Another example is Royal Dutch Shell's OUTPOST Global Network Program.[37] Shell provides assistance to its expatriates and their families in 35 countries through offices and the Internet. The network provides information and professional services on most aspects of life abroad, particularly in the expatriates' specific locations. It provides various guides, newsletters, and information exchange services with other expatriates and facilitates social networking. It also organizes networks of volunteers of many nationalities to welcome new arrivals in a location.

Historically companies provided little, if any, cross-cultural training. But this is an area where change has taken place. More companies are realizing the value of cross-cultural training and providing it to family members. Brookfield found that 81% of its respondents provided cross-cultural training for some or all of its international assignments. However, only 37% provided it for all assignments. Sixty percent offered it for the assignee and his or her family. This was the highest rate reported since the question was first asked in 2005 and was 18% above the historical average.

Adaptation and the Reality of Culture Shock

Despite a strong desire to understand and to adapt to a new environment in order to be effective as a manager, nearly everyone experiences disorientation when entering another culture. This phenomenon, called culture shock[38] or, more appropriately, acculturative stress, is rooted in our psychological processes.[39] The normal assumptions used by managers in their home cultures to interpret perceptions and to communicate intentions no longer work in the new cultural environment. Culture shock is not a shock experienced, for example, from exposure to conditions of poverty. Culture shock is more the stress and behavioral patterns associated with a loss of control and a loss of sense of mastery in a situation. Culture shock, in normal attempts to socialize or in a business context, can result in confusion and frustration. Managers are used to being competent in such situations and now find that they are unable to operate effectively.

An inability to interpret surroundings and behave competently can lead to anxiety, frustration, and sometimes to more severe depression. Most experts agree that some form of culture shock is unavoidable, even by experienced internationalists. People who repeatedly move to new cultures likely dampen the emotional swings they experience and probably shorten the period of adjustment, but they do not escape it entirely. In fact, research on intercultural effectiveness has found that those who eventually become the most effective expatriates tend to report experiencing greater difficulty in their initial adjustment. This is because those who are more sensitive to different patterns of human interaction are likely to be both disrupted by changes in these patterns and likely to become adept at new patterns.

There are generally four modes of responding to a new environment:[40]

- Going Native (assimilation): "acceptance of the new culture while rejecting one's own culture."

- Being a Participator (integration): "adaptation to the new culture while retaining one's own culture."

FIGURE 6.2 Acculturative stress [41]

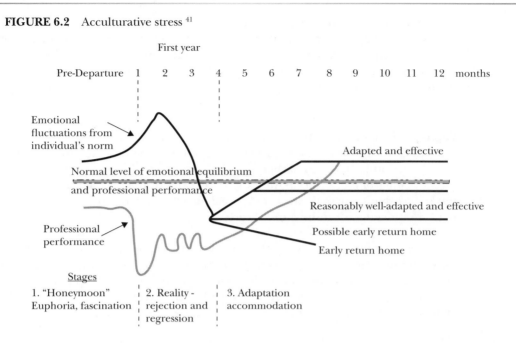

First year

Pre-Departure 1 2 3 4 5 6 7 8 9 10 11 12 months

Emotional
fluctuations from
individual's norm

Adapted and effective

Normal level of emotional equilibrium
and professional performance

Reasonably well-adapted and effective

Professional
performance

Possible early return home

Early return home

Stages

| 1. "Honeymoon" Euphoria, fascination | 2. Reality - rejection and regression | 3. Adaptation accommodation |

- Being a Tourist (separation): "maintenance of one's own culture by avoiding contact with the new culture"; and

- Being an Outcast (marginalization): "the inability to either adapt to the new culture or remain comfortable with one's own culture."

The pattern experienced by people who move into a new culture usually comes in three phases as shown in Figure 6.2: (1) the elation associated with anticipating a new environment and the early period of moving into it; (2) the distress of dealing with one's own ineffectiveness and, as the novelty erodes and reality sets in, the realization that one has to live and function in a strange setting; and (3) the adjustment to and effective coping in the new environment.

During the first and second periods, performance is usually below one's normal level. The time of adjustment to normal or above average performance takes from three to nine months, depending on previous experience, the degree of cultural difference being experienced, and the individual personality.

Frequently observed symptoms of culture shock are similar to most defensive reactions. People reject their new environment as well as the people who live there, often with angry or negative evaluations of "strangeness." Other symptoms include: fatigue; tension; anxiety; excessive concern about hygiene; hostility; an obsession about being cheated; withdrawal into work, family, or the expatriate community; and, in extreme cases, excessive use of drugs or alcohol. The vast majority of people eventually begin to accept their new environment and adjust. Most emerge from the adjustment period performing adequately and some people perform more effectively than before. A smaller percentage either "go native," which is usually not an effective strategy, or experience very severe symptoms of inability to adjust (alcoholism, nervous breakdown, and so on). These types of reactions seem to occur independently of the direction of a move. For example, North Americans going to Russia will probably exhibit patterns similar to Russians coming to North America.

Coping with Culture Shock   Different people have different ways of coping with culture shock. Normal stress management techniques, regular exercise, rest, and balanced diet are helpful. As noted earlier, some use work as a bridge until they adjust. Usually, the work environment does have some similarities to that of one's home culture. But for the nonworking partner who is often left to cope with the new environment on his or her own, the effects can be more severe.

Language training is one very effective way of coping and provides an entry into the host culture. Education about the local history, geography, and traditions of the new culture and then exploration of the new environment also help adjustment. Whatever methods are employed, it is wise to remember that everyone experiences culture shock. Diligent preparation can only moderate the effect, not eliminate it.

Support systems are especially important during the adjustment period. One obvious source of support is the family. Doing more things together as a family, more often, is a way to cope with the pressures. Another is to realize that it is acceptable to withdraw from the new culture, temporarily, for a respite. Reading newspapers from home or enjoying familiar food is a good cultural insulator – if not carried too far. After eight months in Switzerland, an eight-year-old asked her American grandfather to bring her cheddar cheese and a Hershey bar on a visit, even though she had grown to enjoy Swiss fondue and Swiss chocolate! It is important that the use of such temporary interruptions to one's reality be restricted to bridges to the new culture, not as permanent anchors to an old environment.

In company situations, it must be understood that the international manager in a new culture goes through these stresses. Local colleagues should not be surprised at less than perfect performance or strange behavior and can provide crucial support for the managers and their families. When one goes overseas, there are two jobs to accomplish. There is the functional or technical job – for example, the engineering, finance, marketing, or plant management responsibilities. This is obvious. However, too often it is only this job that people identify, focus on, and prepare for. The other job is cultural adaptation. If you cannot adapt successfully, you may be requested to go (or may be sent) home early – often in a matter of months. Such a manager may never get a chance to use his or her technical or functional skills.

You do not have to leave your own country to experience culture shock, as the following demonstrates. A Canadian volunteer on a project in Ghana experienced the symptoms of culture shock, even after participating in an orientation program organized by the sponsoring agency. This same person reported severe symptoms of culture shock on returning to an urban-based MBA program. However, the ultimate culture shock came upon graduating and starting work for a manufacturer located in a small, rural community in one of Canada's Maritime Provinces. In all three experiences, the patterns were the same, and the sharpest disorientation occurred within this person's native country, perhaps because it was least expected. It is important to note that this individual experienced a "reverse culture shock" on the return home.

Return Shock   "Reverse culture shock," "return shock" or "reentry shock" to one's home culture is also an adjustment phenomenon that people experience and for which they need to be prepared. There can be a significant readjustment to one's home country, especially if a manager has been away for a long period of time.

Osland[42] points out that there can be a high degree of uncertainty surrounding one's career upon repatriation that, combined with a loss of prestige and autonomy of being abroad, possibly at the forefront of a company's global strategy, may give an executive pause to think about his or her future career with the company. Both at work and in one's personal life, a returned international assignee may find that others lack interest in their experience. They have grown personally and changed during their assignment, but people at home only want to hear the 30-second sound bite about the experience. Their idealized image of how perfect the home country was and how well everything worked there is often shattered upon return. A person who worked for one of the authors in Nairobi, Kenya often commented about how she could not wait to get back to North America where the copy machines worked. When she returned she discovered that the copiers often broke down there as well. And personally, returned assignees often find that they miss life abroad. All of these factors probably play a role in the attrition rate of returnees discussed in the next section.

Repatriation

The process of selecting the right people, training them properly, and sending them and their families to their foreign posting is not the end of the story. Reintegrating these people into the company after the foreign assignment so that the company can continue to benefit from their experience and expertise is important, and it has also proven to be a problem.

Companies have to contend with failure rates, defined as early return. There are estimates in the literature of failure rates of anywhere from 20–50% for American expatriates but these high estimates have been called into question.[43] Respondents to Brookfield's survey reported an early return rate of 6–7%. However, that number is still high especially given the investment a firm makes in sending an employee and her or his family abroad; and the valuable experience the company loses.

There are many reasons for failure or early return. Various surveys have reported causes such as the inability to demonstrate a global mindset, poor leadership skills, and an aversion to change or a lack of networking skills. Others have found that the key factors of expatriate failure were partner dissatisfaction, family concerns, inability to adapt, poor candidate selection, and the job not meeting the expatriate's expectations. Usually the number one reason prompting early return is family-related issues such as partner/spouse dissatisfaction. This year Brookfield also found a career-related reason and that was employees leaving to join another company.

Expatriate attrition, leaving the company, is a problem. In its 2012 Survey Report, Brookfield found that the turnover rate for expatriates during an assignment was 12%, or similar to the attrition rate of the general employee population, and, of those leaving, it was 24% within the first year after returning. To minimize attrition companies need to think more coherently about career-pathing for their expatriates, so their returnees can use their newly acquired international experience and skills, and provide them with adequate repatriation support and a wider choice of positions after repatriation.

Regardless of the exact numbers on failure rate or attrition, it pays to get the expatriate cycle right – the right people, the right preparation, and the right repatriation. Companies report that they spend anywhere from two to three times an expatriate's annual salary, or more, on an assignment where they move the employee and his or her family for three to five years.[44] These costs include home leave, housing allowances, cost of living allowances, American or international level schooling for children, preparation and language lessons. And these costs do not consider the personal costs to employees and their families from terminating an assignment early. If companies want to retain their internationally experienced managers, they will have to do a better job with their career management processes including the repatriation process. Ways to improve the repatriation process include using the international experience assignees bring home with them, offering job choices upon return, recognition, repatriation career support, family repatriation support, and improving evaluations during an assignment.[45]

An international assignment is an important vehicle for developing global managers; achieving strategic management control; coordinating and integrating the global organization; and learning about international markets and competitors, as well as about foreign social, political, and economic situations. However, the idealized goal of becoming a global, learning organization will only be reached if the right people are selected for foreign assignments, trained properly, repatriated with care, valued for their experience, and then offered assignments that draw on their unique backgrounds.

CHALLENGING DESTINATIONS

There are at least three dimensions on which to categorize countries as challenging destinations: administrative problems for expatriate program managers (government regulations, immigration, work permits, tax issues, locating acceptable housing); cultural difficulty for the assignee and family in adapting to a new country; and personal risk such as security and health issues. Brookfield's 2012 Survey Report identified the USA, China and the United Kingdom as the top destinations for international assignments.[b] China, India and Brazil were reported to be the most challenging destinations for assignees. These three locations plus Russia were found to be the most challenging for international program administrators. In China, administrative issues include suitable housing, immigration issues, bureaucracy, and remote locations. In India and Russia there are similar issues but security is an added concern. Cultural problems for the assignees are common in these three countries and language is also a challenge in China and Russia. In addition to the BRIC countries companies are expanding into new areas that undoubtedly will present administrative and adaptation challenges. Brookfield found that Malaysia, Indonesia, Argentina, Kazakhstan and Colombia were, for the first time this year, mentioned by their respondents as destination countries.

In addition to executing strategy globally under relatively "normal" conditions, executives may find themselves in difficult environments and threatening situations. Today a successful assignment also means a safe assignment. Companies are formalizing programs to ensure the safety and security of their expatriates and families to minimize international assignment turndowns, attrition, early returns, and failures. Since the events of September 11, 2001, we have seen continued economic and political volatility as well as the rise of global terrorism. Kidnapping and piracy have also become all too common phenomena. Executives could be tempted to say: "The world has become a dangerous place and maybe we should concentrate on places like the United States and Western Europe."

We believe that global business is a long-term proposition. Companies cannot succeed by jumping in and out of countries when the going gets tough. Not only is it expensive, but customers and suppliers often remember when they were "deserted."

Nestlé had some of its operations in South America nationalized and later resumed ownership. It then went through a second full cycle of nationalization and renewed ownership. Although the company contested and fought the actions as best it could, the attitude of senior executives was one of patience, knowing that these things happen and that, eventually, the regime would change and the assets would be returned. This company has had a real commitment to its global business and a long-term perspective, both of which have contributed to its unusual success.

Many countries that companies are exploring can be considered difficult places in which to do business and for expatriates to live. It is important to have a realistic attitude toward these situations and to learn to live and work in a world of uncertainty and risk. The more you learn about other countries, the better you understand the risks

---

[b] Recall that 97% of responding companies were headquartered in the West.

involved. This enables better decisions to be made about entering a certain country and the steps necessary to manage the risks in that country.

The following story illustrates this well. One of the authors was having dinner with the president of a British bank's Canadian subsidiary and was describing some of his activities in East Africa to the bank president. The bank president commented about how risky it was to operate in Africa. This comment surprised the author, who understood the difficulties involved but had thought it possible to manage them. The bank president then described all the countries in South America in which the bank was operating and making money. To the author, South America at the time had to be one of the riskiest places to operate, and he said so. The bank president replied, "Not really; the bank has been there for a long time, and we understand the situation." Therein lies the moral: familiarity with, and understanding of a country, provides the necessary perspective for accurately assessing risks, determining acceptable levels of risk, and managing those risks.

Companies need to have strategic and tactical plans for managing risks. Large companies can develop specialists in assessing risks to contribute to informed decision-making, and smaller ones can access specialist firms or consultants for information relevant to specific decisions. All companies are advised to listen to expatriates and locals working in the field when they provide systematic assessments of their environments required periodically as part of the normal business plan by the home office. Individual managers can add to the quality of their own decision-making by reading broadly, by understanding the history of regions in which they operate, and by seeking (and paying attention to) information from international field personnel. As globalization increases, more international representation in the senior ranks of corporate headquarters personnel will also increase the ability to assess risks in specific countries. A global viewpoint, an understanding of the culture, political and social situations, and a long-term commitment to global operations are essential.

Operating globally is different from operating at home, and those differences must be, and can be, understood. The costs of entering the global game can be high. But the experience can be rewarding financially for the corporation, as well as personally and professionally for the manager.

ONGOING TALENT DEVELOPMENT – IMPORTANT FOR ALL INTERNATIONAL COMPANIES

Recent advances in global talent management have been impressive in some companies. We see sophisticated talent pipelines with effective selection and development in many multinational companies.[46] But as we said in the opening of this chapter, as well as earlier in the book, global leaders are more and more important for most companies, even those that don't consider themselves "global." The more companies take talent development seriously, the more we will have a strong ongoing cadre of global leaders to help organizations navigate in this highly complex environment.

Notes

1   This section has been adapted from "Globalization: Hercules Meets Buddha," Lane, H. W., Maznevski, M. L., and Mendenhall, M., *The Blackwell Handbook of Global Management: A Guide to Managing Complexity* (Blackwell Publishers, 2004) 3–25.

2   Wilson, M., Center for Creative Leadership, personal communication.

3   Senge, P., *The Fifth Discipline* (Doubleday, 1990).

4   Weick, K. E. and Van Orden, P., "Organizing on a Global Scale: A Research and Teaching Agenda," *Human Resource Management*, 29(1) (Spring 1990) 49–61.

5   Senge, P. (1990) n. 3 above.

6   Harnden, R. and Leonard, A., *How Many Grapes Went Into the Wine: Stafford Beer on the Art and Science of Holistic Management* (John Wiley & Sons, 1994) 135.

7   Ibid. at 16.

8   Beer, S., *Brain of the Firm: The Managerial Cybernetics of Organization* (John Wiley & Sons, 1981) 356.

9   Ashby, W. R., *Design for a Brain* (London: Chapman Hall Ltd. and Science Paperbacks, 1972) and *Introduction to Cybernetics* (London: Chapman Hall Ltd. and University Paperbacks, 1973).

10 Ashby, 207, n. 9 above.

11 Weick and Van Orden, 49, n. 4 above.

12 Rohwer, J. and Windham, L., "GE Digs into Asia," *Fortune*, October 2, 2000.

13 To understand and keep up to date on what is happening in the corporate world regarding international assignments of executives, we recommend obtaining a copy of the latest Global Relocation Trends published by Brookfield Relocation Services and available at http://www .brookfieldgrs.com/insights_ideas/trends.asp.

14 Chambers, E. G., Foulon, M., Handfield-Jones, H., Hankin, S. M.,and Michaels, E. G., "The War For Talent," *The McKinsey Quarterly* (August 1998).

15 The State of Human Capital 2012. False Summit: Why the Human Capital Function Still Has Far to Go. A Report by McKinsey & Company and The Conference Board; Research Report R 1501-12-RR.

16 Stahl, G. K, Björkman, I., Farndale, E., Morris, S. S., Paauwe, J., Stiles, P., Trevor, J. and Wright, P., "Six Principles of Effective Global Talent Management," *MIT Sloan Management Review*, (Winter 2012) 25–32.

17 Ernst & Young website: http://www.ey.com/GL/en/Issues/Business-environment/ Six-global-trends-shaping-the-business-world—Emerging-markets-increase-their-global-power.

18 Eileen Mullaney (Principal and Leader of PwC's Global Mobility Consulting Practice) International assignment perspectives: *Critical issues facing the globally mobile workforce*, 5 (October 2011) 3.

19 Kwoh. L., "Don't Unpack That Suitcase: These Days, One Foreign Posting Isn't Enough for Managers Who Want Top Jobs," *The Wall Street Journal*, May 8, 2012.

20 Brookfield Global Relocation Services, *Global Relocation Trends*, 2012 Survey Report.

21 For a more in-depth discussion of the issue and challenges of calculating ROI of international assignments see Yvonne McNulty and Helen De Cieri, "Global mobility in the 21st century: Conceptualizing expatriate return on investment in global firm," *Management International Review*, December 2011. See also Yvonne McNulty and Helen De Cieri,

"Do global firms measure expatriate return on investment? An empirical examination of measures, barriers and variables influencing global staffing practices," *International Journal of Human Resource Management*, June 2009.

22   Brookfield Global Relocation Services, *op. cit.*

23   Harzing, A.-W., "Of Bears, Bumblebees, and Spiders: The Role of Expatriates in Controlling Foreign Subsidiaries," *Journal of World Business*, 36(4) (2001) 366–379.

24   Brookfield Global Relocation Services, *op. cit.*

25   Madsen, M. T., and Rask, M., forthcoming. "Global leadership through flexpatriation," in Mendenhal, M. E., Stahl, G. K., and Maznevski, M. L. (eds.), *European Journal of International Management*, special issue on Global Leadership.

26   Miller, E. L., "The International Selection Decision: A Study of Some Dimensions of Managerial Behavior in the Selection Decision Process," *Academy of Management Journal*, 16 (2) (1973) 239–252.

27   Caligiuri, P., *Cultural Agility: Building a Pipeline of Successful Global Professionals* (San Francisco, CA: Jossey-Bass, 2012) 171.

28   Brookfield Global Relocation Services, *op. cit.*

29   Worldwide ERC, *Executive Digest: Support & Retention Strategies for Cross-Border Assignments;* p. 2. http://www.worldwideerc.org/Resources/Research/Pages/SupportandRetentionStrategies-ExecDigest.aspx. Accessed March 18, 2013.

30   Kealey, D. J., *Cross-Cultural Effectiveness: A Study of Canadian Technical Advisors Overseas* (Ottawa: Canadian International Development Agency, 1990). This study was based on a sample of over 1300 people including technical advisors, their spouses, and host-country counterparts.

31   Ibid. at 8.

32   Franke, J. and Nicholson, N., "Who Shall We Send? Cultural and Other Influences on the Rating or Selection Criteria for Expatriate Assignments," *International Journal of Cross Cultural Management*, 2(1) (April 2002).

33   Brookfield Global Relocation Services, *op. cit.*

34   Adler, N. J., "Pacific Basin Managers: A Gaijin, not a Woman," *Human Resource Management*, 26(2) (1987). See also Adler, N. J. and Izraeli, D. N. (eds.), *Women in Management Worldwide* (M. E. Sharpe Inc, 1988). An excellent article is Caligiuri, P. and Cascio, W. F., "Can We Send Her There? Maximizing the Success of Western Women on Global Assignments," *Journal of World Business*, 33(4) (Winter 1998).

35   Mendenhall, M., Dunbar, E. and Oddou, G., "Expatriate selection, training and career-pathing: A review and critique," *Human Resource Management*, 26(3) (Autumn (Fall) 1987) 331–345.

36   Matteau, M., *Towards Meaningful and Effective Intercultural Encounters* (Hull, Canada: Intercultural Training and Briefing Centre, Canadian International Development Agency, 1993).

37   http://www.globaloutpostservices.com/. Accessed March 17, 2013.

38   Some suggested readings on the topic of culture shock include: Torbiorn, I., *Living Abroad: Personal Adjustment and Personnel Policy in the Overseas Setting* (Sussex, England: John Wiley & Sons Ltd, 1982); Adler, N., *International Dimensions of Organizational Behavior*, 5th edn. (Cincinnati, OH: Cengage, 2007); Oberg, K., "Culture Shock: Adjustment to New Cultural Environments," *Practical Anthropology*, 7 (1960) 177–182; Grove, C. L. and Torbiorn, I., "A

New Conceptualization of Intercultural Adjustment and the Goals of Training," *International Journal of Intercultural Relations*, 9(2) (1979).

39 Research on stress and adapting to stressful situations also suggests that there are physiological contributions as well. One reference that links physiology and culture shock is Wederspahn, G., *Culture Shock: It's All in Your Head . . . and Body* (The Bridge, 1981) 10. For these generalizations we are drawing on Torbiorn, *Living Abroad*; the research literature described by Adler in *International Dimensions*; Oberg, K., "Culture Shock," *Practical Anthropologist* 7 (1960) 177–182; and our own experience with numerous executives and students around the world.

40 This framework was developed by Berry, J. W., "Acculturation as Varieties of Adaptation," in Padilla, A. (ed.), *Acculturation: Theory, Model, and Some New Findings* (Washington, D.C.: AAAS, 1980).

41 This figure was adapted from "Psychological Aspects of Environmental Adjustment," Sargent, C., source and date unknown.

42 Osland, J. S., *The Adventure of Working Abroad: Hero Tales from the Global Frontier* (San Francisco, CA: Jossey-Bass Publishers, 1995) 165–192.

43 Harzing, A.-W., "Are our referencing errors undermining our scholarship and credibility? The case of expatriate failure rates," *Journal of Organizational Behavior* 23 (2002) 127–148.

44 "Expatriate costs and assignments," *The Economist* online, July 24 2012. http://www.economist.com/blogs/graphicdetail/2012/07/focus-3. Accessed March 18, 2013.

45 An accessible, practitioner article on repatriation can be found at http://www.relocatemagazine.com/repatriation/repatriation-articles. Accessed March 18, 2013. See also the following articles for further discussions of repatriation: Bossard, A. B. and Peterson, R., "The Repatriate Experience as Seen by American Expatriates," *Journal of World Business* 40 (2005) 9–27; MacDonald, S. and Arthur, N., "Connecting Career Management to Repatriation Adjustment," *Career Development Journal*, 10(2) (2005) 145–159.

46 Caligiuri, P., *Cultural Agility: Building a Pipeline of Successful Global Professionals* (San Francisco, CA: Jossey-Bass, 2012).

CHAPTER 7

Managing Change in Global Organizations[a]

This chapter deals with the implementation of strategic organizational changes. As discussed in Chapter 5, managers have to be able to build global organizations that balance global integration against local responsiveness to effectively serve global customers. As the competitive environment changes, as it seems to do ever faster all the time, they may also have to reformulate their organization's strategy, which, in turn, may necessitate realigning how employees do their work, and revising organizational structures and/or systems to support the new behaviors and the new strategy.

Global organizational change has been defined as "strategically aligned alterations in patterns of employee behavior within organizations operating across national borders."[1] For example, responding to market forces, the manager of a large Swiss-headquartered global chemical company decided that it would switch its European marketing strategy for its resins from selling on volume to increasing profit margins.[2] This strategic change necessitated adjustments in the organizational systems and in employee behaviors across its European subsidiaries. To increase profit margins, the organization had to offer more service to its customers in the form of advanced product know-how. The Swiss-located research and development division of the company possessed such knowledge, but systems had to be developed to share this knowledge across the European subsidiaries. The employee behavior also had to change. The engineers in the research and development division at headquarters now had to provide service to the sales managers

---

[a]We dedicate this chapter to the memory of Al Mikalachki who taught us about organizational change over two decades at the Ivey Business School in London, Canada and on whose work a large part of this chapter is based. We also want to recognize the previous contributions to this chapter by Joe DiStefano and Joerg Dietz. These contributions largely remain in this edition.

of the European subsidiaries. Furthermore, the sales managers in each country location had to attract new customers who valued service over price and were willing to pay a premium for it, and the employees had to provide the service to these customers.

In the above case, being convinced of the ultimate success of his new strategy, the marketing manager neglected to prepare the organization and the employees for the change and instead merely announced it, which might have worked in the company's hierarchy-dominated headquarters in Basel, Switzerland. The employees in the other European subsidiaries overwhelmingly resisted. There were calls for the resignation of the manager, and the early results of the new strategy were poor. Only after the manager started to engage in meetings with the employees, offered employee training on the new service and customer behaviors, and slightly modified the strategy, did the employees adopt the necessary new behaviors. Sometime later the new strategy became a huge success, substantially increasing the profit that the company made in the resin business.

The manager could have avoided, or at least ameliorated, the pains of executing the new strategy if he had paid attention to two issues. First, to be successful, a new strategy has to be the right response to the market and, second, it has to be implemented carefully. Even the "right" strategy will fail if it is not executed properly. Implementing global organizational change is neither a science nor an art, but it is a craft that takes discipline and attention to details.

The above example also highlights four critical elements of our orientation to change:

1　Our focus is strategic change.

2　All change is behavioral. Organizations don't change; people do.

3　Change is a process, not simply an outcome. The final result from a successful change effort may look like and act like a changed organization.

4　Existing systems, structures and/or cultures may need to be modified to reinforce and support the new required behaviors.

This chapter presents a three-stage model that managers can use as a checklist for managing a change process. We will first explain the model and then we will address challenges that managers face in implementing change in global organizations. Before reviewing the model, it is important to recognize that there are at least three different types of change situations, depending on the current performance of the organization: anticipatory, reactive, and crisis, as shown in Figure 7.1.

Ideally companies would like to be able to *anticipate* environmental shifts and make changes through a process of continuous learning and follow the path of renewal. This is not always easy to do when performance is still good and there are no real indicators that there is trouble ahead. Usually not everyone in the company will be looking out into the future far enough or be sensitive to important environmental shifts. The management challenge at this stage is *education* – educating people about the potential

FIGURE 7.1 Strategic change and renewal (adapted from work by our colleagues Peter Killing, Nick Fry, Rod White and Mary Crossan, Ivey Business School and IMD)

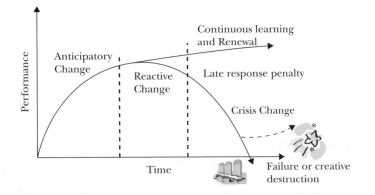

dangers and convincing them that they pose a threat. Anticipatory change generally proceeds at a pretty slow pace.

In the *reactive* stage, as performance begins to suffer after an environmental shift, more managers see the warning signs but they very likely may interpret them differently depending on their roles or functional perspectives. Change initiatives, although still not guaranteed, may move faster now, as more people acknowledge potential threats. The management challenge at this stage is *creating a cohesive picture of the future and achieving agreement* on it.

In the *crisis* stage, the problems are clear for everyone to see and crises generally encourage and permit rapid change. Indeed, organizations require it to survive. History is littered with examples of companies that resisted change or that did not respond fast enough to major changes in their industries. Polaroid missed the shift to digital photography. About the same time, the Boston area was the center of the mini-computer industry that included companies like Digital Equipment, Wang, Prime, and Data General; none of these survived the personal computer revolution. In the American automobile industry, General Motors, in particular, is a good example of the late-response penalty. As we have seen, it took the US government to bailout General Motors. The CEO was fired; the Pontiac Division was shut down; Hummer, Saturn and Saab were sold; and something like 35% of the executives in the United States were let go. Critics had said for years that GM needed to do things like this, but they were never able to muster the management will to do them.

MANAGING CHANGE: PREPARING, INITIATING, REINFORCING

The change model (Figures 7.2, 7.3 and 7.4) serves as a guide for change implementation. The model evolved from many case studies of discontinuous strategic change that altered how an organization conducted its business.[3] The model is applicable for anticipatory and reactive changes that permit executives time for environmental scanning, problem definition, and preparing the organization for change. It describes the steps in the management of one discontinuous strategic change, recognizing that the completion of one change effort becomes the foundation for future changes. Hence, it is a cyclical model. It is not a crisis management model. Crises, such as the bailout and subsequent actions involving GM and Chrysler in 2008–2009, require fast responses that typically may not allow for an extended analysis and the involvement of employees and other stakeholders.

The model illustrates the change process from the beginning to the end of the change cycle. Each step of the process identifies (1) the factors to which managers must attend and (2) the stakeholders that managers ought to involve. It takes into consideration the change phases when employees' old behaviors transition into new behaviors. A period of discomfort and resistance during the transition period occurs in most cases. People have to get used to breaking with the old behaviors while simultaneously learning the new behaviors. Operations during this period are not the most efficient, as the old system is not working as well as it used to and the new system is not yet working as well as it should be. During this period there is a risk of abandoning the change as people question the logic of working harder while performance declines. Understanding and preparing for these difficulties helps managers to guide the organization through the change process. The model encourages managers and other key players to take a planned and organized approach during each step, and keeps everyone aligned throughout the entire change process.

The model recognizes that change occurs in a larger organizational context. If organizations can build a culture for change that becomes part of the organizational mindset, change processes will become more efficient (and the need for crisis management will decrease). Hence, the model can be a tool for creating a perpetual state of change readiness, the first step to the path of continuous renewal. Finally, the model invites revisions to the change process depending on the organizational and cultural context. Although, for example, trust and respect are central to successful change processes, the ways of establishing trust and respect differ among cultures.

In Canadian and American cultures, managers typically gain the trust of their employees by involving them as well as inviting and responding to their feedback. In other cultures this approach is less appropriate. When the Canadian manager of a Guyanese Red Cross children's home applied participatory and team-based practices while leading a change effort, the Guyanese employees did not buy into her ideas.[4] They found her practices dubious and indicative of weakness ("Why would she ask us? Doesn't she know herself?"). They only started to trust and respect her when she finally employed authoritarian means of introducing changes in employee behaviors including punishment. The employees expected to be treated authoritatively and took it as a sign of competent leadership.

Before Implementing: Determining the Required Changes

Presumably, having used the organizational alignment model in Chapter 5 as a diagnostic tool, executives have a good idea of the necessary changes needed in support of a new or modified strategic initiative. Clearly defining and articulating the strategic objective (e.g., increase the market share to 20% in the Chinese market), is important in designing the change process and in communicating the change. Additionally, it motivates employees with a goal. Managers determine the new tasks that the organization will now need to do well (e.g., generate more contacts with buyers) and specify the new employee behaviors (e.g., call buyers during the morning when they are most likely to be available, limit conversations to five minutes per buyer). Behaviors that are specific, concrete, observable, and easy to visualize are a powerful tool for communicating change initiatives to employees. They help employees to focus on what they will do in the future, thereby reducing their uncertainty about the implications of the strategic change. It is important that managers be able to describe strategic objectives, new employee behaviors, and the new systems and structures clearly, in easily understood language. More importantly, employees benefit from understanding how they can contribute towards achieving this goal.

To facilitate the performance of the new behaviors, managers must also consider adjustments in the alignment model. Too often these efforts focus only on changes in the reward system (e.g., a bonus for generating more than 100 new contacts per month). However, most often strategic change and the resulting alterations in employee behavior require much more than changes in the reward system. As discussed in Chapter 5, if employees do not have relevant experience for enacting the new behaviors, managers may need to offer training. Furthermore, new behaviors may necessitate new technology (e.g., advanced phone systems) and a new organizational structure (e.g., change from a structure by product to a structure by client or cross-functional teams).

After doing the analysis and determining what needs to be done, managers are now in a position to design the change process. This is often a neglected step, as managers tend to go right from the "answer," which is the new strategy, to implementation, often with unintended consequences. One example of this "rush to implementation" was the Swiss chemical example described earlier in this chapter. An example that avoided this mistake was the American company Black & Decker.[5] The president of the Asia region wanted to revamp the HR strategy by putting more emphasis on internal feedback. The intent was to help his managers and employees improve their job performance. The president decided to introduce a 360-degree feedback system that had been designed and already implemented successfully in the US. This new system required more assertive feedback behaviors from employees. He even provided specific examples of these new behaviors, such as giving and receiving constructive feedback not only from superiors but also peers and subordinates. However, he immediately met resistance from local Asian managers, who raised concerns that local employees would not accept and use the system because of culturally-engrained attitudes towards staffing, leadership, feedback, and confidentiality. Therefore, the president made adjustments to the system such as using the 360-degree feedback for management-level employees only and rolling out the new system in phases. Had he not taken the time to assess the readiness for change in the organization with his managers, it is likely he would not have been successful.

PHASE 1: APPRAISING THE READINESS FOR CHANGE

An organization's readiness for change is determined by analyzing several factors that affect the support of, or resistance to, the change initiative, such as the visibility of the need for change, the organization's management style, the past history of change processes, and the timing of the change.

How Visible is the Need for Change?

When an organization is doing well and engages in anticipatory change (preparing for future changes in the environment), managers and employees will not necessarily see the need for change. "If it ain't broke, don't fix it," or "Why should we change something that works well?" are common comments in organizations. If, however, changes in the environment have already occurred and the organization engages in reactive change, managers and employees will more easily recognize why the organization's strategy and employees' behaviors have to change.

Diagnosing the visibility of the need for change is important because (1) employees will not partake in the change unless they see the need for change forcing managers to establish it; (2) the more the need for change is visible to employees, the more managers can accelerate the change process.

What is the organization's management style? Employees may be used to a management style that differs from the management style needed to lead the change effort. Many change practitioners in the West advise a participatory style for managing change that involves the employees (change targets). In many cultures, however, employees are used to authoritarian management styles and might be confused if they had a voice in the change process. The example mentioned earlier of the employees in the Red Cross children's home in Guyana was such a situation. Conversely, in reactive change efforts (and even more so in crisis change efforts), the change agent (leader of the change process) may decide on a less participatory style in order to speed up the process.

What is the history of change processes? If change processes went awry in the past, employees may mistrust new change efforts. In the foreign subsidiaries of global organizations, often expatriates come in for limited-term assignments, unleash a major change effort, and then leave after a couple of years, independent of the completion of the change process. This leaves local employees distinctly uncomfortable with the next expatriate's change initiative.

What is the timing? Managers have to assess the timing of the change effort. If the resources of the organization are already stretched to the limit, it does not make sense to launch an anticipatory change effort that will further stretch resources. Such situations can arise during recessions, peak seasons, or when changes occur concurrently with other change efforts (e.g., a product launch).

Top Management Support and Commitment

Employees evaluate the sincerity of a change effort in large part on the basis of top management support and commitment. Hence, the visibility of top management support is critical for implementing change successfully, especially in the early stages of the change process. Top managers, in conjunction with the change agent, should be the initial communicators of the change effort. Employees will be more likely to engage the change effort enthusiastically if top managers make the effort to explain the goals of the change (e.g., new employee behaviors) and the change process. In addition, top management signals the importance of an organizational change through the allocation of resources. Top management support alone will not elicit a change in employee behaviors. However, the absence of top management support might result in resistance or indifference among employees.

Who Will the Change Agents Be?

In selecting a change agent, managers need to ask three questions:

- *Does the change agent have power to implement the change?* Power can be positional, expert, or personal, all relating to the credibility of the change agent. But note that different cultures emphasize different aspects of the bases of power. If employees do not have confidence or trust in the change agent, it will be difficult to motivate them to change.

- *What are the change agent's personal motivations?* The change agent must support the change and act as a positive example for change targets.

- *What are the change management knowledge, skills, and abilities of the change agent?* The change agent should have communication, management, and conflict resolution skills to carry out the change effort. The more cultural boundaries that the change crosses, the greater the need for cross-cultural skills in these areas.

Who is the Target Group for the Change?

The key players in a change process include the obvious, immediate change targets (employees who will have to engage in new behaviors). However, less obvious stakeholders such as unions, suppliers, or customers whose business, systems, or behavior may be affected, need to be considered. Managers need to think about the target group in the broadest possible terms by considering links between the immediate target group and others with whom they may be interdependent.

If a global organization embarks on an organization-wide change effort, both headquarters and foreign subsidiaries are affected. Subsidiaries may differ with regard to effective change processes, depending on local cultural differences, proximity to head-quarters, and the relationship between headquarters and subsidiaries. Hence, managers of global change must understand local differences to determine the processes needed to motivate the expected change in employee behaviors. Furthermore, implementing a strategic change throughout locations in many countries will require a team of change agents. The Swiss-headquartered global chemical company described at the start of this chapter illustrated the different reaction to a strategic change of headquarters and sub-sidiaries. In assessing change targets, two questions are critical.

- First is the *ability* question. Can they do it? What are the knowledge, skills, abili-ties, and resources the change targets need to perform the new behaviors? Even if they support the change, they may not be able to behave appropriately. The fear of inability often leads to anxiety and can undermine support for a change. If employ-ees cannot perform the new behaviors, the change process will have to include employee training and the provision of other resources (e.g., tools and machinery) needed to perform new behaviors. A lack of resources will lead to frustration.

- Second is the *motivation* question. Will they do it? What is the predisposition of employees toward the change? Will they support or resist it? In our opinion, this is the single most important question to assess the organization's readiness for change because high motivation leads people to acquire the needed skills and to exert the extra effort that contributes to success. Managers need to identify opponents as well as supporters and analyze the reasons for the resistance or support.[6] This analysis provides information about how opposition may be turned into support. If change targets resist because, for example, they do not see the need for change, manag-ers could explain the links between the new strategy, the new behaviors, and the improvements for the organization and the employees.

- Are there preemptive problems like previous failed change efforts and a lack of trust that will discourage employees from engaging the change effort? If so, then these issues need to be addressed before moving forward.

Here also is where cultural differences potentially play an important role and manag-ers need to understand cultural differences, especially with respect to expectations of employees about the way managers should go about making changes, and the employees' expected role in any change process. Good knowledge of local ways of expressing agreement and disagreement and about dealing with conflict are also very important. Figure 7.2 is a summary of Phase 1.

Analyzing the readiness for change can be viewed as a gap analysis that assesses an organization's and its employees' current capabilities against the capabilities and behav-iors needed to enact the new strategy. Our advice is that if any of the answers to the questions asked in Figure 7.2 are "no," then it is important to stop and then work to turn those answers into "yes." On the basis of this gap analysis, managers create an ini-tial action plan and select a change agent.

FIGURE 7.2 Assessing the readiness for change

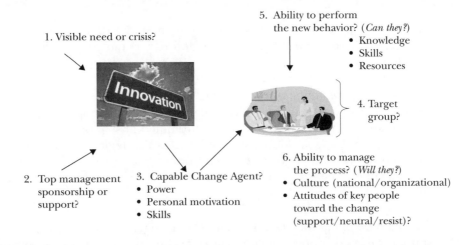

1. Visible need or crisis?

2. Top management sponsorship or support?

3. Capable Change Agent?
- Power
- Personal motivation
- Skills

4. Target group?

5. Ability to perform the new behavior? (*Can they?*)
- Knowledge
- Skills
- Resources

6. Ability to manage the process? (*Will they?*)
- Culture (national/organizational)
- Attitudes of key people toward the change (support/neutral/resist)?

PHASE 2: INITIATING CHANGE AND ADOPTING THE NEW BEHAVIOR

Leading a strategic change is a full-time effort and requires intimate knowledge of the organization, which is why in most cases the change agent is a capable and respected insider. A capable change agent is one who has the requisite power, motivation, and change management skills. These skills include analysis, communication, conflict resolution and, in global organizations, cultural intelligence. Once chosen, he or she needs to initiate the change by making sure the right people are in place for the new tasks and by building support for the change effort.

Training and Selection

To perform new behaviors, employees must be able to do so. If the change calls for behaviors that current employees do not have the potential to perform, managers must select new employees. If current employees have the potential to perform the new behavior, but do not yet possess the ability to do so, the change agent has to find a way to get them the necessary training. Selection and training should occur early because inability to perform the new behaviors causes employees to be frustrated, leading to lowered efforts or resistance.[7]

We want to be clear about our use of the terms "selection" or its opposite, "de-selection." By "de-selection" we do not necessarily mean firing a person. They may be transferred to another job or department, for example. The important point to remember is that if new, required tasks are part of the strategic change, then it is important to have in place people who can perform these new behaviors.

Building Support for the Change

The change agent needs to build commitment and a winning coalition to support the change, establish the need for change, and devise and communicate a roadmap to all stakeholders.

Devise and communicate a road map.   The first priority is to devise a roadmap that shows change participants how to achieve the strategic objectives, new behaviors, and new organizational systems that were determined in step one. The roadmap includes a description of the goals of the change process (strategic objectives, new behavior) and the path towards these goals (e.g., skill training to learn the new behaviors) with specific timelines. The road map serves as a starting point, and the change agent updates it throughout the change process.

Establish the need for change.   The change agent needs to ensure top management support or build support for it as necessary. Top management can provide both direction and resources (e.g., funds) and has the power to remove obstacles. More importantly, top management support signals the importance of the change effort. If top management is not on board, neither the change agent nor the target group will be either. The best way for top management to support the change is to be visibly involved by attending and leading meetings and contributing in task forces. The change agent facilitates the involvement of top management and also makes sure that top management has reasonable expectations. Because of its symbolic value, visible top management support is particularly critical in the early phases of the change process. It is preferable that top management announce the launch of the change process.

Demonstrate that past behavior has been costly and cannot be continued.   Put more positively, it means it is essential to convince the target group that learning the new behaviors will lead to benefits such as improved performance for their organization, recognition for them or, possibly, monetary rewards. Learning new behaviors can be stressful and at first glance seems more costly than sticking with old habits. It is imperative that managers convincingly show that, after a suitable adjustment period, survival and success will follow.

Since change is a complex undertaking that involves many different people and possibly different cultures and many different interpretations of the situation, it is usually difficult to convince people of the need to change with just our words or a memo. We encourage you to use as many different media and types of data as possible. In the case of the Swiss-headquartered chemical company we have been using as an example in this chapter, the manager had to demonstrate that the switch from a volume-oriented to a profit-margin-oriented strategy would improve the bottom line of the subsidiaries. The manager showed that the market was saturated and hence increasing sales volumes would be difficult if not impossible. Understanding this relationship between the new marketing strategy and the bottom line, the subsidiary managers were more willing to learn the new customer-service behaviors. In other words, the manager spoke to the subsidiary managers' self-interest and addressed the question of "What's in it for us?" Customer-service behaviors were instrumental in moving prices up, which in turn improved profit margins and ultimately the compensation of the subsidiary managers. Other types of first-hand data could be generated by visiting customers or suppliers, for example.

Obtain commitment.   Next, the change agent needs to obtain commitment from the target group and build a winning coalition. A clearly communicated and a data-driven new strategy will build commitment as will a diligent assessment of the readiness for change. However, it is most important that the target group is involved in the change process.

Involvement breeds ownership of, and commitment to, the change process and to the solutions. Involvement requires skillful leadership, as people may initially resist a change effort. It also takes time and hence, is hardly feasible in crisis-driven change management. As soon as top management has announced the change effort, you can invite and react to the feedback. Input by the change agent and employees who will be involved, in particular with regard to the new behaviors, increases the likelihood of learning and enacting the behaviors.

Maintain participation in the change effort.   The change agent must ensure that the target group stays involved throughout the change process. This involvement has to give the employees a voice through, for example, meetings, suggestion boxes, and one-on-one conversations. An effective change process typically includes joint discussions between the target group, the change agent, and top management. If the change yields negative outcomes for employees, such as job loss, outside facilitators may join the discussions to assist handling potential hostility.

The benefits of involving the target group are obvious. Employees will know more about the change process and their task-related knowledge is relevant in particular for determining new behaviors. As mentioned before, the most important benefit is a sense of ownership. It also becomes easier for this group to convince their peers to join in the change effort.

In obtaining commitment and gaining participation of employees in the change effort, the *mode* of involvement needs to be appropriate to the cultural norms of the situation. But it is equally important that the assessment of the appropriate mode not be based on stereotypes or assumptions derived from partial or inaccurate information. A good example of this occurred in Argentina when Holcim, one of the top global cement companies with headquarters in Switzerland, bought two competing family companies outside of Buenos Aires.[8] Early in the period after the takeover, the training and development head from Switzerland suggested that one way of helping the managers and supervisors in the acquired firms to understand the business model was to run a tailor-made simulation of Holcim operations (called Ecoman). But when the Argentine-born Swiss CEO and his technical director (also Swiss) offered the opportunity, the local company managers and supervisors declined to attend, citing how busy they were. The CEO then decided to invite the union members and senior workers to attend the training.

At first glance this would seem to clash with the hierarchical sensitivities of Latin managers, and both this technical director and other locals warned the CEO against this move "brought in from outside."

But he understood that the union employees were highly motivated to improve operations (there had already been some lay-offs and the very severe Argentine financial crisis had just devastated the economy), and he knew they were well-educated and thoughtful. It turned out that they not only benefited from better understanding the complexities and imperatives of the business operations, but, stimulated by their new knowledge, they started offering suggestions to significantly improve performance. Soon the CEO and his technical director realized that this was a new way of using the simulation, and they attended the closing sessions of all the programs. It wasn't long afterwards that the managers, who were "too busy" earlier, eagerly joined in the development program themselves. Conventional wisdom in international settings isn't always right.

Adopting New Behaviors

The previous process of selection and training should have put in place employees who are able to engage in the new behaviors. Furthermore, the processes of establishing the need for change and obtaining commitment should have built motivation to engage in the new behaviors. The adoption of new behaviors, in most cases, however, is not a one-day event. It is a process with ups and downs that can be smoothed by using such tools as (1) continuous management of resistance, (2) transition devices to remove obstacles and improve employee performance, and (3) ongoing, open, and honest communication of progress.

Continuous Management of Resistance   In the adoption phase, managers continue to manage resistance by eliminating reasons for resisting change. Even within a single change effort, these reasons likely vary among change targets. Five common reasons for resistance – derailers for change – are poor communication, lack of trust, failure to establish the need for change, ignoring change targets' self-interest, and low tolerance for change.

Derailer 1: Poor communication   In anticipatory change and even reactive change, resistance is most likely a result of different interpretations of the company's situation. The challenge is to establish the most accurate interpretation and to educate the employees.

In the case of Minetti, one of the Argentine cement companies acquired by Holcim, the CEO constantly visited the factories in various locations, talking to the workers as well as the managers about the threats from the financial upheaval as well as the opportunities by becoming the industry leader during the turmoil. This constant communication at all levels and in all locations was a critical element in the success of the changes.

Top management must state the problem that the change is designed to solve (e.g., task duplication or customer complaints), the change goal (expected outcome), the relevance of the problem (e.g., solving the problem will improve market share by 10%), and communicate a first draft of the change process, with a timetable. This draft should include concrete opportunities for target group involvement (e.g., feedback tools and timelines) and a timeline for updates by top management or the change agent.

Often, the initiators of a change forget that the target group is not yet on the same page with regard to the problem, change goal, and change process. In addition, the initiators of the change and the change targets may have different cultural backgrounds. Thus, the change agent has to take into consideration the perspectives of various groups of employees with regard to their knowledge of the change and their preferred mode of communication. Remember, this is the *Bridging* (B) part of the MBI model. If managers are not highly skilled or knowledgeable about the local culture, they may benefit from the use of facilitators and cultural mentors.

The communication strategy should include feedback opportunities such as meetings (town hall and small group), surveys, and suggestion boxes. The purpose is to develop a dialogue. Depending on the cultural background, employees will react differently to feedback devices. In the case of the Red Cross children's home in Guyana, employees did not take advantage of the Canadian change agent's open door policy. When, however, she actively sought feedback and offered alternate solutions, employees did not hesitate to offer their opinion.

Despite a communication strategy, employees may misinterpret the messages because they do not listen openly. In that case, managers have likely failed to identify the true reason for employee resistance. In other cases, it may be the managers themselves who have missed or misinterpreted the employees' messages because the manner of delivering the feedback was unfamiliar. For example, indirect feedback through a trusted third party may be the local way of disagreeing upwards, while simultaneously *seeming* to agree when talking directly to a superior. This can be very confusing to a manager from a culture where disagreement is openly and directly expressed, regardless of different status levels of those involved.

Derailer 2: Lack of Trust Employees may not trust managers. There are three primary reasons for lack of trust:

1 Employees harbor doubts about the ability of the managers and change agent to lead the change successfully. Managers and change agents can overcome these doubts only through their actions. This point illustrates the importance of selecting a capable change agent.

2 Employees are concerned whether top management, managers, and the change agent will "walk the talk." Be careful not to make and then break promises. Instead, act predictably. Change is a time of uncertainty and it is important that those who lead the change help people regain a sense of control which results from knowing what to expect.

3 Employees suspect that top management, managers, and the change agent are not entirely forthcoming and complete in their communication. Overcoming this suspicion is handled by interacting frequently with employees. Frequent interactions in most cases result in more open communication and allow for involvement.

Derailer 3: Failure to establish the need for change   As we said earlier, in anticipatory and reactive change efforts, it may be difficult to establish the need for change. The target group may view a change effort through the lens of current or past successes and ask why something should be fixed that is not broken. Success breeds comfort and inertia. It takes considerable dedication to overcome the negative side effects of success. The key tool for doing this is open dialogue:

• Managers and change agents share and explain all the data that convinced them to launch a change initiative.

• Although top management may initially announce the change, subsequently they, the change agents, and the target group listen and provide input.

• Effective dialogue means that the quality of the ideas, not the status of the sender, determines the contribution to the change effort.

An open dialogue fulfills several purposes. First, it clears the air. Open dialogue initially often leads to the release of built-up emotions. Secondly, it creates involvement. Thirdly, it builds understanding of the problem, the change goal, and the change process. Fourthly, it results in shared and hence credible interpretations of the data and the change process.

Open dialogue takes time, something that managers do not have in crisis change. Instead, they must act quickly. It may be tempting to push through with a change process by creating crises. We do not recommend the use of such a tactic, as employees will either call the manager's bluff or the organization will be exposed to unnecessary risks.

Derailer 4: Self-interest   Whether a change serves the self-interest of the target group is a function of the cost and benefits of the new behaviors in which they will have to engage. Different combinations of costs and benefits suggest different courses of action for managers and change agents:

• If it is anticipated that benefits will outweigh costs, change agents may accelerate the change process by fully involving the target group.

• If the target group anticipates only costs and no benefits, they will likely resist the change. Involvement is counterproductive. In the case of downsizing, for example, managers should downsize first and then work with the remaining employees. The morale of the remaining employees will still suffer from the downsizing. Remember, the process of downsizing is important. How it was done and how the employees who were let go were treated will be important to those who remain. It is also important for the remaining employees to have as clear an idea as possible of the extent of downsizing.

The CEO of Minetti and his team treated the people initially laid off in a generous way and were certain that they had gained the trust of those who remained. But as the economic crisis deepened and continued long past their earlier estimates, the benefits to those who had stayed, only to be laid off later, were much diminished by the devaluation of the currency. The emotional distress caused to them, and to the CEO and his team who initially had actively persuaded some key people to stay, was severe. This lesson may be especially appropriate in the circumstances like those encountered in 2008–2009 when each day seemed to bring more bad news without the expected "bottoming out" of the recession.

If the target group expects a balance of benefits and costs, change agents have to allow for negotiations. Change targets will seek to improve the benefits or reduce the costs of the change. It is imperative that managers and change agents do not abuse their power in negotiations. The abuse of power leads to perceptions of unfairness. It alienates both the other party in the negotiation and observers of the negotiation.

Derailer 5: Low tolerance for change   Three common scenarios are:

- A general fear of changes. Bad experiences in the past or a predisposition against changes can lead to resistance.

- A fear of the specific change. There may be fear because of potential negative consequences. Address general and specific fears by being empathetic and demonstrating with a person-centered perspective (*de-centering*) that the change will have benefits.

- Stress because of too many changes. If too many changes take place in the organization, it makes sense to prioritize change initiatives to avoid organization-wide stress. If the stress stems from other changes outside the organization, managers and change agents are limited in their actions.

When employees show a low tolerance for change, managers and change agents have to be sensitive not to step outside their abilities. It can be helpful to seek outside help. As mentioned earlier, in addition to the continuous management of resistance, managers and change agents use transition devices to improve employee performance on new behaviors.

Transition Devices   Other tools to smooth the ups and downs of the adoption of new behaviors are facilitators, task forces, and allocation of additional resources.

Facilitators can play the role of mediators in negotiations among managers, change agents, and the target group. They can also assist in dealing with individual employees.

Finally, facilitators also may be trainers who improve the target group's knowledge, skills, and abilities.

Task forces are effective in dealing with unforeseen obstacles in the change process. Strategic change is a complex endeavor, and more often than not, additional problems are uncovered as the process unfolds. Alternately, task forces can be a forum for negotiations, for example, between management and unions. Task forces typically bring together a small group of managers and employees to solve a specific problem. A clear mandate and timeline help taskforces succeed.

To adopt the new behaviors, employees must not only be motivated and capable; in addition, they need the **resources** to enact the behaviors. In the Swiss-headquartered global chemical company, for example, subsidiary managers needed access to detailed product information to improve their customer service. The research and development division at headquarters had to make this information available.

Ongoing, Open, and Honest Communication about Progress   Change agents need to "showcase" short-term wins but not declare victory too soon.

Showcasing short-term wins   The sharing of short-term wins, even if they are small, will reduce uncertainty. In the Swiss-headquartered global chemical company, while the early overall results of the new strategy were poor, in some subsidiaries local managers quickly enacted the new customer service behaviors and soon observed that many customers willingly paid a higher price for a commodity product (resins). The sharing of this information indicated that the change goal of moving from a volume-based to a profit-margin-based strategy might work. Moreover, sharing this information showed that management had rewarded employees who engaged in the new behaviors. Managers and change agents can plan for small wins by providing interim performance goals.[9]

It is not sufficient only to benchmark behaviors against strategic goals. The results of the benchmarking have to be made public. They will either represent a new need for change (in the case of negative results) or become a reason for a celebration of success. Showcasing successes is critical because employees appreciate being part of a winning team, which in turn increases commitment and breeds self-confidence.

Not declaring victory too soon[10]   As important as it is to showcase small wins, it is equally important not to confuse achieving interim goals with final success. George W. Bush's premature declaration of the end of major combat operations in Iraq signaled by the huge banner behind him stating "Mission Accomplished" during a televised speech from a US Navy aircraft carrier on May 1, 2003 may be the best modern example of the dangers of this point.

Many writers on the subject of change would argue in favor of the "theory of the small win." It is the small, incremental changes that stand the best chances of success.[11]

FIGURE 7.3   Initiating the change

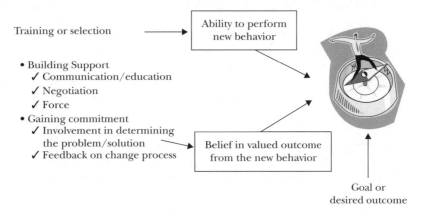

Unless forced by a crisis into making major, system-wide changes, you may be wise to start small and let the change mature and grow. The diffusion of change beyond its initiation depends in large measure on perceived success – continuation of change is fueled by such success and, unless early success is apparent, the chances of realizing your goals are slim.

"Small" wins are not necessarily small but rather they are intermediate changes on the road to a larger strategic change. Keep in mind that they are real and visible success stories that validate your decisions and actions. They build credibility, commitment, and allies, and reduce the power of critics. Our recommendation in planning a change effort is to make sure you have built in some small wins. Figure 7.3 is a summary of Phase 2.

PHASE 3: REINFORCING THE CHANGE

New behaviors are sustainable only if the organization supports and rewards them.

Reward New Behaviors

The first rule is that outcomes you told the target group to expect actually do happen. Recognizing that it is not feasible to control all variables in a change process, this is where the theory of the small win plays an important part. If you design your change plan to incorporate small wins, then you have some control over positive reinforcement that supports the change. Employees will continue to engage in the new behaviors if the rewards (both tangible and intangible) match their expectations. They must see that their behaviors advance the organization's goals and serve their self-interests.

Realign the Organizational Alignment Model

If the existing systems, structures and culture are not aligned with the new required behaviors, managers must adjust them. A new alignment model should be a part of the change goal, but additional modifications may be necessary. For example, as mentioned earlier, in the Swiss-headquartered global company, information systems were put into place to allow the sharing of product information between headquarters and subsidiaries.

This step is critical. Employees respond to signals that systems such as reward and evaluation systems send. It does no good to train employees in new behaviors and then put them back in an organizational system that inhibits these new behaviors.

Benchmark New Behaviors

The new behaviors must contribute to the new strategic goals. Hence, managers and change agents should benchmark the new behaviors against the new strategic goals. In the Swiss-headquartered global company, the manager could benchmark customer service behaviors against profit margin goals. He also could benchmark these behaviors by comparing them to the profit margins of competitors. Figure 7.4 is a summary of Phase 3.

Organizational change efforts are not one-time events. They are processes that require discipline and communication. Skipping a part of the change process can result in failure of the change initiative.[12] The change model focuses on issues that managers have to consider in change efforts. It also suggests actions that they can take. The model, in particular, centers on enabling and motivating employees to engage in the new behaviors.

FIGURE 7.4   Reinforcing the change

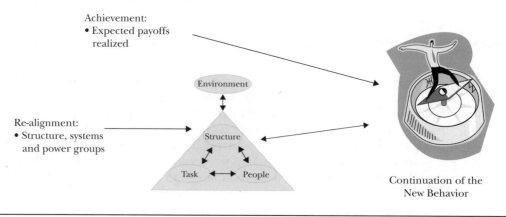

Although the change model suggests a process for completing one change, it should not be interpreted to suggest that change is a one-time effort. It is more meaningful to think about change as a continuous process that can be broken into meaningful phases.

THE CHANGE-READY ORGANIZATION

In Chapter 5, we noted that the role of senior managers was to interpret information from their external environment, combine this with an understanding of the organization's internal strengths and weaknesses, and create alignment to achieve strategic objectives. Organizational scholars traditionally have viewed management models as a means of reducing the variability and increasing the stability of human behavior,[13] and models like total quality management or Six Sigma programs, for example, do that. Global corporations, however, do not operate in stable and predictable environments. The 2008 Global CEO study by IBM characterized it as a frenetic environment – and that the pace of change was increasing.[14] The 2012 study characterized the environment as a "continuous feedback kind of world" requiring an "organizational nimbleness to respond." How were CEOs responding? According to the report:

> They are creating more open and collaborative cultures — encouraging employees to connect, learn from each other and thrive in a world of rapid change. The emphasis on openness is even higher among outperforming organizations — and they have the change-management capabilities to make it happen. As CEOs open up their organizations, they are not inviting chaos. The need for control remains, but it is evolving into a new form — one better suited to the complexity and pace of business today.[15]

In Chapter 6, we pointed out that trying to manage a global company with models and processes designed to reduce variation in an environment that is characterized by dynamic complexity will probably be ineffective or possibly work only in the short term. In responding to dynamic complexity, organizations have to find the right people and to create the appropriate organizational processes for managing the complexity and executing action plans.

Global managers have to develop organizational cultures that create "nimbleness"; cultures that allow for agility, flexibility, and adaptation to changing environmental conditions on the one hand, while fulfilling the traditional task of creating stability and predictability on the other hand.[16]

Below we describe elements of an organizational alignment model for the change-ready organization.

People

Change-ready organizations require change-ready people, and not just at top management levels – people who are motivated to change and who have the knowledge, skills, and abilities to change. With a cadre of change-ready people it is easier to develop a culture of embracing change.

Motivation   The motivation to embrace change may be hard to train. Hence, change-ready organizations assess the change attitudes of job applicants. Westjet Airlines, a Canadian airline, for example, looks for people who seek involvement, are generally positive, have a high tolerance for change, and want to learn.

Knowledge, Skills, and Abilities   Organizations that are change-ready either have change agents who can assume numerous roles throughout the change process or have the ability to involve a set of people who can assume at least one of the roles. Lawrence and his colleagues found that change-ready organizations had four types of change-ready people: evangelists, autocrats, architects, and educators.[17]

Evangelists share ideas and create conditions for employee involvement in change efforts. They are skillful communicators, use diverse influence strategies, and can present messages from different perspectives. Carlos Ghosn, the Chairman and CEO of Renault/Nissan, emphasized the role of communication in managing the French-Japanese merger of Renault and Nissan. When asked about communication, he stated that he communicated 24 hours a day adhering to the notion that "(1) you say what you think, (2) you do what you think, (3) you make sure that it is understood, and (4) you accept that you are going to be measured on what you communicated."

Autocrats are critical for the translation of good ideas into action. Top management support is a critical ingredient for successful change efforts. Although employee involvement is the key to lasting change, the prudent use of authority is needed to move along change processes. Autocrats endorse change ideas and accept accountability. Their key skill lies in understanding when change efforts need a push toward action. At McDonald's Mexico, the Mexican managers and employees were uncertain about the prospects of offering a breakfast menu. The Canadian CEO took a risk and obtained the funds for rebuilding the kitchens. The Mexican managers and employees then moved forward with the breakfast project, which became a solid contributor to revenues.

Architects embed the change into systems and structures by realigning the organization and creating a new organizational alignment model. They make sure that the systems support the new employee behaviors through, for example, information systems or through a redesign of work spaces. Their key skill is a deep understanding of how the organization functions.

Finally, *educators* strive to implant the organizational change into the fabric of the organization. They present data that the new employee behaviors help the organization achieve its strategic objectives. In doing so, they show employees the meaning of their contribution to organizational success and seek to reenergize them for future change efforts.

Tasks

In traditional stable organizations, employees have clearly specified tasks. In change-ready organizations, core tasks are more fluid. Employees engage in the following behaviors to support the change readiness of their organization.

Stay in Touch with the Environment   Organizations that embrace change continuously scan their environment. The early detection of environmental shifts facilitates anticipatory change and possibly results in first mover advantages. The tasks of most if not all employees include contact with the environment, particularly customers. Other contact points include suppliers, members of the surrounding community, and law-makers. IBM, for example, has largely abandoned the separation of the customer contact and design of information technology solutions. Instead, most members of a customer-focused team are in contact with the customer.

Share and Acquire Information   Employees actively search for and share information. Information about environmental shifts is quickly spread throughout the organization. Information acquisition and sharing is particularly important in global organizations because different subsidiaries might have experience in dealing with similar environmental shifts. When the Canadian CEO of McDonald's Mexico led the subsidiary through the 1994 Peso devaluation crisis, he contacted his Brazilian colleague. The Brazilian subsidiary had already experienced a currency devaluation and his colleague recommended that McDonald's Mexico should immediately increase its prices because the government would likely move to freeze prices. The CEO of McDonald's Mexico followed that advice, and indeed shortly thereafter the Mexican government froze the prices.

Seek Involvement   The Change Model suggests that employee involvement is the most powerful means of obtaining commitment to change because it breeds a sense of ownership. In change-ready organizations employees seek out change opportunities. They involve themselves and do not have to be asked to be involved. In these organizations, job descriptions that narrowly define tasks are antithetical. Instead employees look to increase task scope as necessary. Hence, compared to traditional, stable organizations, the responsibility for determining tasks and task scope lies more with the employees than simply with the organizational model.

Continuously Develop Knowledge and Skills   In organizations that are ready to change, learning and training are not occasional events but ongoing activities. Training can help build change management skills and a future-directed orientation. It occurs both systematically and on an ad hoc basis.

Structure

The organization enables people to accomplish their tasks. Without getting into too much detail, we provide examples of the structures and systems in change-ready organizations.

The larger organizations become, the more difficult it is for them to react to environmental changes. Change-ready organizations break their structures into smaller units and push accountability down the line. The result is dispersed leadership that needs to be reconnected through integration mechanisms. Common examples of accountable units are cross-functional teams that address the demands of internal and external customers. Change-ready organizations not only tolerate, but encourage informal structures. Informal structures and networks accelerate the dissemination of information, and they can make up for deficiencies in formal structures. For example, in customer-centric structures, informal networks among product engineers serve as an integration mechanism across products.

Systems

Change-ready organizations use systems that connect their employees with each other and the organization. For example, Procter and Gamble's intranet includes a feature that allows employees to share their ideas for product improvement and new products. The globally-operating consulting firm Accenture uses social networking technologies to connect its 180 000 employees.

For example, take reward systems. Traditionally organizations have paid employees (and most organizations still do so) on the basis of their jobs. Instead of job-based pay, change-ready organizations use person-based pay. Person-based pay recognizes that in change-ready organizations, job descriptions are largely moot, as employees' core tasks may continuously change.[18] Instead, periodic goal-setting meetings and subsequent goal achievement determine person-based pay.

CHANGE IS A CONSTANT

When the IBM study compared the financial performance of the companies in its sample, it found that the change gap, the difference between expected change and the history of successful change, was smaller not because they faced fewer challenges but because they anticipated more changes. The study concluded that "outperformers are simply more successful at managing change."[19]

Changing an organization is easier said than done. Strategic changes of the type we have discussed involve people and the tasks they perform. In our opinion there probably is no such thing as "immaculate" strategic change in which the organization transforms itself without requiring some employees to change their behavior in some way. Organizations do not change, people do, but we can be lulled into thinking about organizational change too remotely and impersonally. Therefore, it is important to remember that *change means behavioral change*. People in key roles have to change their behavior, which is a function of their beliefs, assumptions, perceptions, tasks, and roles; the tasks and roles are reinforced by evaluation, measurement, and reward systems. These do not change easily or quickly. To accomplish strategic change, managers have to work with individuals and groups of people as well as structures, systems, and practices.

Change can be a challenge in any culture, but when trying to make changes in a global company in multiple countries, the challenge can be compounded by different cultural understandings. The MBI (Chapter 3), organizational alignment (Chapter 5), and change models are tools that will give you greater confidence to negotiate the challenges.

Notes

1   Spector, B., Lane, H. W. and Shaughnessy, D., "Developing Innovation Transfer Capacity in a Cross-National Firm: The Challenge of International Organizational Change," *Journal of Applied Behavioral Science* 45(2) (June 2009).

2   Kashani, K., "Alto Chemicals Europe (AR1)," IMD case IMD-5-0484, 2008.

3   Most three-stage models of organizational change like the one we present in this chapter trace their conceptual lineage back to Kurt Lewin. His article "Frontiers in Group Dynamics: Concept, Method and Reality in Social Science; Social Equilibria and Social Change" was published in *Human Relations,* 1(1) (1947). This article presented a three-stage model (unfreeze, move, refreeze) as well as the concepts of constancy and resistance to change, social fields, force fields, and group decisions as a change procedure. Al Mikalachki built on and modified Lewin's work in his development of a model for thinking about and managing organizational change. Mikalachki's complete model was first outlined in Mikalachki, A. M., *Managing organizational change,* unpublished manuscript, Richard Ivey School of Business. University of Western Ontario, 1997. It also appeared in Mikalachki, A. and Gandz, J., *Managing Absenteeism* (London: University of Western Ontario, School of Business Administration, 1980). We are appreciative to Al for his work and support in our teaching at the Western Business School (now Ivey) and want to recognize clearly the intellectual lineage of these ideas about change and the model.

4   Dietz, J., Goffin, M. and Marr, A., "Red Cross Children's Home: Building Capabilities in Guyana (A)," Ivey case 9B02C042, 2002.

5   Morrison, A. and Black, S., "Black & Decker-Eastern Hemisphere and the ADP Initiative (A)," Ivey case 98G005, 1998.

6   For a good, succinct discussion of this topic see Paul Strebel, "The Politics of Change," *IMD Perspectives for Managers,* 2 (February 1997).

7   Mikalachki, n. 3 above.

8   See DiStefano, J. and Ogunsulire, M., "Merging Two Acquisitions: How Minetti Built a High-Performance, Cohesive Organization" (A & B), IMD cases 3-1484 and 3-1485).

9 Kotter, J., "Leading Change," *Harvard Business Review* (March-April 1995).

10 Ibid.

11 Quinn, J. B., "Managing Strategic Change," *MIT Sloan Management Review* (Summer 1980).

12 "Leading Change," n. 9 above.

13 Katz, D. and Kahn, R. L., *The Social Psychology of Organizations* (Hoboken, NJ: John Wiley & Sons, 1978).

14 *The Enterprise of the Future* (IBM, 2008).

15 *Leading Through Connections* (IBM, 2012); p. 4. This report surveyed 1700 CEOs in 18 industries in 64 countries.

16 Worley, C. G. and Lawler, E. E., "Designing organizations that are built to change," *MIT Sloan Management Review* 48(1) (2006) 19–23.

17 Lawrence, T. B., Dyck, B., Maitlis, S. and Mauws, M. K., "The underlying structure of continuous change," *MIT Sloan Management Review* 47(4) (2006) 59–66.

18 Worley and Lawler (2006), n. 16 above.

19 *The Enterprise of the Future*, n. 14 above.

PART 4

CHAPTER **8**

Competing with Integrity in Global Business: Personal Integrity

OVERVIEW

In earlier chapters we discussed how culture affects behavior including its potential impact on strategy and operations. Now, we will examine the issues of personal ethical behavior that you, as managers, may face in your careers. We highlight personal integrity in this chapter because we believe that issues of individual responsibility and ethics do not always receive the attention that they deserve in business courses.

The objective is to challenge you to consider your responsibilities as a business leader more broadly than simply from a financial perspective. There can be social consequences resulting from your decisions as well as financial ones. The human and social impacts of decisions should be considered at the time these decisions are being made. And it is not just the consequences to some faceless group of people in some faraway land that you need to consider. There can be personal consequences to you as well from your decisions.

Following the global mindset framework presented in the beginning of this book (see Table 8.1), we will now consider these issues at the individual level (ethical behavior) in this chapter and at the organizational level (corporate sustainability) in Chapter 9. What is the difference between ethical behavior and corporate sustainability? A possible distinction is that between the decisions and behavior of an individual or a small group of people, and a formal initiative of an organization. It is not a neat dividing line however. There is clearly an overlap in some situations particularly, for example, when certain products (e.g. cigarettes) and monitoring human rights in the supply chain are

TABLE 8.1 Global mindset framework applied to ethics and corporate sustainability

	Individual/Personal	*Organizational*
Self	Clarify and understand my beliefs about ethical behavior.	Clarify and understand my organization's approach to corporate sustainability.
Other	Clarify and understand other beliefs about ethical behavior in the context of other cultures and principal theories of moral philosophy.	Clarify and understand other corporate approaches to sustainability in the context of other industries, other cultures and principal codes of conduct.
Choice	Belief in and commitment to a set of ethical principles.	Belief in and commitment to an approach to corporate sustainability.

involved. Corporate sustainability decisions and programs may involve potential ethical considerations. However, if there are no clear guidelines it is left to each executive to make a decision for him or herself. As companies develop sustainability initiatives and define their approach to corporate sustainability more clearly, the resulting guidelines provide employees with counsel regarding their behavior and decisions about social (people), environmental (planet) and business (profit) tradeoffs.

In this chapter we will explore the distinction between ethical and legal behavior as well as the differences in major ethical frameworks or theories of moral philosophy such as consequential (results focused), rules-based (universal), and cultural relativism. We hope that these discussions of competing with integrity, personal and corporate, help you develop your own way of thinking about competing with integrity.

What is integrity? As Professor Glen Rowe from the Ivey Business School so simply, practically and managerially describes it, "Integrity is *consistency* among what you *believe* in your heart; *think* in your head; what you *say* with your mouth; and what you *do* – your behavior and actions."[1]

De George suggests that executives should act and compete with integrity in international business.[2]

Acting with integrity is the same as acting ethically, but the word integrity does not have the negative connotation, the moralizing tone, or the sense of naïveté that the word "ethics" carries for many people. According to De George: "Acting with integrity means both acting in accordance with one's highest self-accepted norms of behavior and imposing on oneself the norms demanded by ethics and morality."[3]

Competing with integrity means that corporate executives should compete in a way that is consistent with their own highest values and norms of behavior. Although these values and norms are self-imposed and self-accepted, they cannot be simply arbitrary and self-serving; but neither is there a requirement to be perfect. "The imperative to act with integrity cannot insist on moral perfection. It can and does demand taking ethical considerations seriously."[4]

ETHICAL ISSUES

The least clear aspect of managerial responsibility may be in the domain of ethics, which is the "moral thinking and analysis by corporate decision makers regarding the motives and consequences of their decisions and actions."[5] Ethics is the study of morals and systems of morality, or principles of conduct. The study of ethics is concerned with the right or wrong and the "should" or "should not" of human decisions and actions. This does not mean that all questions of right and wrong are ethical issues, however. There is right and wrong associated with rules of etiquette – for example, in which hand to hold your knife and fork, in the use of language and rules of grammar, and in making a computer work. Holding a fork in the wrong hand or speaking ungrammatically does not constitute unethical behavior.

The ethical or moral frame of reference is concerned with human behavior in society and with the relationships, duties, and obligations between people, groups, and organizations. It is concerned with the human consequences associated with decisions and actions, consequences not fully addressed in the pursuit of profits, more sophisticated technology, and larger market share. In this concern for human outcomes, it differs from other perspectives such as financial, marketing, accounting, or legal. An ethical perspective requires that you extend consideration beyond your own self-interest (or that of your company) to consider the interests of a wider community of stakeholders, including employees, customers, suppliers, the general public, and even foreign governments. It also advocates behaving according to what would be considered better or higher standards of conduct, not necessarily the minimum acceptable by law.

Not all problems come neatly labeled. Ethical decisions do not necessarily arise separately from strategy, finance, marketing, or operating decisions, for example, because problems in the real world do not come with neat labels attached: here is a finance problem; here is a marketing problem; and now, an ethical problem. Managers may categorize the issues by functional area or break up a complex problem into components such as those mentioned. Usually policy issues and decisions are multifaceted and simultaneously may have financial, marketing, and production components. They may also have ethical dimensions that managers should consider. However, in considering a typical complex problem with more than one dimension, the ethical dimension may be overlooked as managers focus on the finance or marketing issues for example.

If situations did come with labels on them, a person could apply the techniques and concepts he or she had learned, such as net present value to a financial problem, or market segmentation to a marketing problem. What would happen if a problem labeled "ethical dilemma" arrived? A manager would, more than likely, be in a quandary because he or she most likely would not have a way of analyzing, let alone resolving, this type of problem.

The decision-making tools for this type of situation would probably be lacking. Business schools, traditionally, have not emphasized the teaching of ethics as rigorously as they have the teaching of finance or marketing, for example. Business students and managers generally have not been trained to think about ethical issues as they have been trained in the frameworks and techniques for functional areas of specialization.

However, after numerous scandals in the United States (e.g. Enron, Tyco, WorldCom) and in Europe (e.g. Parmalat in Italy), this has changed as business schools moved to address the issue of managerial ethics.

Some Examples

Over the years, there have been many examples of ethical lapses by executives from many companies and many nations. Some examples included Xerox which in 2002 admitted that its subsidiary in India had made "improper payments" to win government contracts over a period of years;[6] the Norwegian state-run oil group, Statoil, which was involved in a bribery scandal with Iran in 2003; in 2007 Chiquita Brands International, the banana company, pleaded guilty to making $1.7 million in illegal "protection" payments from 1997 to 2004 to *Autodefensas Unidas de Colombia* (AUC) or the United Self-Defense Forces of Colombia, a right-wing paramilitary group.[7]

Unfortunately, executives apparently have not gotten the message and learned from others' mistakes and similar transgressions have continued. In 2010, BAE Systems pleaded guilty to making false statements and accounting practices in a corruption and bribery scandal related to arms deals in Saudi Arabia and Africa.[8] A culture of bribery developed in Siemens over the years.[9] It was a way of doing business and until 1998, under German law, it was not illegal. Peter Solmssen, who is a managing board member and general counsel of Siemens explained:

> It was largely a failure of leadership. It seems employees believed that they had to pay bribes in order to get business.[10]

In 2008, Siemens pleaded guilty to violating the Foreign Corrupt Practices Act (FCPA) and agreed to a fine of $1.6 billion to American and European authorities,[11] a *New York Times* article said:

> Officials said that Siemens, beginning in the mid-1990s, used bribes and kickbacks to foreign officials to secure government contracts for projects like a national identity card project in Argentina, mass transit work in Venezuela, a nationwide cellphone network in Bangladesh and a United Nations oil-for-food program in Iraq under Saddam Hussein.
>
> 'Their actions were not an anomaly,' said Joseph Persichini Jr., the head of the Washington office of the Federal Bureau of Investigation. 'They were standard operating procedures for corporate executives who viewed bribery as a business strategy.'[12]

In 2012 a bribery scandal in Mexico involving Wal-Mart hit the first page of the business section of the *New York Times*.[13,14] An executive of the company in Mexico allegedly paid $52,000 to have a zoning map redrawn of the area around the Teotihuacan pyramids so that it could build a store where one would not have been previously permitted and this, apparently, was not the first instance of such behavior.

Ethical questions can arise in many areas of a business: the type of products produced, marketing and advertising practices, business conduct in countries where physical security is a problem, requests for illegal payments to secure contracts or sales, and protection payments to prevent damage to plants and equipment or injury to employees. Some products are controversial in themselves, such as tobacco or the abortion pill, since they facilitate behavior that some people would consider unethical. Other products such as jeans or rugs may not create dilemmas for the end user, but their production may raise ethical questions.

HUMAN RIGHTS AND SECURITY EXAMPLES

Nigeria   Human rights and fundamental freedoms were issues in Nigeria in November 1995 when Ken Saro-Wiwa was executed by the military government. In 1994, General Sani Abacha had declared the death penalty for "anyone who interferes with the government's efforts to 'revitalize' the oil industry."[15] The declaration was his response to striking oil workers and demands for increased revenue sharing by local communities. Saro-Wiwa was a political activist who was campaigning on behalf of his people, the Ogoni, and against the degradation of the environment by oil spills and pollution caused by Royal Dutch Shell.[16] In 1995, Saro-Wiwa's activities were construed as "interference" and he was executed by the Nigerian government.

Initially, Shell responded defensively with full-page advertisements in major newspapers around the world explaining its position.[17] Later, under pressure from shareholders who filed a resolution at its annual meeting in 1997, it changed the tone of its response dramatically. It named Cor Herkströter, at the time chairman of Royal Dutch (the Dutch half of the company), to be responsible for human rights and environmental issues. Mr Herkströter accepted the criticism that Nigeria Shell should have been more proactive in improving its environmental performance.[18] He also conducted a review of the company's business principles and added commitments to support human rights and sustainable development.

Since 2000, Shell has been actively translating this commitment into practice.[19] The company has conducted intensive training in countries where it operates that have poor human rights records. For example, with the Danish Institute for Human Rights, Shell has trained more than 5900 staff and contractors in Nigeria since 2005 in managing difficult situations, like responding to conflict in local communities.

It also created a training aid, *Human Rights Dilemmas: A Training Supplement*,[20] that provides help in developing competence in managing human rights issues and a series of human rights dilemmas/incidents to help managers understand their responsibilities regarding human rights. It also developed a risk assessment tool to analyze the human rights risks associated with entering or operating in politically sensitive areas. And it became a participant in a new initiative to support human rights, the Voluntary Principles on Security and Human Rights.

The Voluntary Principles on Security and Human Rights were developed through a dialogue among the governments of the US, the UK, the Netherlands, and Norway, companies in the extractive and energy sectors, and nongovernmental organizations (NGOs). All had an interest in human rights and drafted a set of voluntary principles to "guide companies in maintaining the safety and security of their operations within an operating framework that ensures respect for human rights and fundamental freedoms."[21]

Employee Security   Situations in which the physical security of managers could be a problem may present ethical issues for managers and employees. Consider a situation in which British expatriate women working in the Middle East training center of a North American-based bank found themselves. They were en route to conduct a training program in Lagos, Nigeria, and were supposed to be met by one of the bank's local staff who would assist them through difficulties in customs at the airport. When the local staff member failed to appear, the women felt forced to pay bribes to bring legitimate training materials and equipment into the country. Soon after paying the money, their taxi was stopped at the darkened perimeter of the airport and machine guns were jabbed at them through the windows by uniformed men. The women were "shaken down" again and felt very vulnerable, particularly with no foreign currency left. After repeatedly showing their documents and denying that they were violating any laws, they were finally permitted to pass. The women were deeply shaken by the experience and vowed never to travel into that country alone again.[a]

What responsibility did the local management bear for abandoning them? And what was the ethical responsibility of the experienced managers for whom the women worked who sent them into such a situation so ill-prepared? What is a manager's responsibility regarding the implementation of his or her decisions, particularly when the specific action has to be taken by another person?

Unfortunately, in recent years the world has become a more dangerous place and situations in which physical security is a managerial concern are becoming more common for global companies. As we were writing the previous edition of this book, a sophisticated, well-planned and coordinated, large-scale terrorist attack had just ended in Mumbai, India that left more than 170 people dead. A group called Deccan Mujahideen claimed responsibility for the attack and it was learned they had received training from Lashkar-e-Taiba, a group fighting to bring "independence" to Muslims in

[a]One of the previous authors of this text was involved in this training program for this bank which is how he knew about the situation. One of the current authors is involved in a training program for a European based company and has learned that travel to and in Lagos for its executives remains a security concern in 2013. This company has developed elaborate safety procedures for its executives travelling there.

the Indian Kashmir. An American, David Headley, who admitted to helping plan the attack, was sentenced in January 2013 to 35 years in prison.[22] News reports at the time suggested that they were apparently searching for and targeting foreigners, although many more Indians died in the attack than did foreigners. *Business Week* reported that the CEO of Unilever "narrowly escaped death in the massacre at the Taj Mahal hotel where he was dining with colleagues."[23]

Many companies currently are operating in countries where personal security concerns are considerations and/or where political violence and terrorism are issues. On March 11, 2004, terrorists bombed a train in Madrid, killing 191 people and injuring 2000 others.[b] In late May 2004, terrorists killed 22 people in oil company office compounds and in an expatriate housing compound in Saudi Arabia and took over 40 hostages, including Americans and Europeans, while earlier in the month terrorists killed six Westerners and a Saudi in another attack. In India, executives of the Korean company POSCO were kidnapped.[24] In January 2013, terrorists seized an Algerian gas field for four days until the Algerian army liberated it and killed over 30 terrorists. In the process, however, more than 20 hostages from a number of countries were killed by the terrorists.

Piracy   Instances of piracy off the coast of Somalia increased dramatically in the late 2000s and reached a high around 2009. It decreased substantially in 2012 when only 297 ships were attacked compared to 439 in 2011.[25] Although attacks off the coast of Somalia decreased, attacks off West and East Africa increased. On February 3, 2013, a French tanker and its crew were hijacked off the coast of Abidjan, Ivory Coast in what was seen as a new development for that area.[26] It was released a few days later, presumably after its owners paid a ransom. How and why the ship was released was not explained by its owners.

Globally, 174 ships were boarded by pirates in 2012, while 28 were hijacked and 28 were fired upon. The number of hostages taken fell to 585 from 802 in 2011. An additional 26 were kidnapped for ransom in Nigeria. Six crewmembers were killed and 32 were injured or assaulted.[27] It is estimated that the attacks cost the industry and governments $6.9 billion in 2011.[28] There are numerous reasons for the reduction in hijackings including the development of best practices and improved defence measures; use of armed guards by shipping companies; and increased attention to the problem by multiple navies. However, the problem has not disappeared and remains a concern for shipping companies and governments.[29]

The Maersk Alabama was hijacked on April 7, 2009.[30] During the fight, the crew captured the pirate leader and locked themselves in the engine room. They disabled the bridge controls and were able to operate the ship from the engine room. The tanker's captain, Richard Phillips, who had stayed on the bridge, surrendered to the pirates in exchange for his crew's safety. The pirates took Phillips into one of the ship's lifeboats,

[b] A Northeastern University business school exchange student was in Madrid and on his way to the Atocha train station when the bombing took place.

tried to exchange him for their compatriot and later attempted to reach Somalia with Captain Phillips.

On April 9, the American destroyer USS Bainbridge arrived and took control of the situation. The USS Halyburton also arrived and escorted the cargo ship into harbor in Mombasa, Kenya. For days there was a standoff between the pirate-controlled lifeboat and the USS Bainbridge. On Sunday, April 12, the captain of the USS Bainbridge determined that Captain Phillips' life was in immediate danger and ordered a rescue operation. US Navy SEAL snipers on board the Bainbridge shot and killed the three pirates remaining on the lifeboat.

It may be tempting for you to say that the examples above come from industries that you won't be working in. However, you don't have to be working for a global engineering company, a global shipping company, a global oil company or other extractive industry companies that work in difficult areas. You could be a banking, consumer goods executive or consultant in Lagos, Mumbai or Madrid visiting on business.

Where is future company growth going to come from? The answer most likely is from emerging markets. What is a company's ethical responsibility associated with assigning an employee to one of these countries? What should it do regarding training and security for employees who work in difficult areas? What is the responsibility of individuals who agree to work there? Global companies are still looking for ways to grow and new markets to enter.

Managing in difficult markets   Emerging markets are the fastest growing markets and represent about 70% of the world's population. According to Goldman Sachs:

> Emerging market economies have been growing at an annual rate of nearly 11% over the past 10 years, compared to only 5% in developed markets . . . Nowhere has this trend been more apparent than in BRIC nations – Brazil, Russia, India and China – four powerhouses whose combined Gross Domestic Product (GDP) could surpass that of the G7 nations by 2032 . . .[31]

Most likely the reader already has some familiarity about the economic reality of the BRIC countries. But have you heard about the "CIVETS" and the "Next 11"?[32] The Chief Economist at Goldman Sachs, Jim O'Neil, coined the acronym BRIC and has since identified 11 more countries as future major economies. These are Indonesia, Vietnam, Egypt, Turkey, Mexico, South Korea, Bangladesh, Iran, Pakistan, Nigeria, Philippines; with Mexico, Indonesia, South Korea and Turkey being the most promising. The Economist Intelligence Unit identified a different set of economies, the "CIVETS" which are Colombia, Indonesia, Vietnam, Egypt, Turkey and South Africa.

The authors do not have an opinion about which of those countries are the likely economic powerhouses of the future but we do know that they can be difficult places in which to work. The Fund for Peace has created an interactive Failed States Index[33] which can be found on its website. All of the countries listed above fall into a "Warning" category with the exception of South Korea which is rated as "Stable." If these are the countries where growth is likely to come from, what are companies doing to attract, train and manage executives who are able to function effectively, and safely, there?

Bribery and Corruption Examples

Other dilemmas that executives may encounter are requests for bribes or even extortion. For example, mobsters threatened Otis Elevator that they would firebomb its operation in Russia if it did not pay protection money.[34] How should this situation be handled? Otis had a code delineating its view of right and wrong behavior that all executives sign each year. Its response was not to give in to the extortion, but to pay more for security.[35] The Otis example took place in the early 1990s but according to Fey and Shekshnia, writing almost a decade later, corruption is omnipresent in Russia.[36] They counsel that managers need to understand their own ethical standards and the reality and risks they face is good advice.

Another example was Statoil (now Statoil ASA). Operating in Norway's harsh waters demanded a high level of innovation, which helped Statoil to become one of the world's foremost authorities in offshore production. By the end of the century, Statoil faced declining reserves at home and sought to expand through international investment. In 2001, the National Iranian Oil Company (NIOC) sought tenders to develop South Pars, an offshore oil field that held approximately 8% of known world gas reserves, and 40% of Iran's known reserves. In October 2002, NIOC awarded Statoil a 40% stake in the South Pars project. Under the terms of the agreement, Statoil was to invest $300 million over four years as part of its $2.6 billion investment in the Persian Gulf.[37]

Less than one year after being awarded the contract, Statoil's future in Iran appeared to be in jeopardy. The controversy centered on alleged bribes paid by Horton Investments, on Statoil's behalf, in order to secure lucrative petroleum development contracts.

In early 2003, Statoil's internal auditors had uncovered secret payments of $5 million to Horton Investments,[38] a Turks and Caicos Islands registered consultancy thought to be run by the son of a former Iranian president. According to Statoil, Horton Investments was hired to provide "insight into financial, industrial, legal, and social issues associated with business development in Iran."[39] But the Iranian government said that the secret $15 million contract between Horton and Statoil was used to channel bribes to unnamed government officials.

According to the company's web site, Statoil settled with the United States, accepted a fine of US $10.5 million for violating the US Foreign Corrupt Practices Act, and accepted responsibility for the bribery, as well as for accounting for those payments improperly; and for having insufficient internal controls to prevent the payments. The company also paid a fine of US $3 million to Norway for violation of Norway's law.[40]

The Foreign Corrupt Practices Act[41]

In 1977, the United States Congress passed into law the Foreign Corrupt Practices Act (FCPA) in response to investigations that discovered that over 400 US companies had made questionable or illegal payments to foreign government officials, politicians, and political parties for a range of reasons, from facilitating payments to get low-level government officials to just do their jobs, to payments to high officials to secure favorable decisions. Twenty years later, the United States and 33 other countries signed the OECD Convention on Combating Bribery of Foreign Public Officials in International Business Transactions.

Under the FCPA it is illegal for US citizens as well as foreign companies with securities listed in the United States to make a payment to a foreign official to obtain business for or with, or directing business to, any person or company. Since 1998, the rules also apply to foreign firms and persons while in the United States. The Act does contain an exception for "facilitating payments" for "routine governmental actions."

The law also requires companies whose securities are listed in the United States to make and keep records that accurately reflect the transactions of the corporation and to maintain an adequate system of internal accounting controls. It is this part of the Act to which companies that have been caught making improper payments usually plead guilty and pay a fine, rather than plead guilty to the act of bribery.

Bribery and corruption are global problems that are not limited to public officials in a few developing countries. Executives of global corporations headquartered in developed countries are affected, and some have even been implicated in scandals. Global executives should not be smug about assuming that the locus of the problem is elsewhere. There is an old saying, "It takes two to tango."

An organization that has been established to combat the problem of bribery and corruption is Transparency International.

Transparency International[42]   Since 1993 when it was founded, Transparency International (TI) has become the leading NGO combating national and international corruption. TI has developed chapters in approximately 90 countries and has worked with organizations like the OECD, the Organization of American States (OAS), the European Union, and the African Union to develop and monitor anti-corruption legislation and treaties. It analyzes corruption by measuring its occurrence through surveys, and it has created resources and tools used by people around the world in the fight against corruption.

These tools include the Corruption Perceptions Index, Global Corruption Barometer, Global Corruption Report, Bribe Payers Index, and the latest anti-corruption information on TI's web site. TI's Bribe Payers Index (BPI) evaluates the likelihood of firms from the world's 28 largest economies to bribe.[43] Companies from the wealthiest countries generally rank in the top half of the Index, but still routinely pay bribes, and TI saw no improvement from its previous report in 2008 and its latest report in 2011. There is no country that is entirely clean. The Netherlands and Switzerland are the "cleanest" and Mexico, China and Russia are at the bottom of the list.

The Corruption Perception Index[44] ranks 176 countries by their perceived levels of corruption, as determined by expert assessments and opinion surveys. The score ranges between 100 (highly clean) and 0 (highly corrupt). The 10 countries that scored the highest (highly clean) on the 2012 Index were Denmark, New Zealand, Sweden, Finland, Singapore, Switzerland, the Netherlands, Norway, Australia, and Canada. The United Kingdom was tied for seventeenth place with Japan and the United States was nineteenth. Over two-thirds of the countries had scores of lower than 50 indicating serious corruption problems. The countries that scored the lowest (highly corrupt) were Somalia, Sudan, Afghanistan, North Korea and Myanmar.

Product Examples with Ethical issues

Cigarettes According to the Center for Disease Control (CDC) tobacco use causes more deaths than all those combined from HIV, illegal drug use, alcohol use, motor vehicle injuries, suicides, and murders.[45] On average, cigarette smokers die 14 years sooner than nonsmokers and also, it "is estimated that 25 million people currently alive will die prematurely from illnesses related to smoking." And it is not just the smokers who will die. Secondhand smoke kills approximately 50 000 people in the United States annually from lung cancer and heart disease.[46]

The World Health Organization (WHO) claims that six million people annually die from tobacco use including 600 000 from secondhand smoke and that "tobacco use is a risk factor for six of the eight leading causes of deaths in the world."[47] Moreover, WHO states:

> Tragically, the epidemic is shifting towards the developing world, where more than 80% of tobacco-related deaths will occur within a few decades. The shift is caused by a global tobacco industry marketing strategy that targets young people and adults in developing countries. In addition, because most women currently do not use tobacco, the tobacco industry aggressively reaches out to them to tap into this potential new market.

Tobacco use is the leading preventable cause of death in the world. At the current rate, the death toll is projected to reach more than 8 million annually by 2030 and a total of up to one billion deaths in the twenty-first century. WHO notes that "no other consumer product is as dangerous, or kills as many people, as tobacco" and that "tobacco is the only legally available consumer product which kills people when it is used entirely as intended."[48]

The problems associated with smoking are well known now, including disease, deaths, and economic costs. On May 21, 2003, the 192 Member States of WHO adopted the world's first public health treaty, the WHO Framework Convention on Tobacco Control (FCTC). This treaty was designed to reduce tobacco-related deaths and disease around the world. Before it could go into effect, however, countries had to sign and ratify it. Among its measures, the FCTC requires that countries impose restrictions on tobacco advertising, sponsorship, and promotion; and establish new packaging and labeling of tobacco products. Achieving agreement on the FCTC was not easy, and according to a former assistant surgeon general the eventual treaty was significantly "watered down" in large measure due to the actions of the Bush (George W.) Administration.[49]

In a letter to President George W. Bush on April 29, 2003, Democratic Representative Henry Waxman, the ranking minority member of the House Committee on Government Reform, said:

> At the most recent, and final, negotiating session, held from February 17 to February 28, 2003, the United States again attempted to weaken the tobacco control treaty on key issues. Indeed, your negotiators even opposed international efforts to restrict the distribution of free samples and to prohibit the sale of tobacco products to children.[50]

The US, Canada, and Germany all opposed a total advertising ban claiming that their constitutions protect freedom of speech and do not permit them to implement a comprehensive ban. NGOs proposed the adoption of a "constitutional carve out" that allowed the FCTC to have a full ban on tobacco advertising, except for countries whose constitutions would not allow for a full ban.[51]

Does freedom of speech cover cigarette advertising? Are trade and choice more important than public health? Even if there are US Constitutional issues involving tobacco advertising bans, should the United States try to prevent other nations from banning tobacco advertising if it is permitted by their own legal systems?

In 2003, the Government Accounting Office (GAO) found that the Foreign Agricultural Service may have violated Congress' prohibition on the US Department of Agriculture from spending any funds to promote the sale or export of tobacco products.[52] Should one part of the US government spend money to combat smoking in the United States while other parts are spending it to promote cigarette exports to other countries? One side could argue that countries like the United States, Britain, and Japan, where the majority of big tobacco companies are located, are exporting death and disease to the developing world. The other side could counter that cigarettes are not illegal, are manufactured and sold in many countries, and, therefore, manufacturers would not be introducing these items for the first time. They would argue that since manufacturing and selling cigarettes is not illegal, international tobacco companies should have access to the developing world's markets.

At a company level, what obligations should a corporation have regarding advertising in other countries? Should Phillip Morris have a kiosk outside a school in Indonesia or violate the law in Pakistan because, as the executive who was found guilty explained, he didn't believe placing ads in magazines was the same as putting them in the "press."[53]

Should the company follow the local laws, even if they are less restrictive than at home, or would there be a responsibility to advertise that cigarette smoking is hazardous to your health and include all warnings required in the United States or elsewhere, if they are stricter? Should they oppose large warning sizes because they may "infringe" on their trademarks on the packages?

All the issues regarding exporting and advertising cigarettes could be treated simply as considerations in international trade, marketing, or advertising, if one chose. Advertising cigarettes in other countries could also be treated as primarily a legal question, as the US and German governments apparently saw it. Is treating complex situations and decisions that involve harmful consequences to humans primarily as trade, marketing, or legal issues without addressing the ethical implications, a mistake and unethical?

Toys   In August 2007, Mattel recalled almost 20 million toys made in China. On August 2, the company recalled 1.5 million toys because of a fear that hazardous levels of lead paint had been used on them. This recall came shortly after recalls involving toothpaste, tires, and pet food ingredients imported from China. Consumers in the United States and the US government were extremely concerned and there was a popular sentiment developing against dangerous products "made in China." On August 13, Zhang Shuhong, owner of the Lida Toy Company, hanged himself in his factory.

On August 14, Mattel recalled 18 million more toys made in China because they contained small, powerful magnets that could come loose and potentially be swallowed by small children, possibly causing them serious harm – in fact at least three children needed surgery after swallowing them.[54] This was obviously another "made in China" problem. Or was it?

China pushed back and it came to light that all the problems were not Chinese ones. On August 21, Thomas A. Debrowski, executive vice president for Mattel's worldwide operations, apologized to China's product safety chief, Li Changjiang. Mattel had said that many of the toys were recalled because of design problems. It also had blamed some vendors in China for violating Mattel's rules by failing to use safe paint or to run tests on paint. Mattel, in Debrowski's apology, accepted blame for its part in the problem which was that the "vast majority of those products that were recalled were the result of a design flaw in Mattel's design, not through a manufacturing flaw in China's manufacturers."[55]

In a study of the toy recall issue, *Toy Recalls – Is China Really the Problem?* authors Bapuji and Beamish state:

. . . an examination of the reasons for the increase [in toy recalls] shows that the number of defects related to design issues attributable to the company ordering the toys is far higher than those caused by manufacturing problems in China.[56]

Regarding its recall of toys for lead paint, had Mattel failed to act responsibly in its oversight of a supplier? Was the company adequately supervising its foreign vendors? In its recall of the defectively designed toys and its associated press releases, was Mattel trying to blame China for a known company failure and to shift the locus of responsibility or was it taking the blame to help a supplier save face and maybe protect itself from some form of Chinese retaliation? Was the company acting ethically?

Labor and Employment Practices Examples

The previous examples had public health considerations including, in the case of Mattel, supervision of foreign contractors. There are potential ethical issues in managing supply chains that don't involve public health such as with products like jeans and rugs when they are manufactured by or purchased from contractors that abuse human rights.

Clothing   Levi Strauss stopped purchasing from subcontractors in Myanmar and China because of practices such as using child and prison labor to manufacture products.[57] In 1991, the company developed a set of standards which address workplace issues for its partners and subcontractors, and the selection of countries for sourcing products. It was the first apparel company to establish a comprehensive ethical code of conduct for manufacturing and finishing contractors. The company's terms of engagement (TOE) are based on standards set by the United Nations (particularly the Universal Declaration of Human Rights) and include ethical standards, legal requirements, environmental requirements, and community involvement; and specifically address issues of child labor, forced labor, disciplinary practices, working hours, wages and benefits, freedom of association, discrimination, and health and safety.[58]

Its original path-breaking TOE was based on a philosophy of compliance and "do no harm." In 2012 the company decided that compliance, monitoring and reporting progress were not sufficient to really make a difference in the lives of the suppliers' workers and their communities, so the company pioneered a new development-oriented approach focusing on five areas: economic empowerment; health and family well-being; equality and acceptance; education and professional development; and access to a safe and healthy environment.[59]

In cooperation with Ceres, Levi Strauss & Co. engaged its stakeholders in evaluating its plan. Ceres is an advocacy organization for sustainability comprised of a coalition of more than 130 organizations, companies, investors, social and environmental advocacy groups and NGOs.[60] Moving from simply passive reporting to active community involvement and development represents a major shift in corporate thinking and approach to sustainability.

Rugs In the 1980s, attention was drawn to the illegal use of child labor in the hand-woven rug industry by the International Labor Organization (ILO), the US Department of Labor, and human rights groups. In 1994, the RugMark Foundation was established by Kailash Satyarthi with a coalition of nongovernmental organizations, businesses, government entities, and multilateral groups like UNICEF to combat child labor.[61] The first carpets bearing the RugMark label were exported from India at the beginning of 1995, mainly to Germany. Later countries promoting the RugMark label grew to include England, the United States, Canada and Nepal. When RugMark began it was estimated that there were 1 million child workers exploited by the handwoven rug industry in South Asia and now the estimate is 250 000. To date, more than eight million carpets bearing the GoodWeave/RugMark label have been sold in Europe and North America.[62] RugMark is now called GoodWeave.

What is a company's responsibility toward ensuring that its suppliers are not using child labor? Some people would argue that children are better suited to making rugs because of their greater dexterity than adults and that their families, who need the money, would be worse off if the children were not working. Opponents, however, point out that many of the children were found to be victims of debt bondage or forced labor, practices banned by the United Nations and condemned as modern forms of slavery.

Is participating in GoodWeave the only way to counter child labor? Is it ever acceptable to use child labor? Ethical issues, by definition, are never simple. The issue about manufacturing rugs is not as simple as "do not use child labor." We spoke at length with a small business owner who exports rugs from Pakistan and Afghanistan. She visits her manufacturers regularly and encourages community development around the making of rugs. There were many girls as young as eight years who were working in her craft shops:

> If I did not hire these girls, they would not be in school. They would be in the fields. Their life expectancy would be shorter; they would be working alone. In the workshop, they sit together with women of three or more generations, they learn a skill, and they learn about their culture. Because they are in my workshop, I can provide good meals and people and materials to provide at least some education and social support for them. Am I doing the right thing? According to the press and many consumers, definitely not! But I do believe that, in this case, hiring these girls and trying to provide a better environment for them is the right thing.

IKEA also recognizes that child labor abuses exist in countries where its products are manufactured, but it has created its own program to prevent child labor based on the United Nations Convention on the Rights of the Child (1989). It also has a Children's Ombudsman and a code of conduct called "The IKEA Way on Preventing Child Labour" including unannounced visits by an auditor at suppliers and subcontractors. In addition, it now supports a project to eliminate child labor by addressing its root causes such as lack of education, debt, and poverty.[63] The following incident experienced by a group from IKEA touring factories in India illustrates the complexity of the issue.

Some time ago, our team went out to India to monitor how things were happening in the field. The team's host, the owner of a local factory, was taking them to see conditions there. They were in his car, and suddenly he stopped, jumped out of the car and went to talk to a young boy, who was hanging out on the side of the road with some other kids.

When the factory owner returned, he explained: 'That kid used to work in our factory. Now, because of IKEA's strict policies prohibiting child labor, we let him go and he's on the streets selling drugs.' This was a real 'aha' moment for the group, when they decided to go beyond child labor to address the root causes of child labor.[64]

One could ask the question about whether or not the factory owner was living up to his responsibility to children.

Although IKEA appears to have addressed the child labor issue responsibly, it has recently issued apologies for some of its suppliers having used forced prison labor in East Germany in the 1980s[65] and for removing images of women from its catalogs sent to Saudi Arabia.[66] In the former instance the company was criticized for not monitoring its supplier network two decades earlier and in the latter case for its "medieval" approach to gender inequality.[67]

The IKEA examples clearly illustrate that operating globally is complicated and as soon as one issue dies down another appears to take its place.

Responding to Ethical Problems

How might managers respond when they encounter ethical problems such as the examples that we have just seen or work in countries where corruption is rampant and where they may encounter requests for bribes? One of the first things they may do is avoid the ethical dilemma through the process of rationalization. They may focus on some other aspect of the problem. They may transform the ethical problem into a legal or accounting problem, for instance. The reasoning seems to be that, so long as one is behaving legally or in accordance with accepted accounting practices, for example, nothing else is required. As will be discussed later, compliance with laws and professional regulations is a minimum requirement for responsible managers.

Another kind of avoidance behavior is to see the problem as only one small piece of a larger puzzle and to assume that someone higher up in the organization must be looking after any unusual aspects, such as ethical considerations. Alternatively, the decision-maker might turn it into someone else's problem – perhaps a customer, supplier, or person in higher authority – with the comment: "I am following my boss's orders" or "my customer's instructions." When a customer asks for a falsified invoice on imported goods for his or her records with the difference deposited in a foreign bank, and you provide this "service," is it only the customer's behavior that is questionable?

Rationalizing one's behavior by transforming an ethical problem into another type of problem, or assuming responsibility for only one specific, technical component of the issue, or claiming that it is someone else's problem, gives one the feeling of being absolved from culpability by putting the burden of responsibility elsewhere.

Who is responsible for ensuring that managers act ethically? We believe that corporations have a responsibility to make clear to their employees what sort of behavior is expected of them. This means that executives in headquarters have a responsibility, not just for their own behavior, but also for providing guidance to subordinates. A number of companies have corporate codes to do just this. For example, General Electric (GE) has an integrity policy entitled, "The Spirit & Letter" that covers, among other issues, ethical business practices, health, safety, and environmental protection, and equal employment opportunity and is considered a "non-negotiable expectation of behavior." Employees sign a pledge that they will adhere to the policy. Jeffrey Immelt, CEO of GE, in his introduction to this policy, wrote:

> For more than 125 years, GE has demonstrated an unwavering commitment to performance with integrity . . . This reputation has never been stronger. In several surveys of CEOs, GE has been named the world's most respected and admired company. We have been ranked first for integrity and governance.

> But none of that matters if each of us does not make the right decisions and take the right actions. At a time when many people are more cynical than ever about business, GE must seek to earn this high level of trust every day, employee by employee.

> This is why I ask each person in the GE community to make a personal commitment to follow our Code of Conduct. This set of GE policies on key integrity issues guides us in upholding our ethical commitment. All GE employees must comply not only with the letter of these policies, but also their spirit.

> If you have a question or concern about what is proper conduct for you or anyone else, promptly raise the issue with your manager, a GE ombudsperson or through one of the many other channels the Company makes available to you. Do not allow anything – not "making the numbers," competitive instincts or even a direct order from a superior – to compromise your commitment to integrity.

> GE leaders are also responsible not only for their own actions but for fostering a culture in which compliance with GE policy and applicable law is at the core of business-specific activities. Leaders must address employees' concerns about appropriate conduct promptly and with care and respect.

> There is no conflict between excellent financial performance and high standards of governance and compliance – in fact, the two are mutually reinforcing. As we focus on becoming the preeminent growth company of the 21st century, we must recognize that only one kind of performance will maintain our reputation, increase our customers' confidence in us and our products and services, and enable us to continue to grow, and that is performance with integrity.[68]

Although a company has a responsibility to outline what behavior it expects from an employee, the person on the spot facing the decision is ultimately responsible for his or her own behavior, with or without guidance from headquarters. However, an issue that global executives need to consider carefully is whether or not codes of conduct are effective. Donaldson found that effective codes of conduct meet three criteria:[69]

1   Senior management has to be committed to ethical behavior and the codes of conduct; and the codes have to affect "everyday decisions and actions."

2   External or "imposed" codes are not generally effective. Companies have to develop their own and take ownership of their codes.

3   Various important stakeholders (employees, customers, suppliers, nongovernmental organizations) have to be involved in shaping the development and implementation of the codes.

In the cases or stories that you read, develop your own stance on the issues. We encourage you to think carefully about the problems to develop reasoned positions. You may find yourself in a similar situation someday, and you will have to make a critical decision. By working through the decisions in such cases and stories now, you will be better able to deal with similar decisions later.

As we personally encountered ethical dilemmas and heard about others who had experienced them, we wrote cases and developed a managerial framework for thinking about and analyzing the problems. We make no claim that the framework to be presented is a complete or definitive treatment of the topic of ethics. We think it does provide a practical and managerial way to think about the topic.

Ethical versus Legal Behavior

A question always arises as to the distinction between legal and ethical behavior. If one acts legally, in accordance with laws, is that not sufficient? Not all of society's norms regarding moral behavior have been codified or made into law. There can, therefore, be many instances of questionable behavior that are not illegal.[70] It would seem that acting legally is the minimum required behavior for executives. However, society relies on more than laws to function effectively in many spheres of endeavor. In business, trust is essential also. Finally, it should also be recognized that not all laws are moral; an example would be apartheid in South Africa, which was legal but clearly not moral.

Henderson has provided a useful way to think about the relationship between ethical and legal behavior.[71] He created a matrix based on whether an action was legal or illegal and ethical or unethical, similar to that shown in Table 8.2. Assuming that executives want to act legally and ethically (quadrant 4) and avoid making decisions (or acting in ways) that are illegal and unethical (quadrant 2), the decisions that create dilemmas are the ones that fall into quadrants 1 and 3.

TABLE 8.2 Framework for classifying behavior

	Illegal	*Legal*
Ethical	1	4
Unethical	2	3

For example, consider the decision of a chemical company manager who refuses to promote a pregnant woman to an area of the company where she would be exposed to toxic chemicals that could damage her child. In the United States or Canada the manager would probably be acting ethically, but illegally (quadrant 1). Maybe the manager could solve the problem by delaying the promotion, if that was possible. This simple example illustrates that a decision can be ethical but not legal; there may also be solutions that allow a win-win outcome in which the decision is legal and ethical because of the way it is made. What about laws prohibiting same-sex marriage and the unequal treatment of women in some countries, are those legal but unethical?

In quadrant 3, there will be situations like the marketing of infant formula in developing countries. Infant formula, which was misused in many countries with poor sanitation and polluted water and where people were illiterate and could not read directions, was blamed for the deaths of hundreds of thousands of babies each year. This activity was not illegal, but the United Nations considered it unethical[72] and criticized companies for unethical marketing practices.[73] In an interesting twist to this story, studies now have shown that the AIDS virus can be transmitted through breastfeeding and the UN has estimated that one-third of all infants with HIV got it through their mother's milk.[74] Infant formula may now be a way to combat the transmission of HIV. This example also points out that society's notions of ethical behavior may change with the times, and with new conditions and knowledge.

Examples of legal but unethical behavior could include not closely monitoring a global supply chain and manufacturing and selling cigarettes that kill through normal use.

An historical example in quadrant 3 would be apartheid in South Africa. This raises the question about whose laws and values should be followed when there are conflicts. Although it might seem that we are avoiding answers, we believe that these are questions each person and company need to answer for themselves. The challenge is to find ways of operating that are consistent with local laws and high standards of conduct. We believe that this goal is attainable with thorough analysis and carefully considered action. In those situations where such a win-win outcome is not possible, there is always the option of choosing not to operate in that environment.

The decision to walk away and lose the business may seem naïve, but we have met and interviewed a number of executives of very successful companies that have done just that. One described how his company turned down a $50 million contract in a Latin

American country because there was no way to avoid paying a bribe to a government official. Another explained that, in his experience, if a company developed a reputation for acting ethically, it was not usually subjected to unethical demands.

Each person has to make his or her own decision and live with the consequences of his or her actions. The information in the following sections is designed to help you in the decision-making process.

ETHICAL FRAMEWORKS[75]

Moral philosophers have developed frameworks for thinking about moral issues and for analyzing ethical problems, but these frameworks generally have not been included in international business curricula. There are various frameworks for analyzing ethical problems and there are conflicting positions and prescriptions among them. In classes we have observed that people advocate actions representing some of the major frameworks, but without understanding the foundations or the strengths and weaknesses of their positions. Consider the following discussion.

> Person X: "If we don't pay what he is asking we will lose the contract and people back home will lose jobs. Is that ethical when people can't feed their families?"

> Person Y: "I don't care. What you are suggesting is absolutely wrong."

> Person Z: "Now hold on, it doesn't seem to be against the rules there. It is different in that culture. Everyone is doing it. They need the extra money to support their families. Besides, we should not impose our system of morality on other cultures."

You may have heard or have taken part in similar exchanges. The people in the conversation above may not realize it, but they are engaged in a discussion of moral philosophy. However, it is the type of discussion that tends to excite emotions and generate heat and argument, rather than provide insight and a thoughtful course of action.

Since you may likely take part in similar discussions (or arguments) at some time in your career, we think that knowledge of these three frameworks will be useful. The intent is to help you link some everyday reasoning and the positions you might espouse to the ethical frameworks underlying them. In the brief exchange above, one sees elements of Kant's categorical imperative, utilitarianism, and cultural relativism. These are commonly invoked frameworks, which is why they were chosen. Each represents a different moral calculus, a different ethical map.

The main categories of ethical theories can be divided into: consequential (or teleological) theories, which focus on the consequences, outcomes, or results of decisions and behavior; rule-based (or deontological) theories, which focus on moral obligations, duties, and rights; and cultural theories, which emphasize cultural differences in standards of behavior. These are discussed briefly here.

Consequential Theories

Consequential theories focus on the goals, end results, and/or consequences of decisions and actions. They are concerned with doing the maximum amount of "good" and the minimum amount of "harm." Utilitarianism is the most widely used example of this type of moral framework. It suggests doing the best for the greatest number of people. Another example is acting in a way that provides more net utility than an alternative act. It is essentially an economic, cost-benefit approach to ethical decision-making. If the benefits outweigh the costs, then that course of action is indicated.

The limitations of this approach are that it is difficult or impossible to identify and account for all the costs and benefits, and, since people have different utility curves, it is difficult to decide whose curve should be used. In real life, how do you compute this utility curve? Finally, in an effort to weigh the costs and benefits, one relies on quantitative data, usually economic data, and many important variables that should be considered are not quantifiable and, therefore, are often ignored.

Rule-based Theories

Rule-based theories include both absolute (or universal) theories and conditional theories. The emphasis of these theories is on duty, obligations, and rights. For example, if an employee follows orders or performs a certain task, management has an obligation to ensure that the task is not illegal or harmful to that person's health. People in power have a responsibility to protect the rights of the less powerful. These theories are concerned with the universal shoulds and oughts of human existence – the rules that should guide all people's decision-making and behavior wherever they are.

One of the best-known absolute theories is the categorical imperative of Immanuel Kant. Whereas utilitarianism takes a group or societal perspective, the categorical imperative has a more individualistic focus: individuals should be treated with respect and dignity as an end in itself; they should not be used simply as a means to an end. A person should not be done harm, even if the ultimate end is good. The criteria should be applied consistently to everyone. One of the questions to ask is: "If I were in the other person's (or group's or organization's) position, would I be willing for them to make the same decision that I am going to make, for the same reasons?"

A variation on absolute theories is fundamentalism. In this case, the rules may come from a book like the Bible, Koran, or Torah. In these systems, one is dealing with an authoritative, divine wisdom that has been revealed through prophets. Difficult questions arise when considering which book or prophet to follow and whose interpretation of the chosen book to use. Priests, mullahs, or rabbis who may reflect the views of an elite segment of society, or possibly an isolated group, usually interpret the books. There can be conflicting interpretations within the same religion as well. Also, the interpretations may be inconsistent with current social and environmental circumstances, as well as with the beliefs of large segments of a society. The rules that people follow can also be secular as well as religious, as was the case in Nazi Germany.

One shortcoming of these types of prescriptions is that they allow you to claim that you are not responsible for your own behavior: "I was just following orders" is a common excuse. The end result may be the same – you do not have to think for yourself or make a moral judgment, but rather you can avoid it by claiming to be following a higher authority. However, the war crimes trials after World War II established that following orders is not an acceptable legal defense for committing atrocities.

Cultural Theories

With cultural theories, local standards prevail. Cultural relativism is interpreted to mean that there is no single right way; in other words, people should not impose their values and standards on others. The reasoning behind the argument is usually that we should behave as the locals behave. The familiar expression tells us: "When in Rome, do as the Romans do." One problem, however, comes from the fact that the local people we are encouraged to emulate, may not necessarily be the most exemplary. In your own culture, you know that people exhibit different standards of behavior. Does that mean we should advocate that business people coming to the United States act like the people convicted in the accounting scandal at Enron, for example, just because those people were Americans? Or should expatriate managers working in Italy follow the example set by Parmalat executives, because they were Italians? Adopting this philosophy also can encourage denial of accountability and the avoidance of moral choice. Using arguments based on this philosophy, the morality of bribes or actions of repressive regimes, for example, do not have to be examined very closely. These theories are summarized in Figure 8.1.

Perry has described a perspective that provides more insight into relativism arguments that managers may find useful – a process of intellectual and ethical development.[76] Although we should recognize that Perry's ideas reflect a cultural bias towards individualism and were derived from a narrow part of the US population, his ideas can help managers think about their positions on this issue.[77] The first category is dualism, in which a bipolar structure of the world is assumed or taken for granted. According to this perspective there is a clear right and wrong, good and bad, we and they. These positions are defined from one's own perspective based on membership in a group and belief in or adherence to a common set of traditional beliefs.

The next category, posited by Perry as a "more developed" perspective, is relativism, in which the dualistic world view is moderated by an understanding of the importance of context, which helps a person to see that knowledge and values are relative. As we have seen through earlier parts of this book, different people in different parts of the world think and believe differently, and a relativistic mode of making ethical judgments

FIGURE 8.1 Analytical frameworks

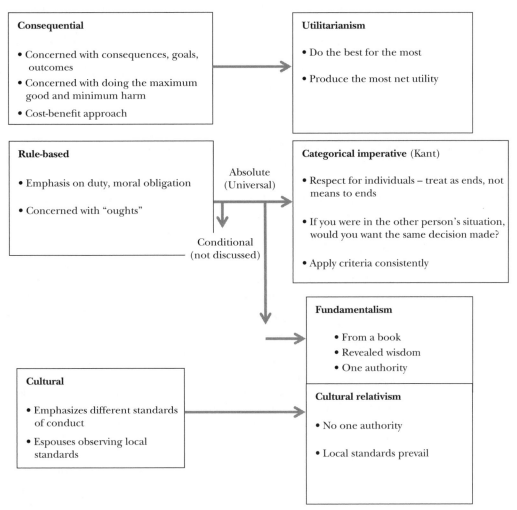

recognizes this fact. As originally observed by Blaise Pascal, Hofstede notes in the preface to his book, *Culture's Consequences*: "There are truths on this side of the Pyrénées which are falsehoods on the other."[78]

In Perry's scheme, the third category is commitment in relativism, in which a person understands the relativistic nature of the world but makes a commitment to a set of values, beliefs, and a way of behaving within this expanded world view. The goal is to arrive at the point where you assume responsibility for your own actions and decisions based upon careful consideration and the application of the "essential tools of moral reasoning – deliberation and justification."[79]

Our inclusion of Perry's ideas is not meant to judge others' choices in this regard, but rather to encourage self-awareness and recognition that simple, cultural relativism is not the highest end point of moral development. Underlying our perspective throughout this book are (1) the assumption that you are interested in developing a relativistic understanding of the world, and (2) the encouragement for you to decide about your own commitments within this relativistic framework. We understand that voicing this position is a reflection of our own values.

Universalism, Relativism, and the "Asian Values" Debate

The previous brief discussion of different theories in moral philosophy provides a context for understanding the underlying ethical positions of what has been termed the "Asian values" debate. At one level it is the age-old debate in moral philosophy about universalism versus relativism. Is there a universal set of rules that should be followed or are morals and ethics all relative depending on the culture? Are one culture's beliefs, values, and practices superior and preferable to those of another? Whose laws, values, or ethics should be followed if and when a disagreement develops, a different course of action is proposed, or a conflict arises? This theoretical debate became more tangible when it turned into an international debate about human rights and economic growth.

In 1948, the United Nations' Universal Declaration of Human Rights was signed.[80] Since that time, there have been discussions and disagreements over which of the human rights specified in its 30 Articles are universal and which are culturally influenced. China, long criticized by the West for human rights violations, issued a White Paper on Human Rights in China in November 1991. Although it "endorsed the language of human rights and praised the development of the international human rights regime . . . [it] argue[d] that the specific contents of human rights vary with 'differences in historical background, social system, cultural tradition, and economic development.'"[81] This proclamation of cultural sovereignty was followed by other pronouncements made by quasi-political bodies and prominent Asian leaders.

In 1993, the Bangkok Declaration was signed by more than 30 Asian and Middle Eastern countries. It presented the view that universal human rights represented statements of Western values and that they were at odds with "Asian values" and not applicable to Asia. This theme was later reiterated by notable Asian leaders.

The imposition of Western values as a form of "cultural imperialism" was alleged by Singapore's Lee Kuan Yew in 1994, when he stated: "It is not my business to tell people what's wrong with their system. It is my business to tell people not to foist their system indiscriminately on societies in which it will not work."[82] In this interview he described some of the differentiators that he saw between East and West:

> The fundamental difference between Western concepts of society and government and East Asian concepts – when I say East Asians, I mean Korea, Japan, China, Vietnam, as distinct

from Southeast Asia, which is a mix between the Sinic and the Indian, though Indian culture also emphasizes similar values – is that Eastern societies believe that the individual exists in the context of his family. He is not pristine and separate. The family is part of the extended family, and then friends and the wider society.[83]

Lee also commented on American society from his viewpoint as an East Asian. While admiring parts of the American system he was critical of other parts:

As an East Asian looking at America, I find attractive and unattractive features.

I like, for example, the free, easy and open relations between people regardless of social status, ethnicity or religion. And the things that I have always admired about America, as against the communist system, I still do: a certain openness in argument about what is good or bad for society; the accountability of public officials; none of the secrecy and terror that's part and parcel of communist government.

But as a total system, I find parts of it totally unacceptable: guns, drugs, violent crime, vagrancy, unbecoming behavior in public – in sum the breakdown of civil society. The expansion of the right of the individual to behave or misbehave as he pleases has come at the expense of orderly society. In the East the main object is to have a well-ordered society so that everybody can have maximum enjoyment of his freedoms. This freedom can only exist in an ordered state and not in a natural state of contention and anarchy.[84]

In 1996 at the 29th International General Meeting of the Pacific Basin Economic Council, Tun Dr. Mahathir bin Mohamad, Prime Minister of Malaysia, continued to defend cultural relativism when he said that there was a belief among many in the West that their values and beliefs were universal and he was concerned about the imposition of the Western values of liberal democracy.[85] Later in 2000, echoing Lee, he said that too much democracy could lead to violence, instability, and anarchy; and that the West was using ideals such as democracy and human rights as tools to recolonize parts of Asia.[86]

In the remarks of Lee and Mahathir one can see the primary values that are in conflict in this debate.

- The East values community and family (collectivism) while the West values the individual. In the East, responsibility towards family and community takes precedence over individual interests and privileges. In the East, people have duties and obligations while in the West they have rights.

- The East values order and harmony while the West values personal freedom, individual initiative, and competition. In the East the values of order and harmony are reflected in respect for age, leaders, persons of authority, hierarchy, and institutions. In the West the values of personal freedom, individual initiative and competition are reflected in democracy, the rights of individuals, and capitalism.

- The West believes in universalism, while the East practices particularism. Universalism emphasizes rules, laws, and generalizations, while particularism emphasizes exceptions, circumstances, and relations. Particularism is often expressed in the East in practices like *guanxi* (the use of interpersonal relationships) in China, which can also be interpreted from a Western perspective as corruption or bribery.

The ethical debate between East and West was later extended from human rights to economic development. In addition to using "Asian values" as the justification for sacrificing political and civil freedoms to maintain social stability, some Asian governments have argued that since not all Asian countries are as economically developed as the West, they cannot be expected to uphold all of the rights in the Universal Declaration. Some have claimed that "Asian values" are supportive of "paternalistic authoritarianism" (such as practiced in Singapore and Malaysia), which has fostered economic development and provided economic security for their people. However, these same values were also cited by Western observers who said they supported "crony capitalism" and contributed to the Asian financial crisis in 1997–1998,[87] while still other observers say these values contributed to the region's quick recovery.[88]

In light of the global financial crisis that occurred in 2008, there is sufficient reason to remind us to be careful about pointing the finger of "crony capitalism" in the direction of the East. It was more than simple greed that led to the unraveling of subprime mortgages and the worldwide consequences that followed. In a 2012 op-ed article in the Wall Street Journal, a Republican, a Democrat and an Independent used that exact term to describe the behavior of politicians in Washington DC.[89]

Encouragement of and cooperation in unwise and perhaps illegal actions could easily be described by the same label of "crony capitalism" that was used to blame the Asian countries for the crisis of 15 years ago. We need to be reminded that a most critical part of the MBI model described in Chapter 3 is "decentering without blame."

Not everyone in Asia agrees and although some Asian political leaders and academics see "Asian values" as different from, and as an alternative to, Western cultural beliefs, others are critical of the way that the idea of special "Asian values" is often invoked.

Asia is not a monolithic, homogeneous area. Critics dismiss the idea that a common set of distinctively Asian principles exists, given Asia's immense cultural, religious, and political diversity. There are regional differences between East, Southeast, and South Asia, and these nations have highly varying historical and religious backgrounds, such as Hindu, Muslim, Confucian, Shinto, and Buddhist.

Critics argue the debate is not so much about cultural values but about maintaining political power and an excuse for autocratic governments that suppress individual rights and dissidents. Human Rights Watch and Amnesty International called China's White Paper a "whitewash."[90]

Not all Asians believe that human rights are an artifact of solely the Western culture. Some of those who disagree with the proponents of the "Asian values" thesis include Nobel Laureate Amartya Sen who has said:

> What about the specialness of "Asian values," about which so much is now being said by the authorities in a number of East Asian countries? These arguments . . . dispute the importance of human rights and press freedoms in Asian countries. The resistance to Western hegemony – a perfectly respectable cause in itself – takes the form, under this interpretation, of justifying the suppression of journalistic freedoms and the violations of elementary political and civil rights on the grounds of the alleged unimportance of these freedoms in the hierarchy of what are claimed to be "Asian values."[91]

The former president of Singapore, Devan Nair has stated, "Human rights and values are universal by any standard, and their violation anywhere is a grievous offence to men and women everywhere."[92] Aung San Suu Kyi, Burmese democracy advocate and winner of the 1991 Nobel Peace Prize, has said:

> Too often we have to try to explain that human rights – which of course include political, civil, social, economic rights – are not a particularly western idea. Human rights are relevant to all human beings. Those who wish to deny us certain political rights try to convince us that these are not Asian values. They try to make us content with what they are prepared to give us.

> When I say "they," I'm referring to authoritarian regimes. Authoritarian regimes all over the world share this desire to convince their people that they don't know what is best for them. That the people do not know what is best for them, but governments do. This is something that we cannot accept.[93]

Some academics have commented that "terms such as 'Asian values' are misleading,"[94] and some have gone so far as to say that "academic moral theory is useless,"[95] and the "Asian values" debate lends credence to that view since the debate does not lead to actionable decision criteria without embracing the beliefs of one side or the other.

There does not seem to be any way to cut through the debate to arrive at the "truth." One is left with either having to impose one's beliefs and values on the other through coercion, or by the conflicting parties agreeing to disagree.[96] Integrative Social Contracts Theory may help find a path forward.

Integrative Social Contracts Theory: A Way to Avoid Ethical Paralysis?[97]

We think that it is important for managers to be able to recognize the basis for their moral and ethical decisions and to be aware, for example, if they are shifting from one theory to another as a way of avoiding tough decisions. However, global executives must make decisions and take action, and they do not have the luxury of simply debating the issue. How do they decide? How does he or she choose among mutually conflicting moral theories?

There is no simple answer to this question. First, the MBI model from earlier in the book can be applied using these frameworks as components of the map (M) portion of the model. If you are dealing with people who use a different moral calculus, Maps (M) of the different moral philosophies provide the basis for the Bridging (B) and

Integration (I) components of the MBI model to communicate across the differences and to manage them.

Another approach for resolving conflicting ethical viewpoints is Integrative Social Contracts Theory (ISCT) developed by Donaldson and Dunfee.[98] We believe that ISCT is a useful approach to resolving conflicting ethical alternatives when making decisions and determining a course of action. However, before showing how one would apply this theory, it is helpful to put it in context with the other theories previously discussed. On a continuum of extreme relativism at one end and extreme universalism at the other end, ISCT is a pluralistic theory and probably is closer to the relativism end of the continuum as shown and described in Table 8.3.

ISCT essentially says that local communities and cultures can determine ethical norms for members of that society but that these norms must be based on the rights of individual members to exercise "voice" and "exit."[99] However, to be legitimate, these local norms or principles must be compatible with macro-level norms, "hypernorms," which are universal precepts. If there is a conflict, the hypernorms take priority.[100]

The challenge, therefore, is to know if a principle has hypernorm status. Donaldson and Dunfee offer 11 types of evidence that support the existence of hypernorm status.[101] The more types of supportive evidence, the stronger the case for hypernorm status.

1 Widespread consensus that the principle is universal.

2 Component of well-known global industry standards.

3 Supported by prominent non-governmental organizations (NGOs) such as the International Labor Organization or Transparency International.

4 Supported by regional governmental organizations such as the EU, OECD, or OAS.

5 Consistently referred to as a global ethical standard by the global media.

6 Known to be consistent with precepts of major religions.

7 Supported by global business organizations such as the International Chamber of Commerce or the Caux Round Table.[102]

8 Known to be consistent with the precepts of major philosophies.

9 Generally supported by a relevant international community of professionals such as accountants or engineers.

10 Known to be consistent with the findings of universal human values.

11 Supported by the laws of many different nations.

One such set of hypernorms would be the Universal Declaration of Human Rights, which can be found at the United Nations web site: http://www.un.org/Overview/rights.html

TABLE 8.3   Integrative Social Contracts Theory

Theory	Position
Extreme relativism	No ethical view, regardless of source or basis, is better than any other.
Cultural relativism	No ethical view held by one culture is better than any other view held by another culture.
ISCT (Pluralism)	There exist a broad range of ethical viewpoints that may be chosen by communities and cultures. The possibility exists that conflicting ethical positions in different communities are equally valid. There are, however, circumstances in which the viewpoint of a particular culture will be invalid due either to a universally binding moral precept or to the priority of the view of another culture or community.
Modified universalism	There exists a set of precepts expressible in many different ethical languages that reflects universally binding moral precepts and that captures many issues of global ethical significance. These precepts rule out the possibility of two conflicting ethical positions in different cultures being equally valid.
Extreme universalism	There exists a single set of precepts expressed only in a single ethical language that reflects universally binding moral precepts and that captures all issues of global ethical significance. These precepts rule out the possibility of two conflicting ethical positions in different cultures being equally valid.

Thomas Donaldson and Thomas W. Dunfee, *Ties That Bind*, Harvard Business School Press, Boston, MA; © 1999 by Harvard Business Publishing; p. 23. All rights reserved.

COMPETING WITH INTEGRITY

Managers have multiple interests that they must consider because they are embedded in a complex network of relationships. The interests, goals, and values of the various actors in any situation can potentially conflict. Identifying these relationships helps in structuring an analysis. To assist in analysis and to promote rational discussion of ethical dilemmas, a series of diagnostic questions and some recommendations are presented below that we hope can serve as a guide for you in the future.

Some Guidelines to Consider

Prepare for Ethical Dilemmas

1 Develop relationships, but with care.

   To the extent possible, enter into strong, trust-based relationships with customers and suppliers. With these relationships you will be able to assess the impact of requests that your contacts make and explain the reason for behaving the way you do. With strong relationships, your stakeholders are more likely to trust your actions, and less likely to push you into behaviors you believe are unethical or irresponsible.

Enter into dependent relationships with care. If you increase dependency on a particular customer or supplier, be certain about the relationship and make certain you retain enough power to maintain your standards.

Don't wait until you are in a crisis situation to reach out to important industry, community, regulatory, and possibly religious groups in a country. Build relationships and social capital with multiple stakeholders as early as possible to enhance your reputation and develop support so as to increase your leverage to follow your own standards if the need arises.

2   Get the best information possible.

Take the time to get the facts – all of them. Avoid fuzzy thinking. Avoid using or being swayed by hearsay or unsubstantiated assertions. These are statements that have no specifics to go with them: "Everybody is doing it," "We'll lose business if we don't do it," or "It's a normal practice." When you hear statements like these, push for the analysis and details. Often, you may find that they are unsubstantiated assertions parading as analysis.

Identify the Impact on Stakeholders

1   Identify all stakeholders.

Remember that a company has multiple groups of stakeholders in addition to the investors in the business, and executives need to be clear about their responsibilities and obligations to all these groups. Who are the stakeholders that have an interest in or will be affected by your decision: shareholders, the home country government, host country governments, customers, suppliers, employees, unions? There are probably others that could be added to that list, but the point is to comprehensively identify the stakeholders and their interests. It can be easy to ignore some of these, particularly when they may be thousands of miles away and may not be able to stand up for their interests and rights. Ethical managers do not avoid them or pretend that they do not exist.

2   Assess your responsibilities and obligations to these stakeholders.

Identify the responsibilities that your organization may have to external stakeholders as well as to stakeholders (employees) in your own organization. For example, a decision about whether or not to shut down operations in a country may involve both external and internal ethical issues.

Take the situation of an insurance company that one of the authors and his colleague had some involvement with. The company was selling life insurance in Uganda during a period of civil war.[103] Years earlier, the company's operation there was nationalized and now was having its ownership restored. The branch in Uganda was not profitable, and a financial analysis showed that it should be shut down.

From a profit-and-loss perspective, the decision may have been easy to make. But what were the company's responsibilities to their managers who ran the company in their interest after it had been nationalized and who were concerned about possible violence to field personnel and to themselves if the company closed its operations? And what were its obligations to its policyholders? The issue may not be whether the company should shut down, but how it should handle its responsibilities, obligations, and commitments to its employees and customers, and shareholders as it shuts down.

Assess and Select Options

1 Identify a broad range of options.

   Some options will jump up immediately, such as pay the bribe or don't pay the bribe. Are there options that have not been identified? In trying to identify possible action, avoid characterizing decisions using false dichotomies – either/or characterizations. Alternatives and options do not have to be win/lose positions. For example, the statement "We need to pay the bribe or lose the business" portrays the situation as win/lose, but it may not be. These positions often develop because the initial analysis was not as complete as it could have been. This mindset can limit the action possibilities open to the manager. Strive for a win-win situation. Is there a way to solve the problem that satisfies all parties and allows you to fulfill your obligations?

2 Analyze the assumptions behind the options.

   What assumptions are being made? What ethical framework is being invoked? Whose utility is being maximized? Whose values are being used? Consider multiple (including opposing) viewpoints, but examine them carefully. Weigh the costs and benefits to all stakeholders.

3 Select an option and develop an action plan.

   If you have followed the steps above you are now in a better position to develop an action plan. Some decision criteria to consider include: do the best for all involved stakeholders; fulfill obligations; observe laws and contracts; do not use deception; and avoid knowingly doing harm (physical, psychological, economic, or social).

Consider Your Own Position Carefully In conducting these arm's-length analyses, it is easy to take ourselves as people – the ones who make the decisions – out of the picture. Remember that there can be personal consequences associated with your decision. People have lost their jobs because someone higher in the organization needed a scapegoat, and some have gone to jail for the actions of others. Don't just think about the decision from your role as a manager. Consider your roles as community leader, husband or wife, parent or global citizen. Ask yourself if you will be acting in accordance with your own highest set of values and norms. Certainly look after the interests of your company in your role as manager, but look after your own interests, also. You may be the only one that does!

1 Make decisions that are your responsibility.

Do not avoid making ethical decisions on issues that are your responsibility, for example, by passing the responsibility on to someone else or waiting until the problem passes.

2 Don't let people put the monkey on your back.

Do not accept responsibility for decisions that are not your responsibility. Some people will try to find a scapegoat to make a particularly difficult, possibly illegal or unethical decision. Do not let them use you. How do you protect yourself? You can ask for the decision or directive in writing or suggest an open meeting with other people present to discuss it.

3 Do not use "culture" as an excuse for not doing things the proper way.

Just because the local company does not treat its toxic waste properly does not mean that it is acting as a role model for that culture. Also, beware of confusing culture and an individual's personality and character. If a person is asking for something that is illegal or unethical, that tells you something about that person's character, not necessarily about his or her culture.

4 Act consistently with your own values.

Consider the "billboard" or the "light-of-day" tests. When you drive to work in the morning, would you be happy to see your decision or action prominently announced on a large billboard for everyone to read and to know about? Or alternatively, would you be willing to discuss your actions in a meeting where you would be subject to questions and scrutiny and have to justify them? Would your actions look as reasonable in the light of day as they did when the decision was made behind closed doors?

A Final Word

As you progress through your international management career, we encourage you to maintain high standards. We suggest that you follow an adage that we have modified, "When in Rome don't do as the Romans do, but rather do as the better Romans do."

Ask yourself, and answer honestly, if you are behaving up to the highest values and expectations of yourself. Are you happy with your answer? If not, you know what to do!

Notes

1 Rowe, Glen; statement made in class during International Week of the EMBA at IPADE in Mexico City, October 2012.

2 De George, R. T., *Competing with Integrity in International Business* (Oxford: Oxford University Press, 1993).

3   Ibid. at p. 6.

4   Ibid. at p. 41.

5   Amba-Rao, S. C., "Multinational Corporate Social Responsibility, Ethics, Interactions and Third World Governments: An Agenda for the 1990's," *Journal of Business Ethics*, 12 (1993) 555.

6   "Xerox admits India pay-offs," July 2, 2002; http://news.bbc.co.uk/2/hi/business/2084382.stm. Accessed February 9, 2013.

7   Leonnig, Carol, "Ex-Chiquita Execs Won't Face Bribe Charges," *The Washington Post*, September 12, 2007. http://www.washingtonpost.com/wp-dyn/content/article/2007/09/11/AR2007091102504.html. Accessed February 9, 2013.

8   "BAE Systems pays $400m to settle bribery charges"; http://www.independent.co.uk/news/business/news/bae-systems-pays-400m-to-settle-bribery-charges-1891027.html. Accessed February 9, 2013.

9   "Siemens Changes Its Culture: No More Bribes," May 12, 2012; http://www.npr.org/2012/05/01/151745671/companies-can-recovery-from-bribery-scandals. Accessed February 9, 2013.

10 Ibid.

11 Lichtblau, Eric and Dougherty, Carter, "Siemens to Pay $1.34 Billion in Fines," *The New York Times*, December 15, 2008. http://www.nytimes.com/2008/12/16/business/worldbusiness/16siemens.html?_r=0. Accessed February 9, 2013.

12 Ibid.

13 "Wal-Mart CEO Knew of Bribery in Mexico since 2005, Emails Show," January 11, 2013. http://latino.foxnews.com/latino/news/2013/01/11/lawmakers-release-documents-on-walmart-bribery/. Accessed February 9, 2013.

14 Barstow, David and Xanic von Bertrab, Alejandra, "The Bribery Aisle; How Wal-Mart Got Its Way in Mexico," *The New York Times,* December 17, 2012. http://www.nytimes.com/2012/12/18/business/walmart-bribes-teotihuacan.html?pagewanted=all. Accessed February 9, 2013.

15 Gordimer, N., "In Nigeria, the price of oil is blood," *New York Times*, May 25, 1997, E 11.

16 "Shellman says sorry," *The Economist*, May 10, 1997, 65.

17 For example in the *Globe and Mail* in Canada on November 21, 1995.

18 "Shellman says sorry."

19 http://www.shell.com/global/environment-society/society/human-rights/training-tools-guidelines.html. Accessed February 10, 2013.

20 http://www-static.shell.com/content/dam/shell/static/environment-society/downloads/management-primers/human-rights-dilemmas.pdf. Accessed February 10, 2013.

21 http://www.voluntaryprinciples.org/files/voluntary_principles_english.pdf.

22 Yaccino, Steven, "Planner of Mumbai Attacks Is Given a 35-Year Sentence," *New York Times*, January 24, 2013; http://www.nytimes.com/2013/01/25/us/david-c-headley-gets-35-years-for-mumbai-attack.html. Accessed February 10, 2013.

23 Srivastava, M. and Lakshman, N., "How Risky Is India?" *Business Week*, December 15, 2008, 25.

24 "How Risky Is India?" n. 23 above, at 24.

25 Statistics are from the International Maritime Board Piracy Reporting Centre (IMB PRC). IMB PRC is a part of the International Chamber of Commerce, an independent non-governmental body established to monitor piracy attacks free of political interference.

http://www.icc-ccs.org/news/836-piracy-falls-in-2012-but-seas-off-east-and-west-africa-remain-dangerous-says-imb. Accessed February 11, 2013.

26 "French tanker, crew hijacked off Ivory Coast freed," *US News & World Report*, February 6, 2013. http://www.usnews.com/news/world/articles/2013/02/06/tanker-crew-hijacked-off-ivory-coast-freed. Accessed February 11, 2013.

27 *Op. cit.* n. 25, above

28 Nightingale, Alaric and Bockmann, Michelle Wiese, "Somalia Piracy Falls to Six-Year Low as Guards Defend Ships," *Bloomberg Business Week*, October 22, 2012; http://www.businessweek.com/news/2012-10-22/somalia-piracy-attacks-plunge-as-navies-secure-trade-route. Accessed February 11, 2013.

29 For an excellent discussion of the piracy problem see McKnight USN (Ret.), Rear Admiral Terry and Hirsch, Michael, *Pirate Alley: Commanding Task Force 151 Off Somalia*, Naval Institute Press, October 2012.

30 For a detailed description and analysis of the Maersk Alabama hijacking and Phillips' kidnapping see *Pirate Alley: Commanding Task Force 151 Off Somalia* (Naval Institute Press, October 2012).

31 World Economic Outlook, International Monetary Fund. GDP CAGR estimated as of December 31, 2009; Global Economics Paper No. 192: The Long-Term Outlook for the BRICs and N-1 Post Crisis. December 4, 2009 as reported in *A Reference Guide to Emerging Markets*, Goldman Sachs, 2010; http://www.goldmansachs.com/gsam/docs/instgeneral/general_materials/primer/reference_guide_to_emerging_markets.pdf. Accessed February 14, 2013.

32 Moore, Elaine, "Civets, Brics and the Next 11," *FT.com*, June 8, 2012; http://www.ft.com/intl/cms/s/0/c14730ae-aff3-11e1-ad0b-00144feabdc0.html#axzz2KuQfj8TB. Accessed February 14, 2013.

33 http://ffp.statesindex.org/http://ffp.statesindex.org/. Accessed February 28, 2013.

34 Drohan, M., "To Bribe or Not to Bribe," *The Globe and Mail*, February 14, 1994, B7

35 Ibid.

36 Fey, Carl and Shekshnia, Stanislav, "The Key Commandments of Doing Business in Russia," INSEAD Working Paper 2008/16/EFE available on SSRN at http://papers.ssrn.com/sol3/papers.cfm?abstract_id=1116663. Also published in *Organizational Dynamics*, 40(1) (2011) 57–66.

37 For a more detailed account of this situation see Lane, H. and Wesley, D., "Statoil Iran," Ivey case no. 9B05C036.

38 Statoil signs Iran gas deal, BBC News, 28 October, 2002. This represented the first of three payments to Horton Investments. The contract was later annulled and no further payments were made.

39 "Statoil Still Afloat Despite Losing Man Overboard," *International Petroleum Finance*, October 8, 2003.

40 Horton Case Settlement, http://www.statoil.com/en/NewsAndMedia/News/2006/Pages/HortonCaseSettlement.aspx. Accessed February 15, 2013.

41 This section has been adapted from the US Department of Justice web site US Department of Justice web site http://www.justice.gov/criminal/fraud/fcpa/. Accessed February 15, 2013). For more detail about the FCPA see the web site.

42 http://www.transparency.org/.

43 See Bribe Payers Index Report 2011, http://bpi.transparency.org/bpi2011/results/. Accessed February 15, 2013.

44 http://cpi.transparency.org/cpi2012/results/. Accessed February 15, 2013.

45 http://www.cdc.gov/tobacco/data_statistics/fact_sheets/health_effects/tobacco_related_mortality/. Accessed February 9, 2013.

46 Ibid.

47 http://www.who.int/features/factfiles/tobacco_epidemic/tobacco_epidemic_facts/en/index.html. Accessed February 9, 2013.

48 An international treaty for tobacco control, August 12, 2003; http://www.who.int/features/2003/08/en/. The latter quote is credited to the Oxford Medical Companion (1994). Accessed February 9, 2013.

49 Russell, S., "Ex-Clinton Official rips White House on tobacco treaty," *San Francisco Chronicle*, February 13, 2003. http://www.sfgate.com/health/article/Ex-Clinton-official-rips-White-House-on-tobacco-2634727.php. Accessed February 9, 2013.

50 http://oversight-archive.waxman.house.gov/documents/20040830122132-63376.pdf. Accessed February 9, 2013.

51 ASEAN inter-sessional meeting 4-7 March 2002, http://www.ash.org.uk/files/documents/ASH_346.pdf.

52 Letter from Durbin & Waxman to USDA (PDF); http://archive.tobacco.org/articles/category/federal/www.cdc.gov/Features/TobaccoEducationCampaign/?starting_at=9375. Accessed February 9, 2013.

53 http://www.tobaccofreekids.org/tobacco_unfiltered/tag/advertising.

54 US Consumer Products Safety Commission web site, http://www.cpsc.gov/cpscpub/prerel/prhtml07/07039.html. Accessed February 9, 2013.

55 Mattel apologizes to China over recalls; http://www.nbcnews.com/id/20903731/. Accessed February 9, 2013.

56 Bapuji, H. and Beamish, P. W., "Toy Recalls – Is China Really the Problem?" Canada-Asia Commentary, September 2007, 1. http://www.asiapacific.ca/canada-asia-agenda/toy-recalls-china-really-problem. Accessed February 9, 2013.

57 See "Human Rights," *The Economist*, June 3, 1995, 58–59; Beaver, W., "Levi's Is Leaving China," *Business Horizons* (March–April 1995) 35–40. See also Cassel, Douglass, "Corporate Initiatives: A Second Human Rights Revolution?" *Fordham International Law Journal*, 19(5) (1995) Article 10.

58 http://www.levistrauss.com/sustainability/people/worker-rights. Accessed February 10, 2013.

59 "Improving Workers' Well-Being: A New Approach to Supply Chain Engagement," April 12, 2012, Levis Strauss & Co. http://levistrauss.com/sites/default/files/librarydocument/2012/4/ceres-lsco-whitepaper-2012-04-17.pdf; p. 4. Accessed February 10, 2013.

60 http://www.ceres.org/about-us. Accessed February 28, 2013.

61 This discussion about GoodWeave USA (formerly the RugMark Foundation USA) and GoodWeave International were taken from the following web sites accessed February 15, 2013. http://www.pbs.org/now/enterprisingideas/RugMarkUSA.html, http://www.goodweave.net/, http://www.goodweave.org/about, http://www.catalogueforphilanthropy-dc.org/cfpdc/nonprofit-detail.php?id=94192

62 http://www.catalogueforphilanthropy-dc.org/cfpdc/nonprofit-detail.php?id=94192.

63   http://www.ikea.com/ms/en_US/about_ikea/our_responsibility/working_conditions/preventing_child_labour.html. Accessed February 15, 2013.

64   Recounted to Elaine Cohen by IKEA Foundation's Head of Communications & Strategic Planning, Jonathan Spampinato. "Banning Child Labor: The Symptom or the Cause?" posted September 20, 2012; http://www.csrwire.com/blog/posts/547-banning-child-labor-the-symptom-or-the-cause. Accessed February 15, 2013.

65   Brown, Stephen, IKEA apologizes for using forced labor to make furniture, Reuters/November 16, 2012, *The Christian Science Monitor*, http://www.csmonitor.com/Business/2012/1116/IKEA-apologizes-for-using-forced-labor-to-make-furniture. Accessed February 15, 2013.

66   Preston, Jennifer, IKEA Apologizes for Removing Women From Saudi Catalog, *New York Times*, October 2, 2012, http://thelede.blogs.nytimes.com/2012/10/02/ikea-apologizes-for-removing-women-from-saudi-catalog/. Accessed February 15, 2013.

67   Ibid. "Medieval" according to Birgitta Ohlsson, the Swedish Minister for European Union Affairs.

68   http://files.gecompany.com/gecom/citizenship/pdfs/TheSpirit&TheLetter.pdf. Accessed February 15, 2013.

69   Donaldson, T., "The Promise of Corporate Codes of Conduct," *Human Rights Dialogue*, 2(4) 2000; http://www.carnegiecouncil.org/publications/archive/dialogue/2_04/index.html/_res/id=sa_File1/HRD_Workers_Rights.pdf. Accessed February 15, 2013.

70   To see examples of this distinction in action in a large Wall Street firm in the 1980s, read Lewis, M., *Liar's Poker* (New York: Penguin Books, 1989).

71   Henderson, V. E., "The Ethical Side of Enterprise," *Sloan Management Review* 23 (1982) 37–47.

72   Ibid.

73   Infant formula contributes to malnourishment – UNICEF, November 6, 2012. http://www.3news.co.nz/Infant-formula-contributes-to-malnourishment–UNICEF/tabid/417/articleID/275577/Default.aspx. Accessed February 15, 2013.

74   Meier, B., "Breast-feeding wisdom in question," *New York Times*, June 8, 1997.

75   This section draws on the following works: Gandz, J. and Hayes, N., "Teaching Business Ethics," Working Paper No. 86-17R, October, 1986, School of Business Administration, The University of Western Ontario; Tuleja, T., *Beyond the Bottom Line* (New York: Penguin Books, 1985); Matthews, J. B., Goodpaster, K. E. and Nash, L., *Policies and Persons: A Casebook in Business Ethics* (New York: McGraw-Hill, 1985).

76   Perry, Jr., W. G., *Forms of Intellectual and Ethical Development in the College Years: A Scheme* (New York: Holt, Rinehart & Winston, 1970).

77   In Perry's full scheme there are nine stages. The authors have chosen to use only the three major positions in the scheme.

78   Hofstede, G. H., *Culture's Consequences* (Beverly Hills: Sage Publications, 1980).

79   Gandz, J. and Nadine Hayes, N., "Teaching Business Ethics," *Journal of Business Ethics* 7 (1988) 659.

80   http://www.un.org/rights/50/decla.htm. Accessed February 21, 2013.

81   http://www.chinesehumanrightsreader.org/reader/intros/52.html. Accessed February 21, 2013.

82   Zakaria, F., "Culture is Destiny: A Conversation with Lee Kuan Yew," *Foreign Affairs*, 73(2) (1994) 109–126 at 110.

83 Ibid., at p. 113.

84 Ibid., at p. 111.

85 http://feeds.archive.org/stream/Mahathir/Mah08_djvu.txt; p. 9. Accessed February 21, 2013.

86 "Mahathir warns against too much democracy," BBC News, Thursday, July 27, 2000. http://news.bbc.co.uk/2/hi/asia-pacific/853673.stm. Accessed February 21, 2013.

87 Fukuyama, F., "Asian Values and Civilization," The ICAS Lectures No. 98-929-FRF. ICAS Fall Symposium September 29, 1998, http://www.icasinc.org/1998/1998f/1998ffrf.html. Accessed February 21, 2013.

88 See, for example, Peerenboom, R., "Beyond Universalism and Relativism: The Evolving Debates about 'Values in Asia,'" Research Paper No. 02-23, UCLA School of Law, October, 31, 2002.

89 Canada, Geoffrey, Druckenmiller, Stanley and Warsh, Kevin, "Generational Theft Needs to Be Arrested," *Wall Street Journal*, (February 14, 2013).

90 http://www.hrw.org/news/2001/04/09/china-white-paper-whitewash. Accessed February 21, 2103.

91 Sen, A., "Satyajit Ray and the Art of Universalism: Our Culture, Their Culture," 11. http://satyajitray.ucsc.edu/articles/sen.html. Accessed February 21, 2013.

92 BBC World Service, http://www.bbc.co.uk/worldservice/people/features/ihavearightto/four_b/casestudy_art30.shtml. Accessed February 21, 2013.

93 Message From Daw Aung San Suu Kyi For Malaysians, 10 Dec 1999; http://groups.yahoo.com/group/harakahdaily/message/145. Accessed February 21, 2013.

94 Jean-Pierre Lehmann, "Asia: Myths and Realities: In Search of a Eurasian Feast of Civilizations," *Bao Review*, (April 2013) 142–143.

95 See Peerenboom, n. 87, at p. 83.

96 See Peerenboom, n. 87, at p. 9.

97 We would like to thank Sheila Puffer and Dan McCarthy of Northeastern University for introducing us to ISCT.

98 Donaldson, T. and Dunfee, T. W., *Ties That Bind* (Boston, MA: Harvard Business School Press, 1999).

99 Ibid., at p. 46.

100 Ibid.

101 Ibid., at p. 60.

102 "The Caux Round Table (CRT) is an international network of principled business leaders working to promote a moral capitalism. The CRT advocates implementation of the CRT Principles for Business through which principled capitalism can flourish and sustainable and socially responsible prosperity can become the foundation for a fair, free and transparent global society. At the company level, the Caux Round Table advocates implementation of the CRT Principles for Business as the cornerstone of principled business leadership. The CRT Principles apply fundamental ethical norms to business decision-making." Taken from About CRT, http://www.cauxroundtable.org/index.cfm?&menuid=2. Accessed February 23, 2013.

103 Burgoyne, D. and Lane, H., "The Europa Insurance Company," Case 9-84-C049 (London: The University of Western Ontario, School of Business Administration, 1984).

CHAPTER **9**

Competing with Integrity in Global Business: Corporate Sustainability[a]

The UN General Assembly created the World Commission on Environment and Development in 1983 to study the impact of human activity on the global environment. The Commission, headed by Gro Harlem Brundtland, then Prime Minister of Norway, issued its report in 1987 and the concept of "sustainable development" came into common usage when the Commission published its report, "Our Common Future." The report defined sustainable development as "development which meets the needs of current generations without compromising the ability of future generations to meet their own needs."[1] To many people this concept became synonymous simply with protecting the environment or being "green." However, it encompasses more than a focus on the physical eco-system and includes concern for economic and social development, the so-called Triple Bottom Line, as well as recognizing the interdependence among the three areas.

There are hundreds of definitions of "sustainability" and "sustainable development."[2] Some writers and companies include ethics in their definitions of corporate sustainability but we have separated that topic out. To be sure, there may be ethical issues associated with some business decisions or a product that will impact the environment or a community. Our reasoning for the separation is that legal and ethical behavior, as discussed in the previous chapter, should be expected by managers in all activities. It also deserves focused attention. Even though corporations may have codes of conduct specifying standards of behavior for their employees, the decision to act legally and ethically is, in the final analysis, a personal decision. As we said in Chapter 8, we are making the distinction between the decisions and behavior of individuals or a small group of people, and a formal initiative of an organization that most likely uses corporate resources to achieve its ends.

[a] The authors would like to acknowledge Andrew Savitz for his comments on this chapter in the last edition and for his contributions to this chapter.

Corporate governance, narrowly conceived as the corporation's relationship with share-holders – well-defined shareholder rights, effective control, transparency and disclo-sure, and an independent, empowered board of directors may also be included in an understanding of sustainability. Some pundits and academics have chosen to talk about environmental, social and governance (ESG) as the best way to evaluate business behav-ior. Again, we believe that the desired relationship with shareholders also should be expected, although in recent years, with examples such as Enron, it has not proven to be the case.

Similarly, sustainability may be considered to be corporate social responsibility or CSR by some writers. All these terms or concepts address the broad notion of aligning companies' activities with society's interests. As it relates to business, sustainability has become the prevailing term for finding the overlap between business interests and soci-ety's interests and we are adopting that convention in this edition.[3]

Sustainability is not simply philanthropy – providing funding for environmental projects or communities in developing countries, for example, to create educational or medical pro-grams, no matter how beneficial they may be. This philanthropy may be a component of a corporation's sustainability efforts but philanthropy alone is not sustainability. *Sustainability is not about how a company spends its money but rather about how a company makes its money.*

Sustainability programs and projects are usually discretionary without necessarily having legal or ethical implications or conforming to the narrower, less inclusive, definition of governance. In this chapter we will focus on the right-hand column of Table 9.1.

The relationship between corporations' interests and society's interests is not a new topic. One writer suggested that serious discussion of the topic in North America started in 1953 with the publication of *Social Responsibilities of the Businessman* and that it turned into a debate later when Milton Friedman asserted that a company's only social respon-sibility was to make a profit for its stockholders.[4] Friedman said:

> . . . there is one and only one social responsibility of business – to use its resources and engage in activities designed to increase its profits so long as it stays within the rules of the game, which is to say, engages in open and free competition without deception or fraud.[5]

However, the history and ideology of corporations having a social responsibility as a management theme can be traced back to 1927. At that time Wallace B. Donham, Dean of the Harvard Business School, advocated greater corporate social responsibility as a way of "aligning business interests with the defense of free-market capitalism against what was depicted as the clear and present danger of Soviet Communism."[6,7] According to Spector, starting in 1946, another Dean of the Harvard Business School, Donald K. David, became a "persistent and consistent voice on behalf of expanding the role of business in American society," a view also supported by the *Harvard Business Review* at the time. But there also were challenges to Donham's and David's position before Friedman's. A notable opponent was a Harvard Business School professor, Theodore Levitt, who in 1958, in a *Harvard Business Review* article, strongly disagreed with it.[8]

TABLE 9.1 Global mindset framework applied to ethics and corporate sustainability

Individual/Personal		Organizational
Self	Clarify and understand my beliefs about ethical behavior.	Clarify and understand my organization's approach to corporate sustainability.
Other	Clarify and understand other beliefs about ethical behavior in the context of other cultures and principal theories of moral philosophy.	Clarify and understand other corporate approaches to sustainability in the context of other industries, other cultures and principal codes of conduct.
Choice	Belief in and commitment to a set of ethical principles.	Belief in and commitment to an approach to corporate sustainability.

TABLE 9.2 The rise of corporate accountability

1950s	1970s	2010s
• MAKE MONEY	• MAKE MONEY	• MAKE MONEY
• Provide philanthropy	• Provide philanthropy	• Provide philanthropy
	• Protect the environment	• Restore the environment
	• Safeguard products	• Safeguard products
		• Promote diversity
		• Protect workers
		• Prevent child labor
		• Foster public health
		• Ensure human rights
		• Alleviate poverty
		• Provide technology
		• Oppose corrupt regimes
		• Patrol supply chain
		• Engage stakeholders
		• Measure and report
		• Continuously improve

Source: *Talent, Transformation, and the Triple Bottom Line: How Companies Can Leverage Human Resources for Sustainable Growth*, Andrew Savitz, Jossey-Bass, 2013. Reproduced with permission of John Wiley & Sons.

Friedman said that corporations had to stay within the rules of the game, which he defined simply as the law and free competition. However, the rules of the game have changed since Friedman wrote. So too has the role of business in society and what society expects of businesses changed over time as Table 9.2 shows. Concerns that were once primarily seen as the responsibility of government have become areas in which businesses are now expected to show leadership.

Although the social responsibility school of thought survived and the topic became incorporated in business schools' curricula, often only as an elective, for decades it was surpassed in the executive mindset by Levitt's and Friedman's viewpoints and encapsulated in the idea of the oft-heard phrase about maximizing shareholder wealth. Lately, however, social responsibility or sustainability has made a comeback and has become a much talked-about and subscribed-to idea.

In 2010, the Economist Intelligence Unit (EIU) of *The Economist* issued a report, *Managing for Sustainability,* which stated:

> Sustainable principles in business were once the preserve of the minority. Over the past decade, these principles have begun moving into the mainstream of business. An increasing number of firms are moving beyond merely cultivating a green image, and are fully embracing sustainability. Many executives see sustainability as the only option, in the long term. Today, it is businesses that have no ambitions in sustainability that form the minority.[9]

Forward-thinking business executives of leading companies are transitioning from "sustainability 1.0 to sustainability 2.0."[10] Sustainability 1.0 tends to be focused on activities such as cost reduction, risk mitigation, brand enhancement and reputational burnishing. Sustainability 2.0 goes beyond those endeavors and looks for opportunities to create value through new products, for example, which address environmental challenges. This might be considered an evolution from efficiency to innovation.

Our purpose here is not to provide a complete treatise on the topic of corporate sustainability, as there are entire books devoted to it, but rather, as in previous chapters, to raise questions about management's responsibility; provide some examples; and offer some ways of thinking about the issues that we have found helpful and hope that you will find useful.

Defining the Domain of Corporate Sustainability

Just as there are numerous definitions of sustainability, similarly there are many organizations, public and private, focusing on sustainability. Numerous international accords and sets of principles have been formulated, adopted, and endorsed in the last half century that provide a base for the development of a transcultural standard of how corporations should behave in the global economy.[11] These accords and principles address the following issues:[12,13]

- **Employment practices and policies**. For example, multinationals should develop nondiscriminatory employment practices, provide equal pay for equal work, observe the right of employees to join unions and to bargain collectively, give advance notice of plant closings and mitigate their adverse effects, respect local host country job standards, provide favorable work conditions and limited working hours, adopt adequate health and safety standards, and inform employees about health hazards. They should not permit unacceptable practices such as the exploitation of children, physical punishment, female abuse, or involuntary servitude.

- **Consumer protection**. MNCs should respect host country laws regarding consumer protection; safeguard the health and safety of consumers through proper labeling, disclosures, and advertising; and provide safe products and packaging.

- **Environmental protection.** MNCs should preserve ecological balance, protect the environment, rehabilitate environments damaged by them, and respect host country laws, goals, and priorities regarding protection of the environment.

- **Political payments and involvement**. MNCs should not pay bribes to public officials and should avoid illegal involvement or interference in internal politics.

- **Basic human rights and fundamental freedoms**. Multinationals should respect the rights of people to life, liberty, security of person, and privacy; and freedom of religion, peaceful assembly, and opinion.

- **Community responsibility**. MNCs should work with governments and communities in which they do business to improve the quality of life in those communities.

We have chosen three leading organizations that have come to the forefront of corporate sustainability to discuss their initiatives briefly: the UN Global Compact, the Global Reporting Initiative (GRI) and the Dow Jones Sustainability Index – one a quasi-governmental organization, one a non-profit, network-based organization and one a private company. An examination of their missions helps to define the domain and scope of sustainability.

The UN Global Compact

The Global Compact was formally launched in July 2000. It is a "platform for the development, implementation and disclosure of responsible and sustainable corporate policies and practices . . . [that] seeks to align business operations and strategies everywhere with 10 universally accepted principles in the areas of human rights, labour, environment and anticorruption."[14] It is the world's largest voluntary corporate sustainability initiative. Its focus is not regulatory but rather transparency and disclosure to achieve public accountability.[15] Many of the participating companies and supporters of the Compact are among the best-known global companies. The *UN Global Compact International Yearbook 2012* provides examples from 42 companies of best practices in core values covered by the Compact.[16]

The UN Global Compact asks companies to embrace, support, and enact, within their sphere of influence, a set of core values in the areas of human rights, labour standards, the environment and anti-corruption:[17]

Human Rights

Principle 1: Businesses should support and respect the protection of internationally proclaimed human rights; and

Principle 2: make sure they are not complicit in human rights abuses.

Labour

Principle 3: Businesses should uphold the freedom of association and the effective recognition of the right to collective bargaining;

Principle 4: the elimination of all forms of forced and compulsory labor;

Principle 5: the effective abolition of child labour; and

Principle 6: the elimination of discrimination in respect of employment and occupation.

Environment

Principle 7: Businesses should support a precautionary approach to environmental challenges;

Principle 8: undertake initiatives to promote greater environmental responsibility; and

Principle 9: encourage the development and diffusion of environmentally friendly technologies.

Anti-Corruption

Principle 10: Businesses should work against corruption in all its forms, including extortion and bribery.

Reproduced with the permission of the United Nations

Do companies participate in the Global Compact simply to bolster their image? Yes, "greenwash[b] is alive and well" according to the *Guardian* with an additional 750 companies likely to be expelled joining over 1000 companies that have already been delisted for not meeting minimum reporting requirements.[18] An analysis of the expelled companies indicated that about 65% were small and medium-size enterprises[19] reinforcing a criticism that the Compact is primarily for large companies that can support the reporting requirements.

In addition to expelling companies in 2010, to cope with these free riders, the Compact introduced a differentiation framework of participants "based on their level of disclosure on progress made in integrating the Global Compact principles and contributing to broader UN goals."[20] These levels are Learner, Active and Advanced. The Advanced level includes a category, "Leadership." The UN created Global Compact LEAD and developed a *Blueprint for Corporate Sustainability Leadership.*[21] Fifty leading companies were invited to participate from many countries including the USA, Canada, Denmark, France, Germany, Japan, Spain, Brazil, India and Russia. The two objectives of LEAD were to:

1 Provide inspiration and role models for companies not as advanced or as far along the sustainability pathway as these leaders, and

2 Encourage these companies to experiment with new practices, products and/or programs to find new ways to increase their performance and impact; and to share their successes and failures and these new best practices.

---

[b] According to the *Collins English Dictionary,* HarperCollins Publishers 2003, greenwash or greenwashing is a "superficial or insincere display of concern for the environment that is shown by an organization".

An impact study of the Compact by Accenture[22] found that awareness of the need for sustainability activities had increased substantially but the real management task remained execution. It also pointed out that a shift was taking place from seeing sustainability from a moral perspective to seeing it as a business opportunity for new products to address sustainability challenges.

Global Reporting Initiative (GRI)

The Global Reporting Initiative (GRI) has become the world's preeminent global, voluntary sustainability reporting system.[23] It has created a non-financial reporting (NFR) system that covers corporate economic, environmental, and social performance indicators. GRI believes that:

> A sustainable global economy should combine long-term profitability with social justice and environmental care. This means that, for organizations, sustainability covers the key areas of economic, environmental, social and governance performance.

GRI's Sustainability Reporting Framework enables all companies and organizations to measure and report their sustainability performance. By reporting transparently and with accountability, organizations can increase the trust that stakeholders have in them, and in the global economy.[24]

The latest guidelines, the G4 Sustainability Reporting Guidelines, focus on *Economic Performance* including direct and indirect economic impact and procurement practices; *Environmental Aspects* to include such items as materials, energy and water usage, biodiversity, emissions and waste; and *Social* which includes sub-categories of Labor Practices and Decent Work, Human Rights, Society and Product Responsibility. A complete listing of the G4 Guidelines and detailed explanations of all the categories can be found on the Global Reporting Initiative's website at: https://www.globalreporting.org/resourcelibrary/GRIG4-Part1-Reporting-Principles-and-Standard-Disclosures.pdf

A listing of which companies have filed reports can be found in a searchable database: http://database.globalreporting.org/

It would be naïve, however, not to acknowledge that companies can be hypocritical in their support of sustainability, social responsibility and ethical behavior in the areas indicated. Endorsing codes such as the GRI or Global Compact is easy to do, but this act alone does not mean that a company is committed to implementing them or managing by them.

Sustainability, its definition, management guidelines to promote it and outcomes are no longer only the concern of international, quasi-governmental organizations or NGOs, but for some private investment companies, as well.

Dow Jones Sustainability Index[25]

The Dow Jones Sustainability Index is a product of RobecoSAM Indices and S&P Dow Jones Indices that track the performance of the world's leading companies in the area of sustainability. S&P Dow Jones Indices LLC is a subsidiary of The McGraw-Hill Companies and is a source of data and indices such as the S&P 500 and the Dow Jones Industrial Average. RobecoSAM is an asset manager and investment specialist in sustainability located in Zurich and Rotterdam. The indices track the stock performance of the world's leading companies in terms of economic, environmental and social criteria. The indices serve as benchmarks for investors who integrate sustainability considerations into their portfolios, and provide an effective engagement platform for companies who want to adopt sustainable best practices.

The Dow Jones Corporate Sustainability Indices are based on the belief that corporate sustainability leaders "create long-term shareholder value by . . . gearing their strategies and management to harness the market's potential for sustainability products and services while at the same time successfully reducing and avoiding sustainability costs and risks . . . [and that] the opportunities and risks deriving from economic, environmental and social developments can be quantified and used to identify and select leading companies for investment purposes." More specific dimensions of the Index can be seen in Figure 9.1.

FIGURE 9.1   Corporate Sustainability Assessment

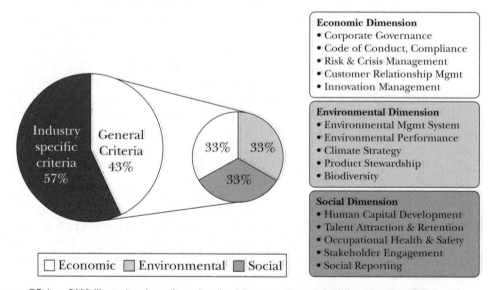

Source: ©RobecoSAM. Illustrative chart: dimensional weights can substantially differentiate from 33% based on aggregated criteria weight; http://www.sustainability-indexes.com/sustainability-assessment/corporate-sustainability-assessment.jsp, accessed January 21, 2013. Reproduced with permission of RobecoSAM.

Each year the world's 2500 largest companies in terms of market capitalization are invited to participate. Questionnaires are completed by these companies and then evaluated according to specified criteria, scored and the data verified. The top companies in each sector are then included in the indices. Not all companies are eligible to be included in the indices. Companies that generate revenue from the following list of activities and products are excluded from the indices: Adult Entertainment, Alcohol, Armaments (for military purposes), Cluster Bombs, Firearms, Gambling, Landmines, Nuclear (power plants, uranium mining) and Tobacco. For the armaments category, if a company earns greater than 5% of its revenues from armaments it is excluded. For all the others the criterion is that they cannot earn any revenue from those activities.

Summary: The Triple Bottom Line – People, Planet, Profits

Although there may be some minor differences in the specific categories, dimensions or values that each of the three organizations use, it is clear that there is convergence around the idea that corporate sustainability encompasses continued, strong economic performance, a broad concept of social justice and a concern for environmental quality; and recognizes the interdependency between the three areas. John Elkington, founder of SustainAbility coined the concept and term, "triple bottom line," in his 1994 book, *Cannibals with Forks*.[26] Sustainability is about performance and progress on the "three pillars" of sustainability – people, planet and profits – and the triple bottom line is a way of measuring and reporting this performance.[27]

Some Examples

Let's look at a couple of brief examples of what some leading global companies in very different industries and countries are doing: a Swedish construction company, a global conglomerate headquartered in the USA, and a Swiss food, beverage and development nutrition company.

Skanska   Skanska is one of the ten largest project development and construction companies in the world with over 57 000 employees. It operates in Europe, the United States and Latin America, and in 2012 it had revenues of approximately $20 billion.[28] It has a strong commitment to sustainability and since 2006 it has been using the Global Reporting Initiative as a guide in developing its sustainability agenda "to better focus strategies and actions that balance the never-ending trade-off between Economic, Social and Environmental considerations." Its Sustainability Agenda is shown in Figure 9.2 and specific details can be found on a presentation on its website.[29]

FIGURE 9.2   Skanska's Sustainability Agenda

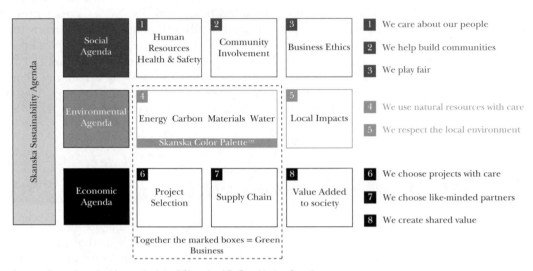

Source: Reproduced with permission of Skanska AB, Stockholm, Sweden.

General Electric   Ben Heineman, former Senior Vice President for law and public affairs at GE, believed that the job of a CEO is to "fuse" high performance with high integrity, which will foster corporate citizenship, and which he defined as:

> Strong and sustained economic performance. Robust and unwavering adherence to the spirit and letter of relevant financial and legal rules. The establishment of, and adherence to, binding global standards – extending beyond the requirements of formal rules – that are in the company's enlightened self-interest because they promote its core values, enhance its reputation, and advance its long-term economic health.[30]

The argument of maximizing shareholder wealth versus corporate social responsibility, or sustainability, has created a specious debate, and both sides have gotten it wrong because, according to Heineman:

> The basic elements of "corporate citizenship" are high performance *and* [emphasis added] high integrity that recognize the long-term interests of shareholders are advanced by responsibly addressing the concerns of other stakeholders.[31]

In the last edition we took our cue from Heineman and used the term, "corporate citizenship" instead of the term "corporate social responsibility" which we felt had a more naïve, almost socialistic, ring to it and was probably overused and very frequently misunderstood. CSR programs are often criticized as not much more than corporate image builders and ways to spend shareholders' money for things governments should be doing.[32]

TABLE 9.3 GE's Areas of Sustainability Focus[33]

People	Planet	Economy

• Helping Our Customers Succeed
  ○ Partnerships on Sustainability
• Keeping Our Employees Confident & Productive
  ○ Health & Safety
  ○ Soliciting Opinions
  ○ Diversity
  ○ Integrity & Privacy
  ○ Labor Relations
  ○ Learning & Development
• Building Enduring Communities
  ○ Volunteerism
  ○ Education
  ○ Health
• Creating Shareholder Value
	• Water Scarcity
	  ○ Management
	  ○ Footprint
	  ○ Products
	• Energy Consumption
	  ○ Management
	  ○ Footprint
	  ○ Products
	• Environment & Resource Management
	  ○ Environment, Health & Safety Program Management
	  ○ Supply Chain
	  ○ Efficiency
	  ○ Supplier Expectations
	  ○ Supplier Program
	  ○ Metrics
	  ○ Resource Optimization
		• Public Policy
		  ○ Rule of Law
		  ○ Human Rights
		  ○ Conflict Minerals
		  ○ Political Activities
		  ○ Climate & Energy
		  ○ Healthcare
		  ○ Strengthening Global Economy
		  ○ Countries of Concern
		• Governance & Compliance
		  ○ Compliance
		  ○ Controllership
		  ○ Government Business
		• Sustainable Systems
		  ○ Water, Energy & Climate
		  ○ Transportation
		  ○ Responsible Lending
		  ○ Accessible Healthcare
		• Job Creation

Source: Reproduced with permission of GE, 2013.

The idea of citizenship is still alive and well at GE. Its web page that focuses on sustainability is titled "GE Citizenship." It states:

> Citizenship at GE is more than a program or a set of good intentions. It is our pledge to improve social, governance, environmental and economic sustainability efforts around the world. Our citizenship and reporting priorities are informed by broad engagement with stakeholders across GE's businesses and the communities where we work. While corporate citizenship is embedded in the fiber of our company, there are key challenges we address that align with the material impacts of our business.[34]

GE's focal areas are shown in Table 9.3.

General Electric is in the Dow Jones Sustainability Index and under CEO Jeff Immelt, it has taken the corporate citizenship credo well beyond Heineman's conceptualization to create a business from sustainability. GE's Ecomagination is a strategic initiative designed to create products that address global environmental problems. It has invested $5 billion in clean technology research that has created products that have created $106 billion in revenue through 2011.[35]

Mark Vachon, former VP in charge of Ecomagination, uses Brazil as a classic case. GE has 40 Ecomagination products and has spent about $2 billion there. These products are treating water, creating biokerosene for Embraer aircraft and turbines fueled by ethanol.[36] Sustainability is not just about reducing waste, energy or water; nor is it simply an effort to remove costs; sustainability can also be a revenue generator, a business. GE has also created a corresponding initiative to improve healthcare, called Healthymagination which is designed to improve access to and affordability of healthcare. Along with StartUp Health, an academy for health entrepreneurs, this three-year program is designed to accelerate growth for consumer health companies. Early-stage consumer health companies will have access to GE's executives and technology experts; training on scaling business operations; and a GE leadership mentor.[37]

Nestlé   Nestlé is in the Dow Jones Sustainability Index, a supporter of the UN Global Compact and an Organizational Stakeholder of the GRI network of companies. Its belief about sustainability can be found on its website:

> We believe that it is only possible to create long-term sustainable value for our shareholders if our behaviour, strategies and operations are also creating value for the communities where we operate, for our business partners and, of course, for our consumers. We call this "Creating Shared Value".

> We are investing for the future to ensure the financial and environmental sustainability of our actions and operations: in capacity, in technologies, in capabilities, in people, in brands, in R&D. Our aim is to meet today's needs without compromising the ability of future generations to meet their needs, and to do so in a way which will ensure profitable growth year after year and a high level of returns for our shareholders and society at large over the long-term.[38]

Nestlé is an example of how a company can focus its efforts in sustainability attempting to achieve maximum benefit for itself and for society. Although Nestlé's Creating Shared Value Summary reports on its activities in areas such as environmental sustainability and human rights, the company has chosen to focus its efforts in sectors that are core to its business: nutrition, water, and rural development.[39] It created the CSV Pyramid as depicted in Figure 9.3.

Sustainability may be viewed as a naïve ideal or as good business practice that produces a positive public image, creates a competitive advantage in business processes, produces environmentally friendly products or solutions and possibly assists in recruiting capable, motivated employees wishing to join companies with which they can identify.[40] The three companies highlighted above show that sustainability is much more than a naïve ideal. But a question remains, does sustainability pay?

Does Corporate Sustainability Pay?

The answer to this question is not completely clear. However, there does seem to be evidence that there is a benefit at least in the long-term. One meta-analysis concluded that

FIGURE 9.3   Nestlé's creating shared value pyramid[41]

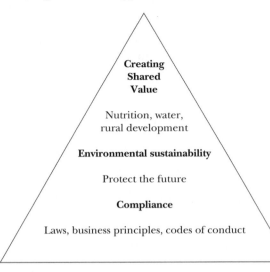

Source: Reproduced with permission of NESTLE ®, a registered trademark of Société des Produits Nestlé S.A., Vevey, Switzerland.

there was a positive association between corporate social performance (CSP) and corporate financial performance (CFP) and that it "supported the validity of enlightened self-interest in the social responsibility arena."[42]

Another meta-analysis of 167 studies of corporate social performance and corporate financial performance found a small correlation between good corporate behavior and good financial results.[43] The authors stated that "companies can do good *and* do well, even if they don't do well by doing good."[44] On the other hand, the research did confirm that corporate misdeeds, if discovered, are very costly to companies.

The Economist Intelligence Unit's (EIU) research, reported in *Doing Good: Business and the sustainability challenge*, found that "sustainability does pay."[45] This was based on interviews with over 1200 senior executives from around the world,[c] in-depth interviews with 28 senior executives including CEOs and heads of sustainability initiatives, plus experts in the field. Fifty-seven percent said that the benefits of corporate sustainability outweighed the costs but 80% of them said that any change in profit would most likely be small. The report stated that:

> . . . sustainable practices can help reduce costs (particularly energy expenditure), open up new markets and improve the company's reputation. Part of this involves a shift away from defensive behavior towards more active exploration of the opportunities sustainability can present . . . the costs of implementation, however, are not to be ignored.[46]

[c] Fifty percent were from the "C Suite" and 26% were CEOs.

The report also suggested a link between sustainability and share price. It stated that the companies in the research with the highest growth in share price in the previous three years were the ones that paid the most attention to sustainability. However, the causal link is not as clear. Do companies that perform better financially pay more attention to sustainability or do companies that pay attention to sustainability perform better financially?

Another EIU report, *Managing for Sustainability*, found that only 24% of the 200 executives in its survey felt that there was a correlation between sustainability and financial performance – in the short term. However, 69% said that the link was stronger in the long term.[47]

A more positive perspective can be found in two reports from the Harvard Business School and MIT. Robert G. Eccles, Ioannis Ioannou and George Serafeim conducted a study in which they compared 90 of what they designated as High Sustainability firms with a matched set of Low Sustainability ones. They found that:

> The High Sustainability firms, in contrast, pay attention to externalities and this is manifested in their relationships with stakeholders such as employees, customers, and NGOs representing civil society. In particular, High Sustainability firms are characterized by distinct governance mechanisms which directly involve the board in sustainability issues and link executive compensation to sustainability objectives; a much higher level of and deeper stakeholder engagement, coupled with mechanisms for making it as effective as possible, including reporting; a longer-term time horizon in their external communications, which is matched by a larger proportion of long-term investors; greater attention to non-financial measures regarding employees; a greater emphasis on external environmental and social standards for selecting, monitoring and measuring the performance of their suppliers; and a higher level of transparency in their disclosure of nonfinancial information.[48]

The study also examined the financial performance of these firms over an 18-year-period and reinforces the view of executives reported above that strong financial performance is a long-term proposition.

> . . . the High Performance firms dramatically outperformed the Low Sustainability ones in terms of both stock market and accounting measures [such as ROI, ROE, etc.]. However, the results suggest that this outperformance occurs only in the long-term.[49]

MIT Sloan Management Review and the Boston Consulting Group reported on their joint study of 2600 executives from companies around the world.[50] They report that sustainability has become a permanent agenda item for many companies and a source of profits for *some* (emphasis added). The percentage of respondents reporting profits increased to 37%, an increase of 23% over 2011.

Creating Sustainable Value

Arguments about the role of sustainability, corporate citizenship, creating shared value or other terminology for the initiatives tend to pit business against society and

TABLE 9.4 Sustainable Value Framework[51]

+	Unsustainable (shareholders lose value and other stakeholders benefit)	Sustainable (both win)
Stakeholder value		
−	Unsustainable (both lose)	Unsustainable (shareholders benefit and other stakeholders lose value)
	− Shareholder value +	

moral actions against profitable ones. One of the major debates is to whom and for what are the management and board of directors of a company primarily responsible – the shareholders or other stakeholders. Unfortunately, this argument, much like the ones we discussed in the previous chapter, generates more heat than light. Positioning shareholders against other stakeholders creates a false dichotomy. Shareholders are a subset of stakeholders, and management should be trying to do the best they can for all groups – aiming for the upper right quadrant of Table 9.4. Let's take a look at some examples of companies represented in the quadrants.

Lower right, shareholders benefit and other stakeholders lose. Monitoring activities of suppliers in a global supply chain can be an enormous and complicated task; and is viewed as the "weakest link" in the sustainability initiatives of companies.[52] Anglo American, the mining company, has 40 000 suppliers and Coca Cola has 100 000.[53] How do companies ensure that their sustainability codes of conduct are adhered to with so many suppliers spread around the world in countries with very different cultures and standards of what are acceptable practices?

Two of the more salient sustainability dimensions related to a global supply chain are potential environmental degradation and human rights abuses. For example, Walmart has over 100 000 suppliers[54] and was criticized for selling clothes made for two of its suppliers in a factory in Bangladesh where 112 workers died in a fire in 2012. The suppliers were using the factory unbeknown to Walmart and the company had previously been taken off the authorized list. The factory apparently had a record of previous fire violations and some workers said barred windows prevented workers from escaping the blaze.[55] As a result Walmart has toughened fire safety standards for its suppliers and requires them to pre-authorize factories they intend to use. Although it is commendable to react to events like the fire to improve surveillance and tighten standards, companies have to be more proactive in policing suppliers and taking preventative measures in order to prevent tragedies such as the building collapse in 2013 in Bangladesh that killed over 1000 workers.

Nike, in the 1990s, was often used as a prime example of all that was wrong with globalization as "greedy" companies eliminated jobs in the United States and took advantage of workers in other countries. It moved production out of the United States into low-wage places such as Korea and Taiwan. When wages increased there and unions became more powerful in Korea, it encouraged suppliers to move again into places like China, Vietnam and Indonesia. It was seen as "the 'poster child' of corporate *in*responsibility in a global economy."[56]

In 1977 Nike started producing shoes in Korea and Taiwan and it became a public company in 1980. Its revenue in 1980 was $270 million and its earnings per share were $0.39. In 1986, two years after signing Michael Jordan to a sponsorship contract, revenue reached $1 billion for the first time. In 1998 at the height of the sweatshop scandal, revenue reached $9.6 billion and earnings were $1.35 per share in what looked like a classic transfer of value from stakeholders to shareholders. At the time it was accused of numerous transgressions such as using toxic, carcinogenic materials, worker abuse, child labor and low wages. There were numerous anti-Nike protest groups, like Team Sweat,[57] that organized against the company to publicize and condemn its activities and held demonstrations at its stores. In 1998, Phil Knight, Chairman and one of Nike's founders, admitted at the National Press Club that, "the Nike product has become synonymous with slave wages, forced overtime, and arbitrary abuse."[58,59]

But that is not the end of the story. In 2000 Nike became active in the UN Global Compact. It participates in the Global Reporting Initiative and in 2012 was invited to participate in the Dow Jones Sustainability Index. That same year it received the SAM Silver Class Designation for companies in the Clothing, Accessories and Footwear Sector.[60,d] The Sector Leader and Gold Class designation went to adidas AG from Germany. A Silver Class distinction means that Nike scored within 1%–5% of adidas AG.

The criteria for these designations include the following:[61]

- **Economic.** Brand Management, Codes of Conduct/Compliance/Corruption & Bribery, Corporate Governance, Risk & Crisis Management.

- **Environmental.** Environmental Policy/Management System, Environmental Reporting, CO_2 from Logistics, Product Stewardship.

- **Social:** Talent Attraction & Retention, Human Capital Development, Stakeholder Engagement, Standards for Suppliers.

Nike can be considered a sustainability turnaround story. Our purpose here is not to explain all its current sustainability initiatives and performance which can be found in detail in its 2012 Sustainability Report.[62] Rather, our intent is to show that sustainability offenders can change and that companies discussed as falling into any of the four quadrants in Table 9.4 represent only a snapshot at a particular point in time. However, it is not simple to turn a company around and requires more than creating a department as Nike learned.[63] Sustainability must become integral to corporate strategy; and people and systems, in addition to structures, must be aligned with the new strategic thrust as was discussed in Chapter 5.

---

[d] As of December 2011. Puma also received a Silver Class designation.

Upper left, Shareholders lose value and stakeholders benefit. An example in the top left quadrant might be Mattel in 2007, discussed in the previous chapter. A lack of attention to its suppliers' practices in China created the need for a large recall. The Chinese firm received value from the Mattel business and customers may have benefited from lower prices for toys made in China, but the result ultimately took value from the Mattel shareholders. From May 1, 2007, before the recall, until a year later, Mattel's share price declined by 34.4%. Meanwhile its major competitor, Hasbro, gained 11% in the same period. However, the earlier caveat applies – it is a snapshot in time. Since then, earnings per share for Mattel have improved from $1.06 in 2008 after the recall, to $2.52 for 2012.

Lower left, both lose. A classic example in which employees and shareholders/owners both lost from what was initially seen as a socially responsible, but economically questionable, decision is Malden Mills.[64] Malden Mills was one of the largest textile mills in New England. The CEO and owner, Aaron Feuerstein, defied conventional wisdom and advice when he did not follow other textile companies in moving operations to lower-cost countries in Latin America or Asia.

Malden Mills declared bankruptcy in 1981 when its main product line, fake fur, went out of fashion. Feuerstein rescued the company by focusing efforts on two popular fabrics the company had developed from recycled plastic products, Polartec and Polarfleece.[e] In 1995 a fire destroyed the factory in Lawrence, Massachusetts. Feuerstein guaranteed all of the workers – more than 3000 – full wages for 90 days and vowed to rebuild the factory in Lawrence instead of moving offshore. In 2001 once again Malden Mills filed for bankruptcy because it could not compete with lower-cost competitors from Asia and because of the heavy debt it had incurred from the rebuilding program. In 2003 the company re-emerged from bankruptcy with 1200 employees. More than 1800 Malden Mills workers in the United States had lost their jobs in the five-plus years since the fire. In 2004 Feuerstein was not retained as CEO and he left the company that his grandfather had founded. It was eventually sold to a private equity firm and renamed Polartec.

More recently, British Petroleum (BP) has been in the news for the Deepwater Horizon oil spill in the Gulf of Mexico on April 20, 2010. Between January 4 and April 19, 2010, BP's share price, adjusted for dividends and splits, fluctuated between $53.43 and $54.14 with average sales volumes ranging from 4.5 to 10.5 million shares. From April 26 to June 21, 2010, the adjusted share price ranged from a high of $47.15 down to $24.84 on average volumes of sales of 37.5 to 147.2 million shares. BP shareholders lost a lot of value. For the period June 26, 2010 to Dec 31, 2012, share prices stabilized in a range of $26.98–$45.94 fluctuating mostly in mid-to-high $30 dollar to low $40 dollar range. On February 1, 2013 the adjusted closing share price was $44.77.[65]

Who else lost? Just about everyone except maybe the lawyers involved in the case. The oil spill, the largest in US waters, lasted for 84 days and was estimated at 206 million

---

[e] An innovation that he never patented. HBS Case 9-410-083, p.2.

gallons or 4.9 million barrels.[66] Eleven men were killed, beaches, fisheries, and wet-lands were damaged and thousands of people's livelihoods were threatened. BP has created a $42 billion reserve for costs and claims related to the oil spill.[67] According to the Congressional Research Service, as of January 2013, BP had paid $14 billion in response costs for the spill.[68] In January 2013, a federal judge approved the agreement between the Justice Department and BP in which it pleaded guilty to 14 criminal charges and paid a fine of $4 billion.[69] The company said it had already paid over $24 billion in claims and cleanup costs.[70] Although this agreement settles the criminal case for BP, it still faces civil penalties resulting from numerous law suits. In addition to the monetary costs, two BP officials were charged with manslaughter and a former VP was charged with obstruction of Congress and making false statements.

Depending on one's perspective, BP can be viewed as a villain; or as a cautionary tale of trying to do too much too soon without changing the organizational culture first;[71] or as a possible example of green spin or greenwashing.[72] BP participates in the Global Reporting Initiative (GRI) but some observers claim that their reporting just "veiled core weaknesses in how the company managed pivotal issues of maintenance and safety."[73] On June 14, 2010, Congressmen Henry Waxman and Bart Stupak, Chairs of Congressional Subcommittees investigating the oil spill, wrote a letter to Tony Hayward, then CEO of BP, prior to his testimony in which they said:

> The Committee's investigation is raising serious questions about the decisions made by BP in the days and hours before the explosion on the Deepwater Horizon. On April 15, five days before the explosion, BP's drilling engineer called Macondo a "nightmare well." In spite of the well's difficulties, BP appears to have made multiple decisions for economic reasons that increased the danger of a catastrophic well failure. In several instances, these decisions appear to violate industry guidelines and were made despite warnings from BP's own personnel and its contractors. In effect, it appears that BP repeatedly chose risky procedures in order to reduce costs and save time and made minimal efforts to contain the added risk.[74]

Prior to the Gulf crisis BP developed a reputation for trading off maintenance and safety in favor of cost savings as critics pointed to the fire and explosion at the Texas City refinery that killed 15 workers, and the North Slope oil spill that was linked to not inspecting and cleaning two pipelines for a period of years.

However, BP's GRI Sustainability Reports presented a very different and positive picture of their sustainability efforts and culture.[75] It is not enough for companies to talk the talk, they also must walk the talk. Where companies want to aim for is in the upper right-hand quadrant, win-win.

Upper right: Both win. Toyota Motor Corporation is an example of a company in the top right quadrant. It has a number of sustainability initiatives such as reducing the amount of waste per vehicle; a battery recovery program for batteries used in its hybrid automobiles; numerous LEED (Leadership in Energy and Environmental Design) certi-fied green buildings.[76] Its star sustainability performer has been the Prius.

Toyota received the SAM Silver Class Designation in its 2013 report and it was named as the top sustainability brand by Interbrand, the global brand consultancy, in its 2012 report.[77] The report stated:

> Holding strong at #1 for the second year in a row – and topping green brand lists all over the world –Toyota continues to demonstrate unparalleled sustainability leadership. Overall, environmental sustainability is deeply ingrained in the company's culture and has been a core management priority since the early 1990s. Since then, Toyota's dedication to sustainability has kept them ahead of the clean vehicle trend and resulted in steady improvements in energy use, water consumption, waste, and toxic emissions year after year. Always looking ahead, Toyota continues to embark on company-wide initiatives to improve environmental performance and builds on its reputation for cutting-edge eco vehicle development through innovation, key partnerships and strategic campaigns. Toyota benefits from a powerful halo effect generated by the success and long-term visibility of the Prius, which, in many people's minds, has become synonymous with the term "hybrid." However, Toyota's outstanding performance on all levels proves that sustainability isn't just about winning hearts and moving product – it's a winning way of doing business.

In terms of business performance, Toyota first passed General Motors (GM) in total sales in 2008 to become the world leader in sales; lost the title in 2011 but regained it in 2012 beating GM and Volkswagen. On February 4, 2013, Toyota raised its profit projection for its fiscal year which ends in March 2013 to a five-year high.[78] With products like Prius, Toyota has proven to be a winner for the environment, its shareholders and its stakeholders. Prius appeared to create a "halo" effect over all Toyota products. Because it was the company to commercially develop and introduce the hybrid, it caused other car companies to play catch-up and many people assume it is the most innovative, has the best engineers, etc. The company's products and, importantly, its employer brand were greatly enhanced. Thus, the Prius had a positive business impact beyond its sales.[79]

Going forward: Embracing Stakeholder Theory

How should a company think about the issue of corporate sustainability? There is no simple answer to that question other than that corporations need to actively address the question in a responsible manner. The answer is not simple because the factors to be considered are complex and it represents a decision resulting from a combination of value judgments and financial analyses that executives of each corporation will have to take for themselves. Stakeholder theory asks two questions that executives need to answer:[80]

1 What is the purpose of the firm?

2 What responsibility do managers have to stakeholders?

Stakeholder theory rejects the separation theory, that shareholders and stakeholders are different and that one group has more rights than the other. It also believes that values are explicitly a part of management. The approach managers choose most likely will depend on the senior executives' and board of directors' values and view of the relationship between business and society. If they believe that society's moral or social values and business objectives are inherently in conflict, or at best totally separate domains of activity, they may favor a stance that resists doing more than the minimum.[81] A paradigm in which business objectives and societal values are in harmony or are complementary will more likely lead to actions deemed as progressive or as leading the way.

Using the courts and the internet, stakeholders can exert a lot of power today. There are many stories from the Brent Spar (Shell versus Greenpeace) to Nike (media/labor frenzy over children working for Nike contractors) to Walmart being unable to get into Boston due to bad behavior, actual or perceived, regarding its workers. There has been a shift in expectations since Ralph Nader and Rachel Carson in terms of what companies are expected to do and in the ability of stakeholders to enforce many of those expectations.[82]

What is clear is that top management must set its desired course for corporate sustainability initiatives. It is also clear that there is a progression of views taking place from a defensive, reactive, seeing sustainability almost as a moral issue, to, at a minimum, a risk management view and on to a proactive, enlightened self-interest and business opportunity that some of the leading global companies now display.

Conclusions

As we conclude this seventh edition of International Management Behavior, it is useful to reflect on how much the world has changed since the original two authors (Henry Lane and Joseph DiStefano) started writing about international business. The first course in intercultural management was launched at the Ivey Business School in London, Canada in the early 1970s. Many business executives wondered why it was being offered; several faculty colleagues remarked that there were so few differences between doing business domestically and "going international" that they wondered what would sustain more than one or two class sessions devoted to the topic. At that time the North American Free Trade Agreement (NAFTA) wasn't on the table, China had not been recognized by Richard Nixon or Pierre Trudeau, and no one was anticipating the rise of the BRIC countries.

Although international business curricula had emerged in some business schools, when the first edition was published in 1988 there weren't many other books like this one, and we were not sure if a sufficient market existed to sustain sales and plan for a second edition. The intervening 25 years have seen an explosion of international activity, even involving some new technology that did not exist when we started our work. And we have gone from the optimism of the "end of history," which asserted that the fundamental values of liberal democracy and market capitalism had emerged triumphant as well as the election of the first multiracial, multicultural president of the United States, to the continuing pessimism of current economic turmoil, terrorism and social disintegration in many countries.

To summarize all these changes we opened this edition with an equation that described the challenge facing global managers: Globalization = Managing Complexity. We said that complexity was reflected in increased interdependence, variety and ambiguity and that these were subject to constant and rapid change or "fast flux." We also said that dealing with this complexity started with developing a global mindset – understanding ourselves and our own organizations, and understanding a diverse set of other people and other organizations.

These *elements* of a global mindset are not different from those we faced when we wrote the first edition: but the complexity of each has certainly increased. But the tools and technology to help us manage the increased complexity have also improved and increased. So we hope that this volume – a *very* different book than the first edition – will help our readers manage the complexity they face during their careers in international business. We have extended our original conceptions and knowledge, added our own international and cross-cultural experiences of teaching and of managing, and borrowed generously from the wisdom of our colleagues and friends. What we have not changed is our excitement about the prospects for you adding to your own rich experience during your international careers and thereby increasing your abilities to contribute to the prosperity of your organizations and society and to the development of peace in the world. We end this seventh edition with warm and sincere wishes for success in your journey.

Notes

1 http://www.un-documents.net/our-common-future.pdf.

2 Johnston, P., Everard, M., Santillo, D. and Karl-Henrik, R., "Reclaiming the Definition of Sustainability," *Environmental Science Pollution Research*, 14(1) (2007) 60–66.

3 Andrew Savitz, author of *The Triple Bottom Line* (San Francisco, CA: Jossey-Bass, 2006) and *Talent, Transformation and the Triple Bottom Line* (Jossey-Bass, 2013); personal communication.

4 Bowen, H. R., *Social Responsibilities of the Businessman* (New York: Harper & Row, 1953) as referred to in Carroll, A. B., "A Three Dimensional Model of Corporate Performance," *Academy of Management Review* 4(4) (1979) 497–505.

5 Friedman, M., "The Social Responsibility of Business is to Increase its Profits," *The New York Times Magazine*, September 13, 1970.

6 Spector, B., "Business Responsibilities in a Divided World: The Cold War Roots of the Corporate Social Responsibility Movement," *Enterprise & Society: The International Journal of Business History*, 9(2) (June 2008) Oxford University Press.

7 Donham, W. B., "Social Significance of Business," *Harvard Business Review*, 5 (July 1927) 406–419; as reported in "Business Responsibilities in a Divided World: The Cold War Roots of the Corporate Social Responsibility Movement," vi. 4 above.

8 Levitt, T., "The Dangers of Social Responsibility," *Harvard Business Review*, 36 (September–October 1958) 41–50.

9 Watts, Christopher, *Managing for Sustainability* (Economist Intelligence Unit, February 2010) 1.

10 Kielstra, Paul. *Doing Good: Business and the Sustainability Challenge* (Economist Intelligence Unit, February 2008) 35.

11   Frederick, W. C., "The Moral Authority of Transnational Corporate Codes," *Journal of Business Ethics* 10 (1991) 165–177.

12   These documents include: The United Nations Universal Declaration of Human Rights (1948), The European Convention on Human Rights (1950), The Helsinki Final Act (1975), The OECD Guidelines for Multinational Enterprises (1976), The International Labor Office Tripartite Declaration of Principles Concerning Multinational Enterprises and Social Policy (1977), The United Nations Code of Conduct for Transnational Corporations. The Caux Roundtable formulated its Principles for Business; the OECD developed its Guidelines for Multinational Enterprises (http://www.oecd.org); and in 1997 the Global Sullivan Principles were created. The Caux Round Table (CRT) (http://www.cauxround-table.org/index.cfm?&menuid=2) is "an international network of principled, senior business leaders working to promote a moral capitalism. The CRT advocates implementation of its code through which principled capitalism can flourish and sustainable and socially responsible prosperity can become the foundation for a fair, free, and transparent global society." In 1977, Reverend Leon Sullivan developed the Sullivan Principles, a code of conduct for human rights and equal opportunity for companies operating in South Africa. The Sullivan Principles are acknowledged to have been one of the most effective efforts to end discrimination against blacks in the workplace in South Africa, and to have contributed to the dismantling of apartheid. To further expand human rights and economic development to all communities, Reverend Sullivan created the Global Sullivan Principles of Social Responsibility in 1997 (http://thesullivanfoundation.org/about/global-sullivan-principles).

13   Frederick, "The Moral Authority of Transnational Corporate Codes," n. 11 above, 166–167.

14   http://www.unglobalcompact.org/docs/news_events/8.1/GC_brochure_FINAL.pdf. Accessed January 19, 2013.

15   Ibid.

16   http://exchange.plant-for-the-planet.org/cpt_nicht_verschieben/global/un_global_compact_yearbook_20121025.pdf

17   http://www.unglobalcompact.org/AboutTheGC/TheTenPrinciples/index.html.

18   Confino, J., "Cleaning up the Global Compact: dealing with corporate free riders," *Guardian Professional Network*, guardian.co.uk, March 26, 2012; http://www.unglobalcompact.org/docs/news_events/in_the_media/Guardian_26.3.12.pdf. Accessed January 20, 2013.

19   http://globalcompactcritics.blogspot.com/2011_01_01_archive.html. Accessed January 20, 2013.

20   http://www.unglobalcompact.org/COP/differentiation_programme.html. Accessed January 20, 2013.

21   http://www.unglobalcompact.org/docs/news_events/8.1/Blueprint.pdf. Accessed January 19, 2013.

22   Lacy, P., Cooper, T., Hayward, R. and Neuberger, L., "A New Era of Sustainability: UN Global Compact-Accenture CEO Study 2010," http://www.unglobalcompact.org/docs/news_events/8.1/UNGC_Accenture_CEO_Study_2010.pdf. Accessed January 20, 2013.

23   Levy, D. L., Szejnwald, H. B. and de Jong, M., "The Contested Politics of Corporate Governance: The Case of the Global Reporting Initiative," *Business & Society*, 49 (2010) 88–117, originally published online 6 October 2009.

24   https://www.globalreporting.org/Information/about-gri/Pages/default.aspx. Accessed January 20, 2013.

25   http://www.sustainability-indexes.com/dow-jones-sustainability-indexes/index.jsp

26   http://www.sustainability.com/history

27   Andrew Savitz, personal communication.

28   http://group.skanska.com/en/About-us/Skanska-in-brief/. Accessed July 24, 2013.

29   http://group.skanska.com/en/Sustainability/Skanska-and-sustainability/. Accessed July 24, 2013.

30   Heineman Jr., B. W., *High Performance with High Integrity*, Memo to the CEO Series (Boston MA: Harvard Business Press, 2008) 20–21.

31   Ibid., at p. 6.

32   "Just Good Business: A Special Report on Corporate Social Responsibility," *The Economist*, January 19, 2008.

33   http://www.gecitizenship.com/focus-areas/. Accessed January 30, 2013.

34   Ibid.

35   http://www.ecomagination.com/leadership. Accessed January 28, 2013.

36   http://www.ecomagination.com/short-reads. Accessed January 28, 2013.

37   http://www.genewscenter.com/Press-Releases/GE-and-StartUp-Health-Partner-to-Accelerate-Consumer-Health-Innovation-3daf.aspx. Accessed April 29, 2013.

38   http://www.nestle.com/aboutus/strategy. Accessed January 30, 2013.

39   http://storage.nestle.com/Interactive_CSV_2011/index.html#/35/zoomed; p. 34. Accessed January 30, 2013.

40   Decant, K. and Alumna, B., "Environmental Leadership: From Compliance to Competitive Advantage," *Academy of Management Executive*, 8(3) (1994) 7–27.

41   http://www.nestle.com/csv/nestle. Accessed January 30, 2013.

42   Orlitzky, M., Schmidt, F. L. and Rynes, S., "Corporate Social and Financial Performance: A Meta-Analysis," *Organization Studies*, 24(3) (2003) 423.

43   Margolis, J. D. and Elfenbein, H. A., "Do Well By Doing Good? Don't Count on It," *Harvard Business Review* (January 2008).

44   Ibid., at p. 1.

45   Kielstra, *op. cit.,* 5–6.

46   Ibid.

47   Watts, *op. cit.,* 2.

48   Eccles, Robert, Ioannou, Ioannis and Serafeim, George, "The Impact of a Corporate Culture of Sustainability on Corporate Behavior and Performance," Working Paper 12-035, Harvard Business School, November 2011, 33. http://papers.ssrn.com/sol3/papers.cfm?abstract_id=1964011. Accessed February 6, 2013.

49   Ibid. p. 34.

50   "The Innovation Bottom Line," *MIT Sloan Management Review* Research Report, Winter 2013.

51   Lazlo, C., Sherman, D. and Whalen, J., "Expanding the Value Horizon: How Stakeholder Value Contributes to Competitive Advantage," *Journal of Corporate Citizenship*, 20 (Winter 2005) 67.

52   Kielstra, *op. cit.,* 5.

53   Ibid. pp. 24–25.

54   http://www.walmartstores.com/sites/responsibilityreport/2011/sustainable_overview.aspx. Accessed February 1, 2013.

55   Steven Greenhouse, "Wal-Mart Toughens Fire Safety Rules for Suppliers After Bangladesh Blaze," *New York Times,* January 23, 2013; p.B3.

56   Spector, Bert, *Implementing Organizational Change: Theory into Practice,* 3rd edn. (Pearson: Boston, 2013) 176.

57   http://www.teamsweat.org/

58   http://www.organicconsumers.org/corp/nikesham.cfm. Accessed February 2, 2013.

59   Sterling, Scott, "How Apple's Foxconn problem is like Nike's sweatshop problem, and why the outcome is the same," *Digital Trends,* Oct 10, 2012. Accessed February 2, 2013.

60   KPMG & SAM, Sustainability Yearbook 2012. http://www.sustainability-index.com/images/sam-yearbook-2012-final_tcm1071-337504.pdf. P. 68.

61   Ibid.

62   http://www.nikeresponsibility.com/report/content/chapter/business-overview. Accessed February 2, 2013.

63   For a discussion of Nike's organizational design changes see Spector, *op. cit.,* 176–178.

64   For a detailed description of the Malden Mills story see the Harvard Business School Cases, *Malden Mills (A),* 9-404-072; *Malden Mills (A) Abridged,* 9-410-083; and *Malden Mills (B),* 9-404-073.

65   Share prices and volume data were obtained at http://finance.yahoo.com/q/hp?s=BP+Historical+Prices. Accessed February 3, 2013.

66   Ramseur, Jonathan L. and Hagerty, Curry L., *Deepwater Horizon Oil Spill: Recent Activities and Ongoing Developments,* Congressional Research Service, http://www.fas.org/sgp/crs/misc/R42942.pdf; January 31, 2013.

67   Krauss, Clifford and Schwartz, John, "BP Will Plead Guilty and Pay Over $4 Billion," *The New York Times,* November 15, 2012.

68   Ramseur, *op. cit.*

69   Krauss, Clifford, "Judge Accepts BP's $4 Billion Criminal Settlement Over Gulf Oil Spill," *The New York Times,* January 29, 2013.

70   Ibid.

71   Andy Savitz, personal communication.

72   Lewis, Sanford, "Learning form BP's 'Sustainable' Self-Portraits: From 'Integrated Spin' to Integrated Reporting," Corporate Disclosure Alert, http://corporatedisclosurealert.blogspot.com/2010/10/from-integrated-spin-to-integrated.html; Accessed February 7, 2013.

73   Ibid.

74   http://thehill.com/blogs/congress-blog/energy-a-environment/103255-letter-to-tony-hayward-chief-executive-officer-of-bp-rep-henry-waxman-and-rep-bart-stupak. Accessed February 7, 2013.

75   Lewis, *op. cit.*

76   Hincha-Ownby, Melissa, "Toyota releases annual sustainability report," *Mother Nature Network,* November 9, 2011. http://www.mnn.com/money/sustainable-business-practices/blogs/toyota-releases-annual-sustainability-report. Accessed February 8, 2013.

77   http://www.interbrand.com/en/best-global-brands/Best-Global-Green-Brands/2012-Report/BestGlobalGreenBrandsTable-2012.aspx. Accessed February 8, 2013.

78 http://www.bloomberg.com/news/2013-02-05/toyota-raises-profit-forecast-as-yen-fuels-japan-inc-revival.html. Accessed February 8, 2013.

79 Andrew Savitz, personal communication.

80 Freeman, R. Edward, Wicks, Andrew C., and Parmar, Bidhan, "Stakeholder Theory and The Corporate Objective Revisited," *Organization Science*, 15(3) (May-June 2004) 364–369.

81 See Barnett, J. H., "The American Executive and Colombian Violence: Social Relatedness and Business Ethics," *Journal of Business Ethics* 10 (1991) 853–861, for a description of the three models: conflict, compartment, and complementarity.

82 Andrew Savitz, personal communication.

Index

Transparency International 226–7
transportation 10–11
triple bottom line 263
Trompenaars, F. 45
trust 103–4, 108–9, 203–4
Turkey, CIVETS countries 224–5

uncertainty *see* Volatile, Uncertain, Complex
       and Ambiguous
understanding, shared 103, 107–9
United Nations (UN) 240, 242, 244,
       259–61, 266
United States (US) 137–8, 220, 225, 226–7
Universal Declaration of Human Rights 240,
       242, 244
universalism 240–3, 245
UN (United Nations) 240, 242, 244,
       259–61, 266
utilitarianism 237, 239

value creation 111
       see also sustainable value
variety 13–14
Vietnam, CIVETS countries 224–5
virtual teams 105–11
       communication 108–9
       complexity 106–7, 111
       discipline 109–10

dispersal configuration 106–7
diversity levels 106
global management 105–11
meeting in person 110–11
organization of 109–10
right technology 110
shared knowledge 107–9
strategy execution 161–2
three challenges 106–7
trust 108–9
value creation 111
virtuous cycles 109–11
Volatile, Uncertain, Complex and Ambiguous
       (VUCA) 12
Voluntary Principles on Security and Human
       Rights 222
VUCA (Volatile, Uncertain, Complex and
       Ambiguous) 12

Wal-Mart 220–1, 269
Western values 240–3
WHO (World Health Organization) 227–8
Wilde *see* Hax and Wilde's Delta model
within-country homogeneity 65–6
women managers 177–8
work units 98–105
World Health Organization (WHO) 227–8
worldviews 39–44